22nd Chinese National Conference on Computational Linguistic (CCL 2023)

Frontier Forum

Harbin, China
3 - 5 August 2023

ISBN: 978-1-7138-8989-2

Printed from e-media with permission by:

Curran Associates, Inc.
57 Morehouse Lane
Red Hook, NY 12571

CURRAN ASSOCIATES INC. proceedings.com

Some format issues inherent in the e-media version may also appear in this print version.

Printed with permission by Curran Associates, Inc. (2024)

For permission requests, please contact the Association for Computational Linguistics at the address below.

Association for Computational Linguistics
209 N. Eighth Street
Stroudsburg, Pennsylvania 18360

Phone: 1-570-476-8006
Fax: 1-570-476-0860

acl@aclweb.org

Additional copies of this publication are available from:

Curran Associates, Inc.
57 Morehouse Lane
Red Hook, NY 12571 USA
Phone: 845-758-0400
Fax: 845-758-2633
Email: curran@proceedings.com
Web: www.proceedings.com

The 22nd Chinese National Conference on Computational Linguistics: Frontier Forum

Proceedings of the Frontier Forum

August 3 - August 5, 2023

Harbin, China

Order copies of this and other CCL proceedings from:

Chinese National Conference on Computational Linguistics (CCL)

Courtyard 4, South Fourth Street, Zhongguancun , Haidian District, Beijing 100190, China

Tel: + 010-62562916

Fax: + 010-62661046

cips@iscas.ac.cn

Introduction

Welcome to the proceedings of the Frontier Forum of the twenty second China National Conference on Computational Linguistics (22nd CCL). The conference were hosted and co-organized by Harbin Institute of Technology, China.

CCL is an annual conference (bi-annual before 2013) that started in 1991. It is the flagship conference of the Chinese Information Processing Society of China (CIPS), which is the largest NLP scholar and expert community in China. CCL is a premier nation-wide conference for disseminating new scholarly and technological work in computational linguistics, with a major emphasis on computational processing of the languages in China such as Mandarin, Tibetan, Mongolian, and Uyghur.

The Program Committee selected 9 overviews for the Frontier Forum of CCL 2023, in order to give a general view of the NLP in the past year and increase the sense of the edge-cutting works for the attendees. The 9 overviews encompass the compelling facets of large language models, including selection, training, evaluation, and integration with the knowledge graph, among others.

We thank the Program and Organizing Committees for helping to make the forum successful, and we hope all the participants enjoyed the CCL conference and a wonderful days in Harbin.

July 2023

Jiajun Zhang

Organizers

Tutorial Chairs

Jiajun Zhang	Institute of Automation, CAS, China

Table of Content

基座模型训练中的数据与模型架构

颜航[*]
上海人工智能实验室
yanhang@pjlab.org.cn

费朝烨[*]
复旦大学计算机学院
zyfei20@fudan.edu.cn

杨小珪
复旦大学计算机学院
yangxg21@m.fudan.edu.cn

高扬
上海人工智能实验室
gaoyang@pjlab.org.cn

邱锡鹏
复旦大学计算机学院
xpqiu@fudan.edu.cn

摘要

ChatGPT以对话形式的交互方式，降低了使用大模型的门槛，因此迅速在全球范围内流行起来。尽管OpenAI并未公开ChatGPT的技术路线，但一些后续的工作宣称已经在开源的基座模型上复现了ChatGPT的性能。然而，尽管这些模型在某些评测上表现出与ChatGPT相似的性能，但在实际的知识量和推理能力上，它们仍然不如ChatGPT。为了更接近ChatGPT甚至GPT4的性能，我们需要对基座模型的训练进行更深入的研究。本文针对基座模型训练的数据以及模型架构进行讨论，首先总结了当前预训练数据的来源以及基本处理流程，并针对目前关注较少的代码预训练数据和中文预训练数据进行了分析；然后对当前已有基座模型的网络架构进行了回顾，并针对这些架构调整背后的动机进行了阐述。

关键词： 基座模型数据 ； 基座模型架构

1 引言

从2022年11月底，美国OpenAI公司推出ChatGPT[1]后，大语言模型（Large Language Model，简称LLM）在学术界和工业界都引起了轰动。ChatGPT可以通过对话的形式完成各种任务，例如撰写代码、整理数据、润色论文等，并且当其没有输出预期结果时，还可以通过多轮对话逐步优化自身输出，这种通过对话交互的方式极大降低了模型的使用门槛，因此ChatGPT迅速在全球范围内出圈，热度扩散到了人工智能领域之外。OpenAI公司并未公开ChatGPT的技术路线，但他们在InstructGPT (Ouyang et al., 2022)论文中提到，可以通过一个基座语言模型，结合人类对齐（Human Alignment）训练来让模型跟随人类的指令完成特定任务。使用InstructGPT中类似的方法，后续的一些工作在开源的基座模型 (Nijkamp et al., 2023b; Touvron et al., 2023)上一定程度复现了ChatGPT的性能 (Sun et al., 2023; Taori et al., 2023)。不过最近来自美国伯克利大学的研究指出，尽管现在这些模型从一些评测上展现出与ChatGPT相似的性能，但从知识量及推理能力方面，它们均不及ChatGPT，只是由于回答形式上接近ChatGPT，才获得了不错的评测性能。为了能够更加接近ChatGPT乃至GPT4的性能，还需要在基座模型的训练上进行更深入的研究 (Gudibande et al., 2023)。

为了得到一个好的基座模型，我们首先需要大量的预训练数据，在图1中我们对比了近年来不同预训练模型的大小与使用的预训练数据大小。从GPT-2(Radford et al., 2019)到PaLM2(Anil et al., 2023)，模型的大小增长了200倍，但是预训练的数据量大小增长了450倍。因此，预训练模型对数据的需求是巨大的。表1中罗列了几个基座模型训练所需要的计算资源。除了对预训练数据进行总结之外，我们也将对比不同的基座模型的网络架构，并对各种基座模型的架构进行归纳。

2 预训练数据

数据是知识的载体，也是大规模预训练模型训练的基础，自深度学习技术发展以来，数据就是决定模型性能的重要因素。对于基座模型的训练而言，预训练数据在一定程度上决定了其能力的边界。Kaplan等人(2020)研究发现，训练基座模型的过程中，模型大小与数据规模是决

[*] 共同一作.

[1] https://chat.openai.com

第二十二届中国计算语言学大会论文集，第1页-第15页，哈尔滨，中国，2023年8月3日至5日。
卷2：前沿综述

模型	训练Token数	计算资源	训练时长
GPT3 (Brown et al., 2020)	300B	10000张V100	14天
GLM-130B (Zeng et al., 2023)	450B	992张A100	60天
LLaMA-65B (Touvron et al., 2023)	1.4T	2048张A100	21天
MPT-7B (Team, 2023)	1T	440张A100	10天

Table 1: 基座模型对训练资源需求

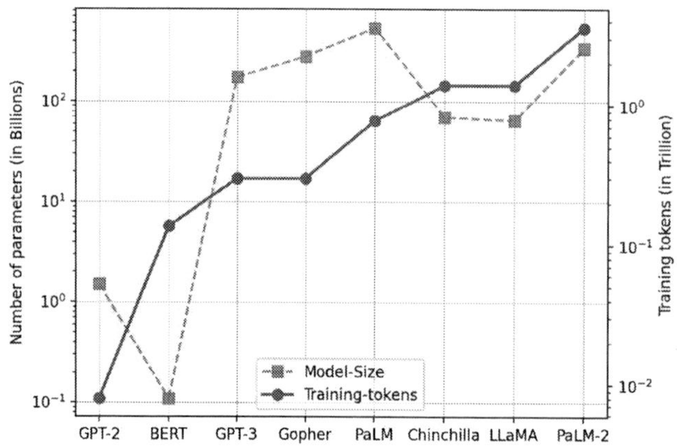

Figure 1: 近年的预训练模型大小以及它们使用的预训练数据大小

定预训练模型的关键因素，这也是GPT-3(Brown et al., 2020)乃至后面ChatGPT成功的理论基础。Hoffmann等人(2022)进行了类似的探究，发现在给定的计算量条件下，所需要的数据量相比较于Kaplan等人预计的要更多，并基于此训练了性能更好的Chichilla模型。本章将从数据入手，总结当前预训练数据的处理流程，并对其问题展开讨论。

2.1 预训练数据的来源

预训练数据的来源直接关系到语料的多样性。不同来源的语料往往是不同的主题，不同的格式以及不同的组织方式，补充不同来源的数据可以很好地提升模型的鲁棒性与泛化性(Longpre et al., 2023)。目前，大规模预训练语料主要来源于互联网中的文本信息。

互联网作为人类信息交换的重要方式，积累了巨量的信息。根据谷歌公司CEO Eric Schmidt预计，整个互联网数据数量高达5000 PB[2]。由于总量巨大且居于此的信息时刻在发生改变，因此如何获取这一份数据是一项巨大的挑战。受益于互联网爬虫计划Common Crawl [3]的开展，研究人员可以更加便利地收集网络中的数据，并将精力集中于数据处理阶段。Common Crawl是一项开放网络爬虫的数据存储库的开源项目，其爬取并保存了自2013年以来开放互联网中的各种数据，为研究人员提供了一个海量、非结构化、多语言的网页数据集。Common Crawl可自动爬取整个互联网上的数据，并采用时间作为刻度，每隔一段时间将会放出一部分数据集，不同时间片的URL以及内容尽量保证不重复。每一个时间片大概存有1.5 Billon个文档，包含该时间段内互联网中更新的绝大部分内容。

Common Crawl 数据集具有总量巨大和来源渠道多样化等特点，但正是这些特点导致从中提取高质量文本变得异常困难。因此，之前的几份工作均引入更多的预处理数据，或针对指定网站的数据进行定向收集。例如，在Brown等人(2020)提到，除了预处理Common Crawl的数据外，他们同样添加了高质量图书数据集以及维基百科等。Pile语料 (Gao et al., 2021)除了Common Crawl收集的数据外，还收集了将近21个站点的数据，其中包括学术论文网站PubMed、Arxiv，代码共享平台Github，编程交流平台Stack Exchange，预处理图书数据集BookCorpus 2、Books3以及其他相关高质量数据集等。悟道 (Yuan et al., 2021)同样的采用

[2] https://www.easytechjunkie.com/how-big-is-the-internet.htm

[3] https://commoncrawl.org/

第二十二届中国计算语言学大会论文集，第1页-第15页，哈尔滨，中国，2023年8月3日至5日。
卷2：前沿综述

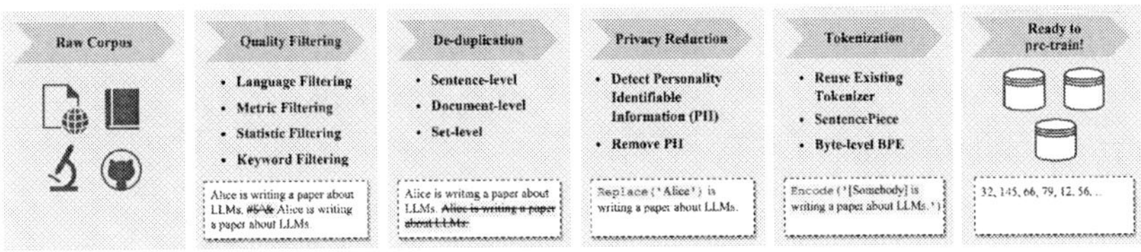

Figure 2: 预训练数据处理流程图示(Zhao et al., 2023)

了大量的网络语料，与前面不同的是，其主要筛选中文语料，并丢弃中文字符少于10个的网页。

此外，经过我们的调查发现，Pile(Gao et al., 2021)作为处理质量较高的数据集在开源后被广泛使用，后续的一系列工作倾向于在预训练语料中加入Pile或者Pile CC，以节省数据处理的时间，同时加入部分更新时间戳下的Common Crawl语料，以保证模型的质量与时效性。

2.2 预训练数据的处理

一般而言，从网页中获取的数据往往不能直接使用。一方面，这一类数据以HTML的格式组织在一起，一般的大语言模型无法通过训练从中提取纯文本信息；另一方面，预训练数据中往往充斥着各种虚假信息，模版信息，广告信息以及黄色暴力内容等，此外还有自动生成的信息，这一类信息我们统称为脏数据。脏数据的引入不利于语言模型对于语言建模任务的学习。因此，目前的主流模型通常会对收集到的网络数据进行处理，以使模型可以更好地学习其语言内部的分布。

如图2所示，预训练数据的处理流程主要分为四部分：质量筛选，数据去重，隐私信息删除与文本词元化。如果获取到的信息为网页信息，还需要对网页信息进行提取，尽量提取纯净的内容数据而避免模版数据。为此，除了采用一些网页信息抽取工具来对Common Crawl的信息进行抽取之外，Common Crawl本身同样提供了纯文本的.WET格式数据。在处理预训练语料的流程中，删除隐私信息可以避免大语言模型泄露隐私，文本词元化将文本转化为token，以作为预训练模型的输入。而数据质量筛选与数据去重将在内容层面直接关系预训练数据的属性与性质，从而影响基座模型的训练。本节将着重介绍数据质量筛选与数据去重，以及目前主流的处理方法。

2.2.1 质量筛选

预训练数据的质量直接关系到大语言模型的性能，而对于数据的质量筛选直接关系到预训练语言模型的性能。目前主流预训练模型采用的质量筛选方案包含两种，分别为规则过滤及训练分类器方法。

规则过滤方法，其最简单的方式是通过URL筛选数据。但由于数据量过于庞大，我们无法遍历所有的URL进行筛选，因此研究人员提出了多种自动化的方法以解决此类问题：

启发式规则过滤方法。人为设计一部分启发式规则，直接对文本进行筛选。C4即采用了这种方法，通过大量启发式规则对数据筛选，包括删除所有非停止符号结尾的段落，根据不良单词列表删除文档，删除过短的语句，删除带有“javascript”字样的段落等 (Raffel et al., 2020)。这一类筛选规则虽可以筛选出一些不流畅的语句以及不良语句，但无法避免数据重复或者广告等问题。为了筛选出重复性的数据，在MassiveText 语料构建过程中，研究人员提出通过计算不同gram的重复性 (Rae et al., 2021)，以及选择不同的筛选阈值来筛选重复性数据。

基于模型的数据过滤方法。之前的工作通常旨在减少直接的脏数据，例如数据中不符合人类规范的，重复多次的数据，带有不良词汇的数据，更多的脏数据可能是混入了HTML模版，机器自动生成的看起来是文字实际是乱码的数据。为了筛选掉这部分脏数据，主流的预训练方法提出引入基于模型的数据过滤方法。例如，GPT-3通过Wiki等高质量数据集训练了一个简单的分类器，并通过分类器对数据进行筛选，LLaMA等工作训练了一个KenLM的小型统计语言模型，用以筛选出脏数据。

2.2.2 数据去重

在网页数据中，数据可能会存在重复，Lee等人(2022)主张通过n-gram结合MinHash的方式

第二十二届中国计算语言学大会论文集，第1页-第15页，哈尔滨，中国，2023年8月3日至5日。
卷2：前沿综述

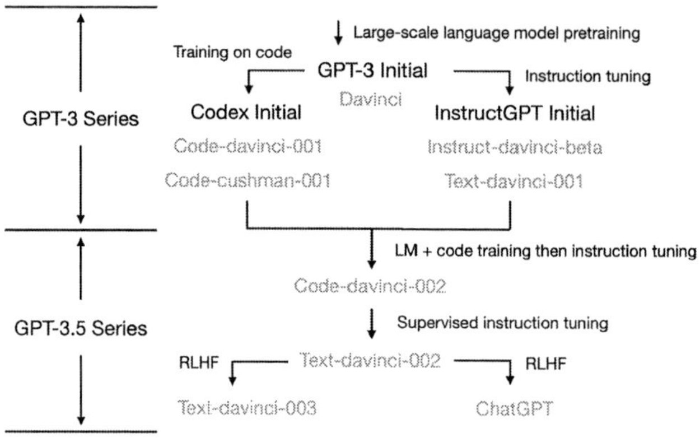

Figure 3: 符尧(2022)等人整理的OpenAI模型进化图

来删除数据中的重复数据，删掉重复数据可以让训练更加有效。Hernandez等人(2022)指出如果训练数据中存在10%的重复数据，将导致模型的有效大小减半，即400M参数量的模型其效果仅相当于一个200M参数量的模型。除此之外，PaLM模型(Chowdhery et al., 2022)也在论文中提到在新数据上训练将更有可能让模型获得更好的性能。尽管数据去重已经成为了基座训练中的标准一环(Zhang et al., 2022; Zeng et al., 2023; Scao et al., 2022; Touvron et al., 2023)，但也有研究表明适当的重复使用数据不会对模型的性能造成很严重的问题，在T5论文(Raffel et al., 2020)中，作者尝试了重复使用数据，模型的性能并没有受到特别严重的损害，不过由于作者使用的模型是编码器-解码器架构，其规律可能与语言模型的规律不一致。Muennighoff等人(2023)在9B参数量的语言模型上测试了重复数据对模型的影响，他们发现数据重复量只要在4次以内，就几乎不会对模型造成性能损害。综上所述，数据去重应避免留下重复过多次的数据，但如果重复量控制在4次以内，对训练产生的影响应该都不致命。

2.3 代码数据的引入

传统的大语言模型对于代码的关注度并不高，而对于训练纯文本模型十分感兴趣。OpenAI的CodeX (Chen et al., 2021)模型中首次将代码引入大模型预训练中。根据符尧等人(2022)的观察，引入代码，使得OpenAI的GPT系列模型有了重大性能突变。不过目前还没有非常直接的证据可证实这个猜想，但由于让语言模型能够生成代码本身也是一种非常重要的特性，且该方式也提供了一种未来大模型与现实世界发生交互的接口，因而将代码数据加入到预训练中也非常有必要。

在之前的模型训练中，代码数据的处理均较为粗粒度 (Touvron et al., 2023; Nijkamp et al., 2023b)，他们都只在代码文件粒度进行了去重，但实际上由于各种脚手架代码不断重复，代码数据中存在非常严重的重复问题。为了更好地使用代码数据，Li等人 (2023)发现，对于代码的精细化处理，可以使模型更好地学习代码中蕴含的能力与知识。例如，其筛选了一部分的Github中的数据，并对其分语言进行处理，处理了Jupyter Notebook，使其更符合人类语言的特点等，诸如此类的操作使得他们的模型在代码任务上的性能得到了显著提高。进一步地，Gunasekar等人(2023)认为大部分的代码是无用且低效的，他们提出，一个好的代码数据集应该是清晰的、独立的、有启发性的和平衡的。由此，他们对The Stack数据集 (Kocetkov et al., 2022)进行了过滤，同时采用ChatGPT生成了一部分数据，使其具有更强的启发性。

2.4 中文预训练数据

尽管之前已有部分工作开源了部分中文语料，例如Wudao (Yuan et al., 2021)、Yuan 1.0T (Wu et al., 2021)，但这部分数据一方面是时效性不足，另一方面是数量和质量都还不足以训练一个性能较好的基座模型，因此需要获取更多的中文语料。受到Pile语料的启发，我们也对中文语料进行了分类，并尝试寻找对应的数据来源，结果如表2所示。

我们对中文互联网上的数据进行了粗略的估计，结果如表3中所示，我们发现，目前可获取的中文token不足1T，对于目前动辄上T token级别的预训练，中文数据还是非常缺乏。除此

第二十二届中国计算语言学大会论文集，第1页-第15页，哈尔滨，中国，2023年8月3日至5日。
卷2：前沿综述

数据类别	英文来源	中文对照数据来源
Pile-CC	https://commoncrawl.org/the-data/	WuDao、CC中抽取中文数据
PubMed Central	https://pubmed.ncbi.nlm.nih.gov/	各类医学网站、开源数据库
Books3	https://bibliotik.me	豆瓣阅读、Kindle电子书、sobooks
OpenWebText2	https://www.reddit.com/	微博、百度贴吧、小红书
ArXiv	https://arxiv.org/	
Github	https://github.com/	
FreeLaw	https://www.freelaw.in/	中国法院网、北大法宝、威科先行法律信息库
Stack Exchange	https://stackexchange.com/	中文问答社区、百度知道、头条问答
USPTO Backgrounds	https://www.uspto.gov/	中国专利信息网、壹专利、开源专利数据库
PubMed Abstracts	https://pubmed.ncbi.nlm.nih.gov/	各类医学网站、开源数据库
EuroParl	https://www.statmt.org/europarl/	翻译数据
Gutenberg (PG-19)	https://www.gutenberg.org/	古典文学网、中国古典文学、古书房
OpenSubtitles	https://www.opensubtitles.org/en	字幕库、SubHD、诸神字幕组
Wikipedia(en)	https://www.wikipedia.org/	中文维基百科、百度百科、MBA智库百科
DM Mathematics	https://github.com/deepmind/mathematics_dataset	作业帮、各类数学题网站
Ubuntu IRC	https://webchat.freenode.net/	微博超话在线聊天、各类聊天机器人、多轮对话数据集
BookCorpus2	https://www.smashwords.com/	起点中文网、纵横中文网
HackerNews	https://news.ycombinator.com/	36氪、极客公园、虎嗅网
Youtube Subtitles	https://www.kaggle.com/datasets/wadzim/youtube-subtitles	Subscene网站
PhilPapers	https://philpapers.org/	哲学中国网、学术·哲学_爱思想、中国哲学书电子化计划
NIH Grant Abstracts	https://reporter.nih.gov/exporter/abstracts	财政部公开信息
Enron Emails	https://www.cs.cmu.edu/∼enron/	互联网中免费共享的电子邮件数据库

Table 2: Pile中的各类语料对应的中文来源

第二十二届中国计算语言学大会论文集，第1页-第15页，哈尔滨，中国，2023年8月3日至5日。
卷2：前沿综述

之外，处理难度较大也是困扰中文大语言模型训练的一大难题。目前主流的数据清洗代码大都支持英文而不支持中文，需重新适配，例如上述提到的启发式规则，对于中文数据需要重新编写。中文数据中的广告处理相对于英文数据也存在难点，中文数据中，广告通常存在于语句内部，比较难将其筛选出来。

来源	Token数量
古文诗词	0.8B
百科	5B
各类小说	120B
社区问答	200B
新闻	100B
中文专利	9.5B
法律判决	90B
博客	64B
学术论文	9.5B
总计	598.8B

Table 3: 中文不同类型数据Token数量粗略统计

2.5 预训练语料质量的评估

由于大语言模型的训练成本巨大，对于处理好的预训练语料，研究人员希望对其进行质量评估。Gopher(Rae et al., 2021)论文中采用训练一个1.4B左右的语言模型的方式来评估不同处理流程对于下游任务的影响。他们发现，随着数据清洗与处理的不断深入，经由这些数据训练得到的模型的效果也越好。在经过质量筛选与数据去重之后，得到的数据训练的模型相比于原始数据与开源数据（OpenWebText与C4）在语言建模任务上性能存在明显的上升。采用同样的方法，Longpre等人(2023)在1.5B模型的基础上，研究了不同质量的数据对于大语言模型在处理不同下游任务上的性能差异。研究人员不仅希望评估语料质量对于模型训练的影响，更希望探究不同质量语料对于模型不同维度能力激发之间的差异。

这种采用小模型进行验证的方法成本较低，且可以在正式训练之前发现数据存在的诸多问题，以及对于基座模型的训练进行预测。但由于大语言模型涌现现象的存在，可能在某些能力上，模型需要达到一定量级才可以看出性能的差异。另外，生成式模型的能力评估也十分困难，由于Prompt的引入，评测本身也带有一定的不确定性，表4中展示了在评测过程中，如果使用不同的Prompt进行评测，得到的结论会大相径庭。因此，如何低成本地评估预训练语料的质量与不同数据对于模型能力的影响，仍然是自然语言处理社区活跃的研究问题。

训练Token数	验证集损失	Prompt #1	Prompt #2
20B	1.335	66.5	71.55
40B	1.334	65.6	73.88
60B	1.329	64.2	74.37
80B	1.328	64.8	76.17
100B	1.324	64.7	77.09

Table 4: 随着训练的进行，验证集损失在不断下降。如果使用Prompt #1的结果作为判断，模型的性能在变差，但如果使用Prompt #2的结果，则性能在变好。

2.6 开源预训练数据集

随着大语言模型在自然语言处理领域的广泛应用，高质量的开源模型与预训练数据集的需求迅速增长。正如Together公司[4]宣称的那样："AI正在迎来Linux时代"，高质量大规模的开源

[4]https://together.ai/blog/redpajama

第二十二届中国计算语言学大会论文集，第1页-第15页，哈尔滨，中国，2023年8月3日至5日。
卷2：前沿综述

模型	位置编码	自注意力	归一化层位置	归一化层类型	损失函数
GPT3-175B	Absolute	Standard	PreNorm	LayerNorm	LM(+FIM) Loss
CodeGen-16B	RoPE	Standard	ParallelLayer	LayerNorm	LM Loss
PaLM-540B	RoPE	Multi-Query	ParallelLayer	LayerNorm	LM(+UL2) Loss
OPT-175B	Absolute	Standard	PreNorm	LayerNorm	LM Loss
GLM-130B	RoPE	Standard	PostNorm	LayerNorm	GLM+LM Loss
BLOOM-176B	ALiBi	Standard	PreNorm	LayerNorm	LM Loss
LLaMA	RoPE	Standard	PreNorm	RMSNorm	LM Loss
CodeGen2-16B	RoPE	Standard	ParallelLayer	LayerNorm	LM Loss
MPT-7B	ALiBi	Standard	PreNorm	LayerNorm	LM Loss
StarCoder	Absolute	Multi-Query	PreNorm	LayerNorm	LM+FIM Loss
Falcon	RoPE	Multi-Query	ParallelLayer	LayerNorm	LM Loss
ChatGLM2-6B	RoPE	Multi-Query	PreNorm	RMSNorm	-

Table 5: 各种基座模型

预训练数据集已经成为自然语言处理领域重要的基础设施与关键资源。2019年，Google开源了用于训练T5的C4数据集 (Raffel et al., 2020)，该数据集从Common Crawl中提取并对其进行了抽取与启发式的质量筛选。2020年，EleutherAI开源了Pile数据集(Gao et al., 2021)，该数据集不仅处理了Common Crawl的部分数据分片，还获取了部分高质量英文数据用以提升预训练数据的质量与多样性。此后，一些开源模型（如OPT (Zhang et al., 2022)和GLM-130B (Zeng et al., 2023)）均采用此数据集进行基座模型的训练。

受到LLaMA模型 (Touvron et al., 2023)的启发，Together公司处理并开源了一份大约3TB的预训练数据集RedPajama(Computer, 2023)。RedPajama采用了CCNet流水线处理方式 (Wenzek et al., 2020)，涵盖了2017年至2020年间的Common Crawl数据分片，并补充了如C4、Wikipedia等高质量开源数据集。借助RedPajama数据集，Together公司训练出了3B至7B参数规模的完全开源模型[5]。随后，在RePajama数据集的基础上，Together公司采用了更严格的数据处理方法得到了一个约600B Token的更高质量的SlimPajama数据集 (Soboleva et al., 2023)。此外，Falcon组织整理了2008年至2023年初的所有Common Crawl数据分片，并形成了一个约5T tokens的RefinedWeb数据集(Penedo et al., 2023)，其中600B数据子集可以公开获取到[6]。

此外，代码数据集也引起了NLP领域的广泛关注。开源社区组织的BigCode项目对预训练所需的代码数据进行了深入思考，他们收集并处理了网络中的开源代码库，对特殊代码，如Jupyter，Github issue等进行了特殊处理，并最终开源了大小达到6TB、包含358种编程语言的开源代码预训练数据集The Stack(Li et al., 2023)。

OpenLLaMA项目尝试了使用RedPajama、RefinedWeb和The Stack数据进行预训练，发现结合这三类数据可以取得很好的预训练效果 (Geng and Liu, 2023)。

3 基座模型架构

在这一节中，我们主要对当前的基座模型的模型架构进行讨论。在表5中对最近的基座模型的几个重要部件进行汇总，然后针对不同的部件进行简要介绍。

3.1 位置编码

位置编码从大类上来说可以分成绝对位置编码(Vaswani et al., 2017)和相对位置编码(Shaw et al., 2018; Su et al., 2021)两类。其中绝对位置编码一般有两类，正余弦函数的位置编码和可学习的位置编码，其中可学习的位置编码在之前的预训练模型中被广泛采用，例如BERT(Devlin et al., 2019)、RoBERTa(Liu et al., 2019)和GPT2(Radford et al., 2019)等，Wang (2020)将这几个预训练模型的位置编码两两位置计算了相似度，其结果如图4所示，可以看出不同位置

[5]https://huggingface.co/togethercomputer/RedPajama-INCITE-7B-Base
[6]https://huggingface.co/datasets/tiiuae/falcon-refinedweb

有一定的邻域关系，越靠近的两个位置，相似度也会越大，因此在Transformer中引入相对位置编码来体现这种归纳偏执应该是有益的。Shaw等人(2018)提出了相对位置编码的概念，苏剑林等人 (2021)从虚数的角度出发推导了乘性位置编码RoPE，这种位置编码提出之后便被广泛使用到了基座模型训练之中。尽管RoPE可以高效地表示相对位置，但是它的外推能力较差，即模型只能在训练数据长度以内的数据表现得不错，超出这个长度性能便大幅下降，如图5所示。ALiBi (Press et al., 2022)首先提出了相对位置编码应该具备良好外推性的概念，通过使用ALiBi可以实现在较短的训练语料上训练但在较长的语料上测试，使用ALiBi位置编码的MPT模型 (Team, 2023)甚至可以支持到65,000个词元的输入。

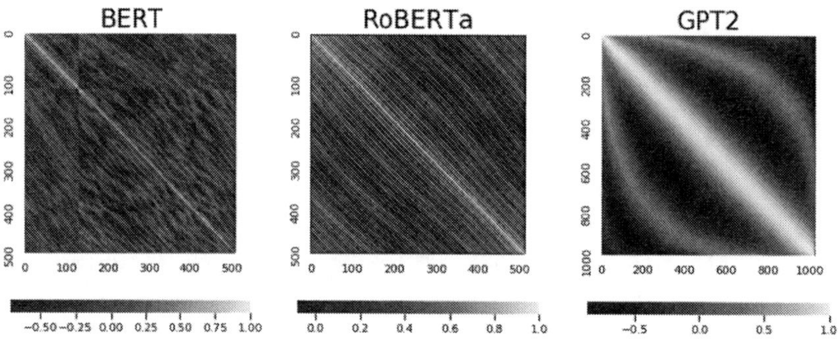

Figure 4: 不同预训练模型位置嵌入中两两位置的相似度

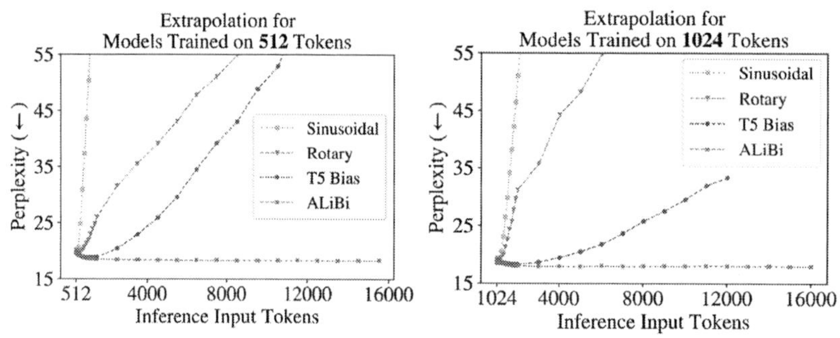

Figure 5: 不同位置编码在长度外推时的性能表现，ALiBi位置编码可以在训练时没有见过的长度上取得良好的性能

3.2 自注意力

自注意力是Transformer模型的核心模块，但其计算复杂度为$O(L^2)$，导致了其计算效率随着输入长度的增加二次增长，之前的工作提出了很多高效自注意力机制(Tay et al., 2023a)，例如Longformer(Beltagy et al., 2020)、Linformer(Wang et al., 2020)等。但在基座模型中这一类直接改良计算复杂度的工作没有被广泛采用，可能的原因有两个，第一个是这类高效Transformer一般都需要引入稀疏计算，这导致它们的计算可能不是GPU友好的，而预训练又是对计算效率非常敏感的任务；第二个原因是现在的预训练模型的隐藏层维度一般都是好几千以上，而目前的基座模型上下文多是两千左右，因此数据长度带来的二次增长，实际上并没有主导模型的计算量。

在基座模型中采用较多的用来降低计算量的方法是Multi-Query方法，Multi-Query方法通过在不同注意力头之间共享自注意力中的Key值和Value值减少显存占用，Multi-Query如图6所示。由于现在的基座模型大部分都是从左到右生成的语言模型，因此在生成过程中，需要使用KV缓存来缓存前面词元的Key值和Value值，在Multi-Query场景下，由于不同注意力头共享

第二十二届中国计算语言学大会论文集，第1页-第15页，哈尔滨，中国，2023年8月3日至5日。
卷2：前沿综述

了Key值和Value值，因此可以只保留一份缓存。这种方式可以极大地减少在推理过程中的显存占用，我们以65B模型为例，在图7中展现了在推理过程中Multi-Query的显存占用和常规自注意力的对比。随着输入长度的增加，常规自注意力机制的显存占用增长显著高于Multi-Query方案，因此未来如果想要将基座模型的输出长度扩充到更大长度，Multi-Query方法值得尝试。

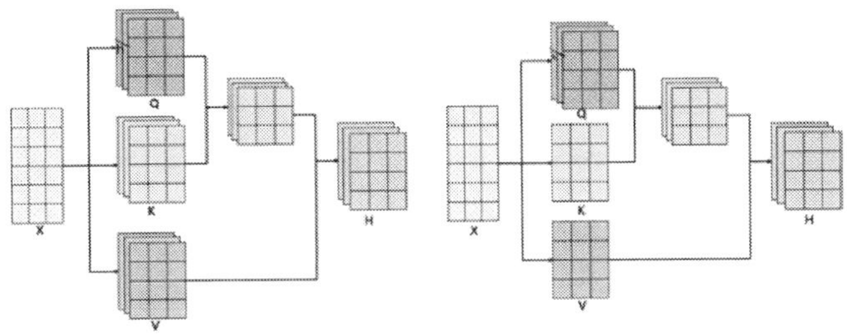

Figure 6: 常规自注意力和Multi-Query自注意力

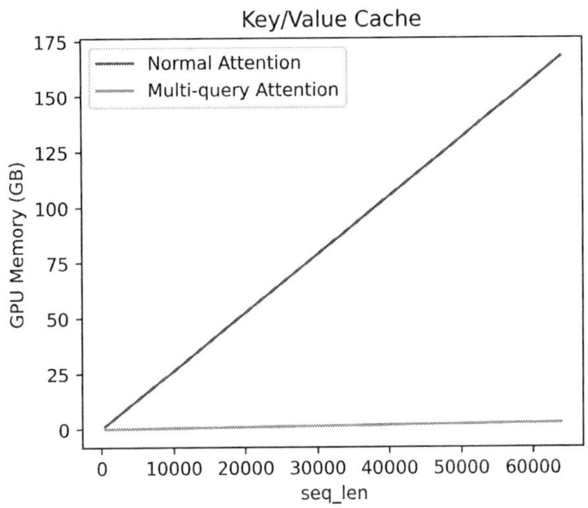

Figure 7: 常规自注意力和Multi-Query自注意力在推理时显存占用的对比

3.3 归一化层

不同的基座模型一方面在归一化层的位置上有所区别，另一方面也会使用不同的归一化层类型。目前基座模型使用的归一化层位置主要有三类，这三类的区别如图8所示。PreNorm在语言模型中被广泛采用(Radford et al., 2019; Brown et al., 2020)；PostNorm则是在BERT(Devlin et al., 2019)、RoBERTa(Liu et al., 2019)等编码器模型中采用较多；Parallel Layer由于将自注意力计算和前馈神经网络并行计算，因此在计算的时候，可以将两个模块的计算同步进行，这样可以让训练的速度更快。归一化层的类型在LLaMA模型发布之前大部分模型都采用的是LayerNorm层归一化，而在LLaMA之后，类似于ChatGLM2[7]、Baichuan[8]等都开始尝试RMSNorm (Zhang and Sennrich, 2019)的方案。

3.4 损失函数

目前大部分的基座模型都使用了语言模型损失作为优化的损失函数，但也有一些其他的尝试。

[7]https://github.com/THUDM/ChatGLM2-6B
[8]https://github.com/baichuan-inc/Baichuan-7B

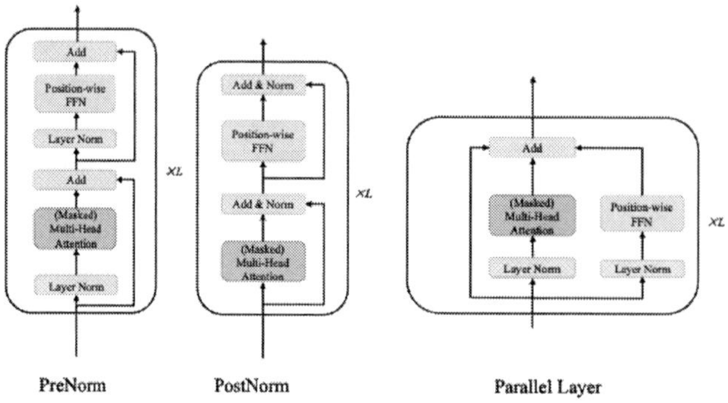

Figure 8: 三种不同的归一化层位置示例

在代码补全场景中存在给定上下文补齐中间代码的场景，因此有研究人员提出FIM（Fill in the Middle）损失函数(Bavarian et al., 2022)，该损失函数在训练的时候会将正常文本进行打乱，首先将文档随机分成三段，例如"document: (prefix, middle, suffix)"，之后在训练阶段将输入顺序调整为"(prefix, suffix, middle)"，这样即可让语言模型学会通过上下文预测中间缺失的地方。尽管这种训练损失函数和语言模型不一致，但加入这种损失并未影响语言模型的正常训练。不过近期也有论文指出，加入FIM损失函数会导致语言模型性能下降(Nijkamp et al., 2023a)。

Tay等人 (2023b)融合了编码器、解码器以及编码器-解码器预训练模型的损失函数，提出了一种融合的损失函数，这种损失函数包含了GPT (Radford et al., 2019)、BERT(Devlin et al., 2019)、T5(Raffel et al., 2020)、UniLM(Bao et al., 2020)等各种预训练模型的损失函数。通过这种损失函数的设计，作者发现可以训练得到性能最好的预训练模型。同时，在后续的研究中，作者发现如果将这种损失函数应用到一个已经训练过的语言模型上，可使得该语言模型仅需少量训练便大幅提升下游性能 (Tay et al., 2022)。

3.5 新的架构

除了基于Transformer的尝试，还有一些其他架构的尝试。例如基于状态空间模型（State Space Model，简称SSM）的模型(Gu et al., 2022; Dao et al., 2023)，这一类模型提出的目标是实现超长文本输入，仅需卷积神经网络量级的计算复杂度即可完成训练（避免了Transformer的二次计算复杂度），而在推理阶段只需固定的计算量，类似于循环神经网络（Transformer的计算量随着长度的增加而增加）。从数学上和实际效果上，状态空间模型在拟合长序列方面确实较Transformer有优势，但目前缺乏更大规模的模型验证，不确定能否成为新的基座模型。除了状态空间模型外，Peng等人(2023)提出了RWKV的方案，RWKV结合了RNN的思想，在Transformer状态更新的时候会融合上一个时刻的状态，在注意力计算过程中，模型将不再进行Query值和Key值的内积计算，而是设计为一个随着距离衰减的函数计算，从而在推理阶段，模型可将过去所有时刻的状态进行累加，无需进行类似于Transformer将Query值与过去的每个Key值做内积的计算，实现了推理时常数级计算复杂度。

总体而言，关于基座模型的架构选择方案仍未确定。一方面，即使是基于经典Transformer架构的基座模型，其在每个单元构件的设计上也并非一致，当前并未有实验表明哪种架构选型是性能更好的；另一方面，在Transformer之外的架构中，在当前的上下文长度下（10,000词元以内），还没有架构能够在运算效率以及性能上都达到与Transformer类模型匹配的效果。由于预训练的代价非常高，因此基座模型架构的运行效率非常关键；此外，由于自注意力机制的二次计算复杂度，未来针对超长序列，我们也许需要更高效的架构设计。

4 总结

本文首先对基座模型训练中的数据进行了回顾，介绍当前基座模型常用的数据来源，并讨论了这些数据的清洗方式，然后针对代码数据处理中的问题进行了讨论，此外，我们简要汇总了一些可能的中文预训练数据来源。如何评估这些收集到的数据质量是一个开放性的问题，不

第二十二届中国计算语言学大会论文集，第1页-第15页，哈尔滨，中国，2023年8月3日至5日。
卷2：前沿综述

同的评测Prompt可能使得结论发生反转，因此在选取数据质量评估方式时需格外小心。同时，我们还汇总了当前不同的预训练基座以及对应的模型架构，并针对这些架构做了初步说明，以期让读者可较快地把握当前基座模型架构的发展方向。

参考文献

Rohan Anil, Andrew M. Dai, Orhan Firat, Melvin Johnson, Dmitry Lepikhin, Alexandre Passos, Siamak Shakeri, Emanuel Taropa, Paige Bailey, Zhifeng Chen, Eric Chu, Jonathan H. Clark, Laurent El Shafey, Yanping Huang, Kathy Meier-Hellstern, Gaurav Mishra, Erica Moreira, Mark Omernick, Kevin Robinson, Sebastian Ruder, Yi Tay, Kefan Xiao, Yuanzhong Xu, Yujing Zhang, Gustavo Hernández Ábrego, Junwhan Ahn, Jacob Austin, Paul Barham, Jan A. Botha, James Bradbury, Siddhartha Brahma, Kevin Brooks, Michele Catasta, Yong Cheng, Colin Cherry, Christopher A. Choquette-Choo, Aakanksha Chowdhery, Clément Crepy, Shachi Dave, Mostafa Dehghani, Sunipa Dev, Jacob Devlin, Mark Díaz, Nan Du, Ethan Dyer, Vladimir Feinberg, Fangxiaoyu Feng, Vlad Fienber, Markus Freitag, Xavier Garcia, Sebastian Gehrmann, Lucas Gonzalez, and et al. 2023. Palm 2 technical report. *CoRR*, abs/2305.10403.

Hangbo Bao, Li Dong, Furu Wei, Wenhui Wang, Nan Yang, Xiaodong Liu, Yu Wang, Jianfeng Gao, Songhao Piao, Ming Zhou, and Hsiao-Wuen Hon. 2020. Unilmv2: Pseudo-masked language models for unified language model pre-training. In *Proceedings of the 37th International Conference on Machine Learning, ICML 2020, 13-18 July 2020, Virtual Event*, volume 119 of *Proceedings of Machine Learning Research*, pages 642–652. PMLR.

Mohammad Bavarian, Heewoo Jun, Nikolas Tezak, John Schulman, Christine McLeavey, Jerry Tworek, and Mark Chen. 2022. Efficient training of language models to fill in the middle. *CoRR*, abs/2207.14255.

Iz Beltagy, Matthew E. Peters, and Arman Cohan. 2020. Longformer: The long-document transformer. *CoRR*, abs/2004.05150.

Tom B. Brown, Benjamin Mann, Nick Ryder, Melanie Subbiah, Jared Kaplan, Prafulla Dhariwal, Arvind Neelakantan, Pranav Shyam, Girish Sastry, Amanda Askell, Sandhini Agarwal, Ariel Herbert-Voss, Gretchen Krueger, Tom Henighan, Rewon Child, Aditya Ramesh, Daniel M. Ziegler, Jeffrey Wu, Clemens Winter, Christopher Hesse, Mark Chen, Eric Sigler, Mateusz Litwin, Scott Gray, Benjamin Chess, Jack Clark, Christopher Berner, Sam McCandlish, Alec Radford, Ilya Sutskever, and Dario Amodei. 2020. Language models are few-shot learners. *CoRR*, abs/2005.14165.

Mark Chen, Jerry Tworek, Heewoo Jun, Qiming Yuan, Henrique Pondé de Oliveira Pinto, Jared Kaplan, Harrison Edwards, Yuri Burda, Nicholas Joseph, Greg Brockman, Alex Ray, Raul Puri, Gretchen Krueger, Michael Petrov, Heidy Khlaaf, Girish Sastry, Pamela Mishkin, Brooke Chan, Scott Gray, Nick Ryder, Mikhail Pavlov, Alethea Power, Lukasz Kaiser, Mohammad Bavarian, Clemens Winter, Philippe Tillet, Felipe Petroski Such, Dave Cummings, Matthias Plappert, Fotios Chantzis, Elizabeth Barnes, Ariel Herbert-Voss, William Hebgen Guss, Alex Nichol, Alex Paino, Nikolas Tezak, Jie Tang, Igor Babuschkin, Suchir Balaji, Shantanu Jain, William Saunders, Christopher Hesse, Andrew N. Carr, Jan Leike, Joshua Achiam, Vedant Misra, Evan Morikawa, Alec Radford, Matthew Knight, Miles Brundage, Mira Murati, Katie Mayer, Peter Welinder, Bob McGrew, Dario Amodei, Sam McCandlish, Ilya Sutskever, and Wojciech Zaremba. 2021. Evaluating large language models trained on code. *CoRR*, abs/2107.03374.

Aakanksha Chowdhery, Sharan Narang, Jacob Devlin, Maarten Bosma, Gaurav Mishra, Adam Roberts, Paul Barham, Hyung Won Chung, Charles Sutton, Sebastian Gehrmann, Parker Schuh, Kensen Shi, Sasha Tsvyashchenko, Joshua Maynez, Abhishek Rao, Parker Barnes, Yi Tay, Noam Shazeer, Vinodkumar Prabhakaran, Emily Reif, Nan Du, Ben Hutchinson, Reiner Pope, James Bradbury, Jacob Austin, Michael Isard, Guy Gur-Ari, Pengcheng Yin, Toju Duke, Anselm Levskaya, Sanjay Ghemawat, Sunipa Dev, Henryk Michalewski, Xavier Garcia, Vedant Misra, Kevin Robinson, Liam Fedus, Denny Zhou, Daphne Ippolito, David Luan, Hyeontaek Lim, Barret Zoph, Alexander Spiridonov, Ryan Sepassi, David Dohan, Shivani Agrawal, Mark Omernick, Andrew M. Dai, Thanumalayan Sankaranarayana Pillai, Marie Pellat, Aitor Lewkowycz, Erica Moreira, Rewon Child, Oleksandr Polozov, Katherine Lee, Zongwei Zhou, Xuezhi Wang, Brennan Saeta, Mark Diaz, Orhan Firat, Michele Catasta, Jason Wei, Kathy Meier-Hellstern, Douglas Eck, Jeff Dean, Slav Petrov, and Noah Fiedel. 2022. Palm: Scaling language modeling with pathways. *CoRR*, abs/2204.02311.

Together Computer. 2023. Redpajama: An open source recipe to reproduce llama training dataset.

第二十二届中国计算语言学大会论文集，第1页-第15页，哈尔滨，中国，2023年8月3日至5日。
卷2：前沿综述

Tri Dao, Daniel Y. Fu, Khaled K. Saab, Armin W. Thomas, Atri Rudra, and Christopher Ré. 2023. Hungry Hungry Hippos: Towards language modeling with state space models. In *International Conference on Learning Representations.*

Jacob Devlin, Ming-Wei Chang, Kenton Lee, and Kristina Toutanova. 2019. BERT: pre-training of deep bidirectional transformers for language understanding. In Jill Burstein, Christy Doran, and Thamar Solorio, editors, *Proceedings of the 2019 Conference of the North American Chapter of the Association for Computational Linguistics: Human Language Technologies, NAACL-HLT 2019, Minneapolis, MN, USA, June 2-7, 2019, Volume 1 (Long and Short Papers)*, pages 4171–4186. Association for Computational Linguistics.

Yao Fu, Hao Peng, and Tushar Khot. 2022. How does gpt obtain its ability? tracing emergent abilities of language models to their sources. *Yao Fu's Notion.*

Leo Gao, Stella Biderman, Sid Black, Laurence Golding, Travis Hoppe, Charles Foster, Jason Phang, Horace He, Anish Thite, Noa Nabeshima, Shawn Presser, and Connor Leahy. 2021. The pile: An 800gb dataset of diverse text for language modeling. *CoRR*, abs/2101.00027.

Xinyang Geng and Hao Liu. 2023. Openllama: An open reproduction of llama, May.

Albert Gu, Karan Goel, and Christopher Ré. 2022. Efficiently modeling long sequences with structured state spaces. In *The Tenth International Conference on Learning Representations, ICLR 2022, Virtual Event, April 25-29, 2022*. OpenReview.net.

Arnav Gudibande, Eric Wallace, Charlie Snell, Xinyang Geng, Hao Liu, Pieter Abbeel, Sergey Levine, and Dawn Song. 2023. The false promise of imitating proprietary llms. *CoRR*, abs/2305.15717.

Suriya Gunasekar, Yi Zhang, Jyoti Aneja, Caio César Teodoro Mendes, Allie Del Giorno, Sivakanth Gopi, Mojan Javaheripi, Piero Kauffmann, Gustavo de Rosa, Olli Saarikivi, Adil Salim, Shital Shah, Harkirat Singh Behl, Xin Wang, Sébastien Bubeck, Ronen Eldan, Adam Tauman Kalai, Yin Tat Lee, and Yuanzhi Li. 2023. Textbooks are all you need. *CoRR*, abs/2306.11644.

Danny Hernandez, Tom B. Brown, Tom Conerly, Nova DasSarma, Dawn Drain, Sheer El Showk, Nelson Elhage, Zac Hatfield-Dodds, Tom Henighan, Tristan Hume, Scott Johnston, Benjamin Mann, Chris Olah, Catherine Olsson, Dario Amodei, Nicholas Joseph, Jared Kaplan, and Sam McCandlish. 2022. Scaling laws and interpretability of learning from repeated data. *CoRR*, abs/2205.10487.

Jordan Hoffmann, Sebastian Borgeaud, Arthur Mensch, Elena Buchatskaya, Trevor Cai, Eliza Rutherford, Diego de Las Casas, Lisa Anne Hendricks, Johannes Welbl, Aidan Clark, Tom Hennigan, Eric Noland, Katie Millican, George van den Driessche, Bogdan Damoc, Aurelia Guy, Simon Osindero, Karen Simonyan, Erich Elsen, Jack W. Rae, Oriol Vinyals, and Laurent Sifre. 2022. Training compute-optimal large language models. *CoRR*, abs/2203.15556.

Jared Kaplan, Sam McCandlish, Tom Henighan, Tom B. Brown, Benjamin Chess, Rewon Child, Scott Gray, Alec Radford, Jeffrey Wu, and Dario Amodei. 2020. Scaling laws for neural language models. *CoRR*, abs/2001.08361.

Denis Kocetkov, Raymond Li, Loubna Ben Allal, Jia Li, Chenghao Mou, Carlos Muñoz Ferrandis, Yacine Jernite, Margaret Mitchell, Sean Hughes, Thomas Wolf, Dzmitry Bahdanau, Leandro von Werra, and Harm de Vries. 2022. The stack: 3 TB of permissively licensed source code. *CoRR*, abs/2211.15533.

Katherine Lee, Daphne Ippolito, Andrew Nystrom, Chiyuan Zhang, Douglas Eck, Chris Callison-Burch, and Nicholas Carlini. 2022. Deduplicating training data makes language models better. In Smaranda Muresan, Preslav Nakov, and Aline Villavicencio, editors, *Proceedings of the 60th Annual Meeting of the Association for Computational Linguistics (Volume 1: Long Papers), ACL 2022, Dublin, Ireland, May 22-27, 2022*, pages 8424–8445. Association for Computational Linguistics.

Raymond Li, Loubna Ben Allal, Yangtian Zi, Niklas Muennighoff, Denis Kocetkov, Chenghao Mou, Marc Marone, Christopher Akiki, Jia Li, Jenny Chim, Qian Liu, Evgenii Zheltonozhskii, Terry Yue Zhuo, Thomas Wang, Olivier Dehaene, Mishig Davaadorj, Joel Lamy-Poirier, João Monteiro, Oleh Shliazhko, Nicolas Gontier, Nicholas Meade, Armel Zebaze, Ming-Ho Yee, Logesh Kumar Umapathi, Jian Zhu, Benjamin Lipkin, Muhtasham Oblokulov, Zhiruo Wang, Rudra Murthy V, Jason Stillerman, Siva Sankalp Patel, Dmitry Abulkhanov, Marco Zocca, Manan Dey, Zhihan Zhang, Nour Moustafa-Fahmy, Urvashi Bhattacharyya, Wenhao Yu, Swayam Singh, Sasha Luccioni, Paulo Villegas, Maxim Kunakov, Fedor Zhdanov, Manuel Romero, Tony Lee, Nadav Timor, Jennifer Ding,

Claire Schlesinger, Hailey Schoelkopf, Jan Ebert, Tri Dao, Mayank Mishra, Alex Gu, Jennifer Robinson, Carolyn Jane Anderson, Brendan Dolan-Gavitt, Danish Contractor, Siva Reddy, Daniel Fried, Dzmitry Bahdanau, Yacine Jernite, Carlos Muñoz Ferrandis, Sean Hughes, Thomas Wolf, Arjun Guha, Leandro von Werra, and Harm de Vries. 2023. Starcoder: may the source be with you! *CoRR*, abs/2305.06161.

Yinhan Liu, Myle Ott, Naman Goyal, Jingfei Du, Mandar Joshi, Danqi Chen, Omer Levy, Mike Lewis, Luke Zettlemoyer, and Veselin Stoyanov. 2019. Roberta: A robustly optimized BERT pretraining approach. *CoRR*, abs/1907.11692.

Shayne Longpre, Gregory Yauney, Emily Reif, Katherine Lee, Adam Roberts, Barret Zoph, Denny Zhou, Jason Wei, Kevin Robinson, David Mimno, and Daphne Ippolito. 2023. A pretrainer's guide to training data: Measuring the effects of data age, domain coverage, quality, & toxicity. *CoRR*, abs/2305.13169.

Niklas Muennighoff, Alexander M. Rush, Boaz Barak, Teven Le Scao, Aleksandra Piktus, Nouamane Tazi, Sampo Pyysalo, Thomas Wolf, and Colin Raffel. 2023. Scaling data-constrained language models. *CoRR*, abs/2305.16264.

Erik Nijkamp, Hiroaki Hayashi, Caiming Xiong, Silvio Savarese, and Yingbo Zhou. 2023a. Codegen2: Lessons for training llms on programming and natural languages. *CoRR*, abs/2305.02309.

Erik Nijkamp, Bo Pang, Hiroaki Hayashi, Lifu Tu, Huan Wang, Yingbo Zhou, Silvio Savarese, and Caiming Xiong. 2023b. Codegen: An open large language model for code with multi-turn program synthesis. In *The Eleventh International Conference on Learning Representations, ICLR 2023, Kigali, Rwanda, May 1-5, 2023*. OpenReview.net.

Long Ouyang, Jeffrey Wu, Xu Jiang, Diogo Almeida, Carroll L. Wainwright, Pamela Mishkin, Chong Zhang, Sandhini Agarwal, Katarina Slama, Alex Ray, John Schulman, Jacob Hilton, Fraser Kelton, Luke Miller, Maddie Simens, Amanda Askell, Peter Welinder, Paul F. Christiano, Jan Leike, and Ryan Lowe. 2022. Training language models to follow instructions with human feedback. In *NeurIPS*.

Guilherme Penedo, Quentin Malartic, Daniel Hesslow, Ruxandra Cojocaru, Alessandro Cappelli, Hamza Alobeidli, Baptiste Pannier, Ebtesam Almazrouei, and Julien Launay. 2023. The refinedweb dataset for falcon LLM: outperforming curated corpora with web data, and web data only. *CoRR*, abs/2306.01116.

Bo Peng, Eric Alcaide, Quentin Anthony, Alon Albalak, Samuel Arcadinho, Huanqi Cao, Xin Cheng, Michael Chung, Matteo Grella, Kranthi Kiran G. V., Xuzheng He, Haowen Hou, Przemyslaw Kazienko, Jan Kocon, Jiaming Kong, Bartlomiej Koptyra, Hayden Lau, Krishna Sri Ipsit Mantri, Ferdinand Mom, Atsushi Saito, Xiangru Tang, Bolun Wang, Johan S. Wind, Stanislaw Wozniak, Ruichong Zhang, Zhenyuan Zhang, Qihang Zhao, Peng Zhou, Jian Zhu, and Rui-Jie Zhu. 2023. RWKV: reinventing rnns for the transformer era. *CoRR*, abs/2305.13048.

Ofir Press, Noah A. Smith, and Mike Lewis. 2022. Train short, test long: Attention with linear biases enables input length extrapolation. In *The Tenth International Conference on Learning Representations, ICLR 2022, Virtual Event, April 25-29, 2022*. OpenReview.net.

Alec Radford, Jeff Wu, Rewon Child, David Luan, Dario Amodei, and Ilya Sutskever. 2019. Language models are unsupervised multitask learners.

Jack W. Rae, Sebastian Borgeaud, Trevor Cai, Katie Millican, Jordan Hoffmann, H. Francis Song, John Aslanides, Sarah Henderson, Roman Ring, Susannah Young, Eliza Rutherford, Tom Hennigan, Jacob Menick, Albin Cassirer, Richard Powell, George van den Driessche, Lisa Anne Hendricks, Maribeth Rauh, Po-Sen Huang, Amelia Glaese, Johannes Welbl, Sumanth Dathathri, Saffron Huang, Jonathan Uesato, John Mellor, Irina Higgins, Antonia Creswell, Nat McAleese, Amy Wu, Erich Elsen, Siddhant M. Jayakumar, Elena Buchatskaya, David Budden, Esme Sutherland, Karen Simonyan, Michela Paganini, Laurent Sifre, Lena Martens, Xiang Lorraine Li, Adhiguna Kuncoro, Aida Nematzadeh, Elena Gribovskaya, Domenic Donato, Angeliki Lazaridou, Arthur Mensch, Jean-Baptiste Lespiau, Maria Tsimpoukelli, Nikolai Grigorev, Doug Fritz, Thibault Sottiaux, Mantas Pajarskas, Toby Pohlen, Zhitao Gong, Daniel Toyama, Cyprien de Masson d'Autume, Yujia Li, Tayfun Terzi, Vladimir Mikulik, Igor Babuschkin, Aidan Clark, Diego de Las Casas, Aurelia Guy, Chris Jones, James Bradbury, Matthew J. Johnson, Blake A. Hechtman, Laura Weidinger, Iason Gabriel, William Isaac, Edward Lockhart, Simon Osindero, Laura Rimell, Chris Dyer, Oriol Vinyals, Kareem Ayoub, Jeff Stanway, Lorrayne Bennett, Demis Hassabis, Koray Kavukcuoglu, and Geoffrey

第二十二届中国计算语言学大会论文集，第1页-第15页，哈尔滨，中国，2023年8月3日至5日。
卷2：前沿综述

Irving. 2021. Scaling language models: Methods, analysis & insights from training gopher. *CoRR*, abs/2112.11446.

Colin Raffel, Noam Shazeer, Adam Roberts, Katherine Lee, Sharan Narang, Michael Matena, Yanqi Zhou, Wei Li, and Peter J. Liu. 2020. Exploring the limits of transfer learning with a unified text-to-text transformer. *J. Mach. Learn. Res.*, 21:140:1–140:67.

Teven Le Scao, Angela Fan, Christopher Akiki, Ellie Pavlick, Suzana Ilic, Daniel Hesslow, Roman Castagné, Alexandra Sasha Luccioni, François Yvon, Matthias Gallé, Jonathan Tow, Alexander M. Rush, Stella Biderman, Albert Webson, Pawan Sasanka Ammanamanchi, Thomas Wang, Benoît Sagot, Niklas Muennighoff, Albert Villanova del Moral, Olatunji Ruwase, Rachel Bawden, Stas Bekman, Angelina McMillan-Major, Iz Beltagy, Huu Nguyen, Lucile Saulnier, Samson Tan, Pedro Ortiz Suarez, Victor Sanh, Hugo Laurençon, Yacine Jernite, Julien Launay, Margaret Mitchell, Colin Raffel, Aaron Gokaslan, Adi Simhi, Aitor Soroa, Alham Fikri Aji, Amit Alfassy, Anna Rogers, Ariel Kreisberg Nitzav, Canwen Xu, Chenghao Mou, Chris Emezue, Christopher Klamm, Colin Leong, Daniel van Strien, David Ifeoluwa Adelani, and et al. 2022. BLOOM: A 176b-parameter open-access multilingual language model. *CoRR*, abs/2211.05100.

Peter Shaw, Jakob Uszkoreit, and Ashish Vaswani. 2018. Self-attention with relative position representations. In Marilyn A. Walker, Heng Ji, and Amanda Stent, editors, *Proceedings of the 2018 Conference of the North American Chapter of the Association for Computational Linguistics: Human Language Technologies, NAACL-HLT, New Orleans, Louisiana, USA, June 1-6, 2018, Volume 2 (Short Papers)*, pages 464–468. Association for Computational Linguistics.

Daria Soboleva, Faisal Al-Khateeb, Robert Myers, Jacob R Steeves, Joel Hestness, and Nolan Dey. 2023. SlimPajama: A 627B token cleaned and deduplicated version of RedPajama. `https://www.cerebras.net/blog/slimpajama-a-627b-token-cleaned-and-deduplicated-version-of-redpajama`.

Jianlin Su, Yu Lu, Shengfeng Pan, Bo Wen, and Yunfeng Liu. 2021. Roformer: Enhanced transformer with rotary position embedding. *CoRR*, abs/2104.09864.

Tianxiang Sun, Xiaotian Zhang, Zhengfu He, Peng Li, Qinyuan Cheng, Hang Yan, Xiangyang Liu, Yunfan Shao, Qiong Tang, Xingjian Zhao, Ke Chen, Yining Zheng, Zhejian Zhou, Ruixiao Li, Jun Zhan, Yunhua Zhou, Linyang Li, Xiaogui Yang, Lingling Wu, Zhangyue Yin, Xuanjing Huang, and Xipeng Qiu. 2023. Moss: Training conversational language models from synthetic data.

Rohan Taori, Ishaan Gulrajani, Tianyi Zhang, Yann Dubois, Xuechen Li, Carlos Guestrin, Percy Liang, and Tatsunori B. Hashimoto. 2023. Stanford alpaca: An instruction-following llama model. `https://github.com/tatsu-lab/stanford_alpaca`.

Yi Tay, Jason Wei, Hyung Won Chung, Vinh Q. Tran, David R. So, Siamak Shakeri, Xavier Garcia, Huaixiu Steven Zheng, Jinfeng Rao, Aakanksha Chowdhery, Denny Zhou, Donald Metzler, Slav Petrov, Neil Houlsby, Quoc V. Le, and Mostafa Dehghani. 2022. Transcending scaling laws with 0.1% extra compute. *CoRR*, abs/2210.11399.

Yi Tay, Mostafa Dehghani, Dara Bahri, and Donald Metzler. 2023a. Efficient transformers: A survey. *ACM Comput. Surv.*, 55(6):109:1–109:28.

Yi Tay, Mostafa Dehghani, Vinh Q. Tran, Xavier Garcia, Jason Wei, Xuezhi Wang, Hyung Won Chung, Dara Bahri, Tal Schuster, Huaixiu Steven Zheng, Denny Zhou, Neil Houlsby, and Donald Metzler. 2023b. UL2: unifying language learning paradigms. In *The Eleventh International Conference on Learning Representations, ICLR 2023, Kigali, Rwanda, May 1-5, 2023*. OpenReview.net.

MosaicML NLP Team. 2023. Introducing mpt-7b: A new standard for open-source, commercially usable llms. Accessed: 2023-05-05.

Hugo Touvron, Thibaut Lavril, Gautier Izacard, Xavier Martinet, Marie-Anne Lachaux, Timothée Lacroix, Baptiste Rozière, Naman Goyal, Eric Hambro, Faisal Azhar, Aurélien Rodriguez, Armand Joulin, Edouard Grave, and Guillaume Lample. 2023. Llama: Open and efficient foundation language models. *CoRR*, abs/2302.13971.

Ashish Vaswani, Noam Shazeer, Niki Parmar, Jakob Uszkoreit, Llion Jones, Aidan N. Gomez, Lukasz Kaiser, and Illia Polosukhin. 2017. Attention is all you need. In Isabelle Guyon, Ulrike von Luxburg, Samy Bengio, Hanna M. Wallach, Rob Fergus, S. V. N. Vishwanathan, and Roman Garnett, editors, *Advances in Neural Information Processing Systems 30: Annual Conference on Neural Information Processing Systems 2017, December 4-9, 2017, Long Beach, CA, USA*, pages 5998–6008.

第二十二届中国计算语言学大会论文集，第1页-第15页，哈尔滨，中国，2023年8月3日至5日。
卷2：前沿综述

Yu-An Wang and Yun-Nung Chen. 2020. What do position embeddings learn? an empirical study of pre-trained language model positional encoding. In Bonnie Webber, Trevor Cohn, Yulan He, and Yang Liu, editors, *Proceedings of the 2020 Conference on Empirical Methods in Natural Language Processing, EMNLP 2020, Online, November 16-20, 2020*, pages 6840–6849. Association for Computational Linguistics.

Sinong Wang, Belinda Z. Li, Madian Khabsa, Han Fang, and Hao Ma. 2020. Linformer: Self-attention with linear complexity. *CoRR*, abs/2006.04768.

Guillaume Wenzek, Marie-Anne Lachaux, Alexis Conneau, Vishrav Chaudhary, Francisco Guzmán, Armand Joulin, and Edouard Grave. 2020. Ccnet: Extracting high quality monolingual datasets from web crawl data. In Nicoletta Calzolari, Frédéric Béchet, Philippe Blache, Khalid Choukri, Christopher Cieri, Thierry Declerck, Sara Goggi, Hitoshi Isahara, Bente Maegaard, Joseph Mariani, Hélène Mazo, Asunción Moreno, Jan Odijk, and Stelios Piperidis, editors, *Proceedings of The 12th Language Resources and Evaluation Conference, LREC 2020, Marseille, France, May 11-16, 2020*, pages 4003–4012. European Language Resources Association.

Shaohua Wu, Xudong Zhao, Tong Yu, Rongguo Zhang, Chong Shen, Hongli Liu, Feng Li, Hong Zhu, Jiangang Luo, Liang Xu, and Xuanwei Zhang. 2021. Yuan 1.0: Large-scale pre-trained language model in zero-shot and few-shot learning. *CoRR*, abs/2110.04725.

Sha Yuan, Hanyu Zhao, Zhengxiao Du, Ming Ding, Xiao Liu, Yukuo Cen, Xu Zou, Zhilin Yang, and Jie Tang. 2021. Wudaocorpora: A super large-scale chinese corpora for pre-training language models. *AI Open*, 2:65–68.

Aohan Zeng, Xiao Liu, Zhengxiao Du, Zihan Wang, Hanyu Lai, Ming Ding, Zhuoyi Yang, Yifan Xu, Wendi Zheng, Xiao Xia, Weng Lam Tam, Zixuan Ma, Yufei Xue, Jidong Zhai, Wenguang Chen, Zhiyuan Liu, Peng Zhang, Yuxiao Dong, and Jie Tang. 2023. GLM-130B: an open bilingual pre-trained model. In *The Eleventh International Conference on Learning Representations, ICLR 2023, Kigali, Rwanda, May 1-5, 2023*. OpenReview.net.

Biao Zhang and Rico Sennrich. 2019. Root mean square layer normalization. In Hanna M. Wallach, Hugo Larochelle, Alina Beygelzimer, Florence d'Alché-Buc, Emily B. Fox, and Roman Garnett, editors, *Advances in Neural Information Processing Systems 32: Annual Conference on Neural Information Processing Systems 2019, NeurIPS 2019, December 8-14, 2019, Vancouver, BC, Canada*, pages 12360–12371.

Susan Zhang, Stephen Roller, Naman Goyal, Mikel Artetxe, Moya Chen, Shuohui Chen, Christopher Dewan, Mona T. Diab, Xian Li, Xi Victoria Lin, Todor Mihaylov, Myle Ott, Sam Shleifer, Kurt Shuster, Daniel Simig, Punit Singh Koura, Anjali Sridhar, Tianlu Wang, and Luke Zettlemoyer. 2022. OPT: open pre-trained transformer language models. *CoRR*, abs/2205.01068.

Wayne Xin Zhao, Kun Zhou, Junyi Li, Tianyi Tang, Xiaolei Wang, Yupeng Hou, Yingqian Min, Beichen Zhang, Junjie Zhang, Zican Dong, Yifan Du, Chen Yang, Yushuo Chen, Zhipeng Chen, Jinhao Jiang, Ruiyang Ren, Yifan Li, Xinyu Tang, Zikang Liu, Peiyu Liu, Jian-Yun Nie, and Ji-Rong Wen. 2023. A survey of large language models. *CoRR*, abs/2303.18223.

第二十二届中国计算语言学大会论文集，第1页-第15页，哈尔滨，中国，2023年8月3日至5日。
卷2：前沿综述

Unleashing the Power of Large Models:
Exploring Human-Machine Conversations

Yuhan Liu[1], **Xiuying Chen**[2], **Rui Yan**[1*]
[1]Gaoling School of Artifical Intelligence, Renmin University of China, Beijing, China
[2]King Abdullah University of Science and Technology, Thuwal, Saudi Arabia
yuhan.liu@ruc.edu.cn, xiuying.chen@kaust.edu.sa, ruiyan@ruc.edu.cn

Abstract

In recent years, large language models (LLMs) have garnered significant attention across various domains, resulting in profound impacts. In this paper, we aim to explore the potential of LLMs in the field of human-machine conversations. It begins by examining the rise and milestones of these models, tracing their origins from neural language models to the transformative impact of the Transformer architecture on conversation processing. Next, we discuss the emergence of large pre-training models and their utilization of contextual knowledge at a large scale, as well as the scaling to billion-parameter models that push the boundaries of language generation. We further highlight advancements in multi-modal conversations, showcasing how LLMs bridge the gap between language and vision. We also introduce various applications in human-machine conversations, such as intelligent assistant-style dialogues and emotionally supportive conversations, supported by successful case studies in diverse fields. Lastly, we explore the challenges faced by LLMs in this context and provide insights into future development directions and prospects. Overall, we offer a comprehensive overview of the potential and future development of LLMs in human-machine conversations, encompassing their milestones, applications, and the challenges ahead.

1 Introduction

In recent years, there has been a remarkable surge in the interest and impact of LLMs across diverse domains (Rodriguez, 2022; Khan et al., 2023). These models have revolutionized various fields, and the ability of LLMs to generate coherent and contextually relevant responses has opened up new possibilities for human-machine interaction (OpenAI, 2023). Within this expansive landscape, the realm of human-machine conversations has emerged as a particularly dynamic and rapidly evolving domain. The ability to engage in natural and meaningful dialogue with machines has long been a goal of AI research, and big models have played a pivotal role in making this aspiration a reality.

LLMs are sophisticated artificial intelligence systems that have the ability to process and understand human language at a remarkable scale. These models, such as GPT-3.5(Lin, 2023) and GPT-4 (OpenAI, 2023), are designed to generate text that is coherent and contextually relevant, making them valuable tools for a wide range of applications. In the context of human-machine conversations, LLMs excel at engaging in a natural and interactive dialogue with users. They can comprehend and respond to questions, provide information, offer suggestions, and even simulate human-like conversations. These models leverage vast amounts of pre-existing textual data to learn patterns and generate responses that mimic human conversation, enabling them to understand user input, adapt to different conversational styles, and provide meaningful and coherent answers. The characteristics of LLMs, including their immense size, computational power, and training on diverse datasets, contribute to their ability to generate accurate and contextually appropriate responses, making them valuable assets in enhancing human-machine interactions.

† Corresponding author.

Proceedings of the 22nd China National Conference on Computational Linguistics, pages 16-29, Harbin, China, August 3 - 5, 2023.
Volume 2: Frotier Forum
(c) Technical Committee on Computational Linguistics, Chinese Information Processing Society of China

To comprehend the significance of big models in human-machine conversations, it is essential to understand their background and evolution. We provide a diagram to help readers familiarize the overall structure (Figure 1). Section 2 gives a comprehensive overview of the development and milestones of LLMs, tracing their origins from neural language models to the transformative impact of the Transformer architecture on conversation processing. The rise of large pre-training models and their utilization of contextual knowledge at an unprecedented scale will also be explored. Furthermore, this section discusses the scaling to billion-parameter models, pushing the boundaries of language generation and paving the way for more advanced conversational capabilities. One key aspect that will be addressed is the advancement of LLMs in facilitating multi-modal conversations, bridging the gap between language and vision understanding. This opens up opportunities for more natural and immersive interactions between humans and machines. Section 3 focuses on two prominent areas: intelligent assistant-style dialogues and emotionally supportive conversations. Through successful case studies, we demonstrate how LLMs can assist users in various tasks and provide emotional support in sensitive contexts. Despite the promising potential, LLMs face challenges in the context of human-machine conversations as mentioned in Section 4. Ethical concerns, biases, and the need for interpretability are some of the key challenges that need to be addressed to ensure the responsible deployment of these models. Lastly, Section 5 highlights the future directions of development.

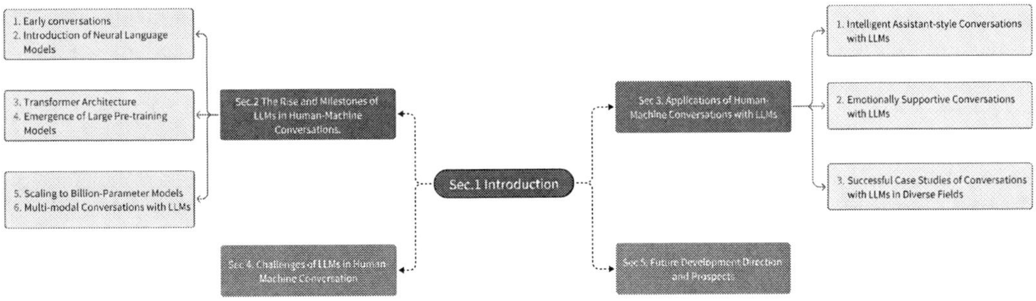

Figure 1: The overall diagram of this article

2 The Rise and Milestones of LLMs in Human-Machine Conversations

2.1 Early Conversations: Tracing the Roots of Conversational AI

Early conversations, such as ELIZA (Weizenbaum, 1966) and ALICE(Marietto et al., 2013), were pioneers in the field of human-machine conversations. However, these early systems had limitations. They could not truly understand the meaning of the user's input and relied heavily on pre-defined rules and patterns. Consequently, these systems often provided generic and impersonal responses.

Despite their shortcomings, early conversations paved the way for advancements in natural language processing and machine learning techniques. Researchers realized the need for more sophisticated models that could learn from data and context, leading to the development of modern LLMs like GPT-3.5.

2.2 Neural Language Models: Opening the Doors to Language Understanding

Neural Language Models (NLMs) have revolutionized the field of human-machine conversations, enabling more dynamic and contextually aware conversations, which leverage deep learning techniques, such as recurrent neural networks (RNNs), to process and understand human language (Sutskever et al., 2014). By training on large-scale datasets, these models learn the statistical patterns and semantic relationships within the language, allowing them to generate more natural and contextually relevant responses. The integration of NLMs into human-machine conversations has significantly improved the quality and naturalness of conversations. These models can consider the context of the conversation, understand nuances, and generate coherent and contextually appropriate responses. Furthermore, they

Proceedings of the 22nd China National Conference on Computational Linguistics, pages 16-29, Harbin, China, August 3 - 5, 2023.
Volume 2: Frotier Forum

can also exhibit a sense of personality, empathy, and adaptability, which enhances user engagement and satisfaction.

While there are still challenges to overcome, such as handling ambiguous queries and maintaining privacy, NLM-based conversations have become invaluable tools for various applications in natural language understanding and interaction. Their ability to generate human-like responses and engage in meaningful conversations opens up new possibilities for human-machine conversations.

2.3 Transformer Architecture: Revolutionizing Conversation Processing

The Transformer (Vaswani et al., 2017) architecture has emerged as a breakthrough in the field of artificial intelligence, particularly in the realm of human-machine conversations. The Transformer model revolutionized the way neural networks process and generate human language. Unlike earlier recurrent neural networks (RNNs) that relied on sequential processing (Sutskever et al., 2014), the Transformer introduced a novel attention mechanism that allowed for parallel processing of words in a sentence. In addition, this architectural innovation overcame the limitations of sequential models, enabling the Transformer to capture long-range dependencies and contextual relationships more effectively. In the context of human-machine conversations, the Transformer architecture has proven highly effective. It excels at understanding and generating coherent responses, exhibiting a level of contextual awareness that makes conversations feel more natural and engaging. Furthermore, the Transformer's architecture allows for parallel processing, making it highly efficient for large-scale training and inference. This scalability has played a pivotal role in training LLMs, such as GPT-3.5, which have pushed the boundaries of human-machine conversations by generating human-like responses across a wide range of topics.

The transformer has significantly improved the quality and coherence of responses, allowing dialogue models to engage in more interactive and contextually aware conversations. With its scalability and versatility, the Transformer architecture continues to drive advancements in natural language understanding and conversational AI systems.

2.4 Emergence of Large Pre-training Models: Harnessing Contextual Knowledge at Scale

Large pre-training models have emerged as game-changer in the field of artificial intelligence, particularly in the domain of human-machine conversations. In the context of human-machine conversations, large pre-training models have shown tremendous potential, which possesses the ability to engage in natural and interactive dialogues with users, simulating human-like conversations.

Model	Publishing Agency	#Parameters	Architecture
BERT (Devlin et al., 2019)	Google AI	110M/340M	Encoder
RoBERTa (Liu et al., 2019)	Facebook	123M/354M	
SpanBERT (Joshi et al., 2020)	Stanford	110M/340M	
ERNIE (Sun et al., 2019)	Baidu	110M	
ERNIE-2.0 (Sun et al., 2020)	Baidu	110M/340M	
ALBERT (Lan et al., 2020)	Google	12M-235M	
DistilBERT (Sanh et al., 2019)	Hugging Face	66M	
ELECTRA (Clark et al., 2020)	Google	14M/110M	
SqueezeBERT (Iandola et al., 2020)	Hugging Face	62M	
GPT (Radford et al., 2018)	OpenAI	117M	Decoder
XLNet (Yang et al., 2019)	CMU & Google	110M/340M	Encoder/Decoder
UniLM (Dong et al., 2019)	Microsoft	340M	
BART (Lewis et al., 2020)	Facebook	140M,406M	Encoder-Decoder
PEGASUS (Zhang et al., 2020)	Google	223M,568M	

Table 1: Overview of Large Pre-training Models

In large pre-training models, as shown in Table 1, we can categorize them into three types based

Proceedings of the 22nd China National Conference on Computational Linguistics, pages 16-29, Harbin, China, August 3 - 5, 2023.
Volume 2: Frotier Forum

on their model architectures: Encoder-Only, Encoder-Decoder, and Decoder-Only. The Encoder-Only models primarily focus on encoding input data, which transforms textual or other forms of input data into semantic vector representations, where the encoder is responsible for encoding the input information into high-dimensional representations. The Encoder-Decoders model combines the functionalities of both an encoder and a decoder. The encoder encodes the input data into high-dimensional vector representations, while the decoder generates output based on the semantic information provided by the encoder. The Decoder-Only model specializes in generating task-related outputs. This model generates appropriate output sequences by utilizing a decoder based on given conditions or context.

- **Encoder-Only**: BERT (Bidirectional Encoder Representations from Transformers) (Devlin et al., 2019) pioneered this trend by leveraging Transformer-based pre-training and utilizing masked language model (MLM) to generate deep bidirectional language representations for comprehensive contextual understanding. Subsequently, RoBERTa (Liu et al., 2019) improved upon BERT by enlarging the dataset, increasing model parameters and batch size, as well as removing the next sentence prediction (NSP) task, leading to enhanced performance through improved text encoding and dynamic masking. SpanBERT (Joshi et al., 2020) introduced novel pre-training objectives specifically designed to better represent the context and establish long-distance dependencies.

  In parallel, Baidu introduced two pre-training models, ERNIE (Sun et al., 2019) and ERNIE 2.0 (Sun et al., 2020), which leveraged large-scale Chinese corpora such as Baidu Baike, Baidu Search, Baidu Zhidao, along with the English Wikipedia, for pre-training. ERNIE 2.0 (Sun et al., 2020) further incorporated a continuous learning semantic understanding framework that continuously learns from massive data and knowledge using techniques like deep neural networks and multi-task learning. ALBERT (Lan et al., 2020), on the other hand, is a lightweight version of BERT that reduces model size while maintaining high performance through parameter factorization of word embeddings and cross-layer parameter sharing.

  The development of these pre-training language models is closely related to the advancements in conversation models. By better understanding context, effectively representing language, and establishing long-distance dependencies, these models provide a foundation and inspiration for conversation construction and optimization. From the lightweight model DistilBERT (Sanh et al., 2019) to the adversarial training-based ELECTRA (Clark et al., 2020) and the smaller and faster SqueezeBERT, these models have not only achieved breakthroughs in performance but also significantly reduced model size and computational costs. They have made important contributions to both academic research and practical applications in the field of human-machine conversation.

- **Encoder-Decoder**: XLNet (Yang et al., 2019), UniLM (Dong et al., 2019), BART (Lewis et al., 2020), and PEGASUS (Zhang et al., 2020) are pre-training models closely related to the development of human-machine conversation. XLNet (Yang et al., 2019) significantly improves text understanding by freely capturing contextual information through a "permutation-based training" prediction approach. UniLM (Dong et al., 2019), combining the BERT encoder structure with diverse pre-training tasks, demonstrates excellent performance across various natural language processing tasks, making it highly applicable to human-machine conversation research. BART, with its combination of bidirectional encoders and autoregressive decoders, possesses broad adaptability and efficiency, effectively addressing the generation models in conversational systems. PEGASUS (Zhang et al., 2020), utilizing the Transformer architecture and employing the Gap Sentences Generation pre-training objective, comprehends context by generating missing sentences and leverages the Fine-tuning with an Easy Data Selection method for performance enhancement. The introduction of these models has provided new insights and techniques for the development of human-machine conversations, leading to improved performance and efficiency in dialogue modeling, including enhanced contextual processing and generation capabilities.

- **Decoder-Only**: The GPT series (Radford et al., 2018), proposed by OpenAI, is a powerful pre-training language model that achieves remarkable performance in complex NLP tasks without re-

Proceedings of the 22nd China National Conference on Computational Linguistics, pages 16-29, Harbin, China, August 3 - 5, 2023.
Volume 2: Frotier Forum

quiring supervised fine-tuning. By increasing the scale of training data and the number of network parameters, the GPT series continually improves its model capacity, thus demonstrating the effectiveness of continuously enhancing model capacity and corpus size.

As a result, large pre-training models have revolutionized human-machine conversations by providing a powerful tool for generating high-quality and contextually appropriate responses.

2.5 Scaling to Billion-Parameter Models: Pushing the Limits of Language Generation

In this paper, we refer to large pre-training models with billion-parameter parameters as LLMs. Billion-parameter models represent a significant milestone in the development of LLMs and have ushered in a new era of human-machine conversations. These models are characterized by their immense size and computational power, pushing the boundaries of what was previously thought possible. It are built upon the foundations of their predecessors, such as GPT-3.5, but with significantly increased capacity. They are trained on vast amounts of textual data from diverse sources, allowing them to capture a wide range of linguistic patterns and semantic relationships. The sheer scale of these models grants them a deeper understanding of human language, resulting in more accurate and contextually appropriate responses.

In the domain of human-machine conversations, billion-parameter models have demonstrated remarkable capabilities. They can engage in natural and interactive dialogues, understand complex queries, and generate highly coherent and contextually relevant responses. These models have the potential to provide users with more personalized and tailored experiences, as they can adapt to different conversational styles and preferences.

Similar to the pre-training models mentioned in the subsection 2.4, as shown in Table 2, billion-scale language models are primarily divided into Encoder-Decoder architectures and Decoder-only architectures. Moreover, as the model size increases, the model structures tend to become more standardized.

- **Encoder-Decoder**: The large-scale language models, namely T5 (Raffel et al., 2020), ERNIE-3.0 (Sun et al., 2021), ERNIE-3.0 Titan (Wang et al., 2021), PaLM-2 (Google, 2023), and GLM-130B (Zeng et al., 2022), which adopt the Encoder-Decoder architecture, play a significant role in the human-machine conversation. Google's T5 (Raffel et al., 2020) approaches all NLP tasks as "text-to-text" problems, which grants it excellent adaptability when dealing with human-machine conversation tasks. Baidu's ERNIE-3.0 (Sun et al., 2021) and ERNIE-3.0 Titan (Wang et al., 2021) demonstrate outstanding performance in knowledge enhancement and self-supervised learning, making them particularly effective in handling knowledge-driven human-machine conversations. Google's PaLM-2 (Google, 2023), with its advanced reasoning capabilities, is especially well-suited for handling complex human-machine conversation scenarios. On the other hand, Tsinghua University's GLM-130B model (Zeng et al., 2022), as a bilingual model, is particularly suitable for addressing cross-lingual human-machine conversation tasks. The development and application of these models have greatly enhanced the capabilities of human-machine conversation in understanding, reasoning, and generating dialogue content, thereby significantly improving the performance and user experience of such systems.

- **Decoder-Only**: Large-scale pre-training models such as GPT2 (Brown et al., 2020), GPT3 (Ye et al., 2023), GPT3.5(Lin, 2023), FLAN (Wei et al., 2022), InstructionGPT (Ouyang et al., 2022), PaLM (Chowdhery et al., 2022), OPT (Zhang et al., 2022), Bloom (Scao et al., 2022), FLAN-PaLM (Chung et al., 2022), and LLaMA (Touvron et al., 2023) have played a crucial role in various domains, including human-machine conversation, natural language understanding, and generation. The GPT series models from OpenAI (Brown et al., 2020; Ye et al., 2023; Lin, 2023), along with OPT (Zhang et al., 2022) and LLaMA(Touvron et al., 2023) from Meta AI, leverage their extensive parameters and complex model structures to provide robust semantic understanding and response generation capabilities for human-machine conversation. Google's FLAN and FLAN-PaLM enhance the model's handling of unknown questions and generalization abilities in human-machine conversation through instruction fine-tuning techniques. The InstructionGPT (Ouyang et al., 2022)

Proceedings of the 22nd China National Conference on Computational Linguistics, pages 16-29, Harbin, China, August 3 - 5, 2023.
Volume 2: Frotier Forum

optimizes GPT-3 to address toxic language and misinformation issues that may arise in human-machine conversation. The PaLM (Chowdhery et al., 2022), trained by Google using large-scale datasets and a distributed training architecture, enables the handling of complex human-machine conversation tasks. Bloom (Scao et al., 2022), as an open-source model with extensive parameters that supports multiple languages, offers powerful support for multilingual human-machine conversation scenarios.

Model	Publishing Agency	#Parameters	Architecture
T5 (Raffel et al., 2020)	Google Brain	220M-11B	
ERNIE-3.0 (Sun et al., 2021)	Baidu	10B	
ERNIE-3.0 Titan (Wang et al., 2021)	Baidu	260B	Encoder-Decoder
PaLM-2 (Google, 2023)	Google	1.04B-2.7B	
GLM-130B (Zeng et al., 2022)	Zhipu.AI	100M-515M	
GPT-2 (Brown et al., 2020)		1.5B	
GPT-3 (Ye et al., 2023)	OpenAI	2.6B-200B	
GPT-3.5 (Lin, 2023)		-	
FLAN (Wei et al., 2022)	Google	137B	
InstructGPT (Ouyang et al., 2022)	OpenAI	1.3B-175B	
PaLM (Chowdhery et al., 2022)	Google	8B-540B	Decoder
OPT (Zhang et al., 2022)	Meta AI	6.7B-175B	
Bloom (Scao et al., 2022)	HuggingFace	560M-176B	
FLAN-PaLM (Chung et al., 2022)	THUNLP	250M-11B	
LLaMA (Touvron et al., 2023)	Stanford	780M-65B	

Table 2: Overview of Large Laguage Models

Nevertheless, billion-parameter models hold tremendous promise for the future of human-machine conversations. As they continue to evolve, they have the potential to revolutionize various domains, including customer support, virtual assistants, education, creative writing, and more. Their ability to generate human-like responses and engage in meaningful interactions opens up new possibilities for enhancing user experiences and pushing the boundaries of conversational artificial intelligence.

2.6 Multi-modal Conversations with LLMs: Bridging Language and Vision

Multi-modal conversation in LLMs represents an exciting frontier in the field of artificial intelligence, particularly in the context of human-machine conversations. Traditionally, language models have focused primarily on text-based interactions. However, with advancements in computer vision and multi-modal learning, there is a growing interest in incorporating visual and other modalities into conversations.

In recent years, a major focus in the field of artificial intelligence has been on multi-modal large-scale pre-training models, as shown in Table 3, which goal is to enable machines to understand and generate various modalities of human conversations, including text, images, and sound. These models have played a crucial role in making human-machine conversations more natural, rich, and intelligent. For example, the PaLM-E (Driess et al., 2023), jointly developed by Google and the TUB, is an embodied vision and language model. It is a generative model that takes multi-modal sentences as input to generate text, providing natural and coherent responses for human-machine conversations. OpenAI's CLIP (Radford et al., 2021), on the other hand, employs contrastive learning to enable machines to understand the relationship between images and text, providing a powerful tool for understanding user-provided image inputs and generating relevant descriptions.

DeepMind's Flamingo (Alayrac et al., 2022) and Google's CoCa (Yu et al., 2022) establish connections between visual and language modalities. They are capable of processing and understanding both visual and textual data, providing support for image understanding and description in human-machine conversations. The Flamingo, in particular, can handle arbitrary interleaved sequences of visual and

Proceedings of the 22nd China National Conference on Computational Linguistics, pages 16-29, Harbin, China, August 3 - 5, 2023.
Volume 2: Frotier Forum

textual data, seamlessly processing image or video inputs. Google's PaLI (Chen et al., 2022a) and Alibaba DAMO Academy's OFA (Wang et al., 2022a), both with multilingual and multi-modal capabilities, support multiple languages and understand inputs from various modalities, allowing them to adapt to different human-computer dialogue environments and requirements.

Microsoft's BEiT-3 (Wang et al., 2022b) and Salesforce Research's BLIP (Li et al., 2022) and BLIP-2 (Li et al., 2023) establish deeper connections between visual and language modalities. Through their deep understanding and generation of images and text, these models provide richer and more accurate responses. The KOSMOS-1 (Huang et al., 2023b), a multi-modal large-scale language model, has a Transformer-based causal language model as its backbone. It can integrate inputs from language, vision, and other modalities, enabling it to consider information from multiple modalities when understanding user input and generating responses.

Finally, OpenAI's GPT-4 (OpenAI, 2023) is a novel language model that has been improved in terms of creativity, visual input, and longer contexts, which allows it to generate more natural, coherent, and relevant responses. Overall, these multi-modal large-scale pre-training models have their unique advantages and characteristics, and they have all contributed to the advancement of human-machine conversations to varying degrees.

Model	Publishing Agency	#Parameters
PALM-E (Driess et al., 2023)	Google & TUB	562B
CLIP (Radford et al., 2021)	OpenAI	428M
Flamingo (Alayrac et al., 2022)	DeepMind	3B-80B
CoCa (Yu et al., 2022)	Google	383M-2.1B
PaLI (Chen et al., 2022a)	Google	3B-17B
OFA (Wang et al., 2022a)	DAMO Academy, Alibaba	33M-930M
BEiT-3 (Wang et al., 2022b)	Microsoft	1.9B
BLIP (Li et al., 2022)	Salesforce	446M
BLIP-2 (Li et al., 2023)	Salesforce	474M-1.2B
KOSMOS-1 (Huang et al., 2023b)	Microsoft	1.6B
GPT-4 (OpenAI, 2023)	OpenAI	-

Table 3: Overview of Multimodal LLMs

Multi-modal conversation in LLMs also holds promise for applications such as virtual assistants, interactive storytelling, and social chatbots. For instance, a virtual assistant equipped with multi-modal capabilities can process both text and images to provide more accurate and contextually relevant responses. Multi-modal dialogue in LLMs has the potential to reshape the landscape of human-machine conversations, creating more immersive and context-aware interactions that better align with human communication modalities. The integration of multi-modal capabilities in LLMs enables them to comprehend not just the text but also the contextual visual information, allowing for more contextually appropriate responses. This opens up new possibilities for more dynamic and engaging human-machine interactions.

3 Applications of Human-Machine Conversations with LLMs

The application of LLMs for human-machine conversations is revolutionizing various industries by harnessing the capabilities of intelligent assistant systems and emotionally supportive conversations. In the field of intelligent assistant-based human-machine conversation, LLMs have significantly improved user experiences through natural language interactions and personalized recommendations. Another notable application of human-machine conversation with LLMs is emotional support conversations. These systems aim to establish empathy with users, provide emotional support, and engage in meaningful conversations. By analyzing user inputs and offering appropriate responses, emotional support dialogues can help individuals cope with stress, anxiety, or loneliness. Such systems have shown promising results in supporting mental health by providing users with a safe and confidential environment to express their

Proceedings of the 22nd China National Conference on Computational Linguistics, pages 16-29, Harbin, China, August 3 - 5, 2023.
Volume 2: Frotier Forum

feelings and receive guidance. Successful cases of LLMs in human-machine conversation have emerged across various domains, demonstrating their transformative impact.

3.1 Intelligent Assistant-style Conversations with LLMs

Intelligent Assistant-Style Human-Machine conversations system, exemplified by popular platforms such as Siri, Alexa, and ChatGPT, has revolutionized the way users interact with technology. These systems are primarily designed to address information needs and provide personalized assistance to users. With a deep understanding of various business processes, they can offer comprehensive responses and fulfill a wide range of user inquiries. Their rich knowledge base allows them to handle tasks such as answering questions, providing recommendations, and assisting with navigation, making them invaluable tools for traditional customer service products.

Modern Human-Machine conversations system are rapidly advancing, giving rise to a series of remarkable models. OpenAI's GPT-4 (OpenAI, 2023) is a large-scale multi-modal model that accepts both image and text inputs and produces text outputs. While its capabilities still fall short of humans in certain real-world scenarios, GPT-4 has demonstrated human-level performance on many professional and academic benchmarks, particularly in the domains of creativity, visual input processing, and understanding longer contexts. Furthermore, OpenAI has developed an AI chatbot called ChatGPT (Lin, 2023), based on GPT-3.5 and GPT-4 architectures. It engages in text-based interactions and leverages reinforcement learning techniques to provide useful outputs.

In contrast, Google's Bard (bar, 2023) is a chatbot built on the large language model LaMDA. Its lightweight version extends to a broader user base while collecting and applying user feedback to continuously improve model performance. Claude (Bai et al., 2022), developed by Anthropic, is another large-scale language model designed to detect and avoid pitfalls such as logical errors and inappropriate content that ChatGPT may encounter. The model emphasizes usefulness and harmlessness, employing the RLAIF algorithm.

For the Chinese-English bilingual environment, ChatGLM-6B (Du et al., 2022) from Tsinghua University is a language model with billions of parameters optimized specifically for Chinese. It supports local deployment on consumer-grade graphics cards. Baidu's ERNIE Bot (Sun et al., 2021) is a generative dialogue product built on the ERNIE model series, leveraging the power of the large language model ERNIE 3.0-Titan, showcasing excellent text understanding and generation capabilities. Finally, MOSS (mos, 2023) from Fudan University, as the first large-scale language model in China similar to ChatGPT, offers enhanced functionalities through plugins, such as support for search engines, image generation, calculators, equation solvers, and more, providing a richer interactive experience.

3.2 Emotionally Supportive Conversations with LLMs

Emotionally Supportive Human-Machine conversations have revolutionized the field of human-machine interaction by focusing on emotions and social interaction. These systems aim to provide users with information, emotional support, and engaging conversations. With rich emotions, knowledge, and personality as their main characteristics, these conversations can empathize with users, understand their emotional states, and respond accordingly.

In the field of emotion-aware human-machine conversations, leading technology giants and academic institutions such as Google, Meta, and Baidu have developed various outstanding models. Google's Meena (Adiwardana et al., 2020), a chatbot developed with 2.6 billion parameters and trained on 341GB of social media conversation text, demonstrates human-level coherence and specificity in its responses. Meta's BlenderBot (Roller et al., 2021), on the other hand, is an open-domain dialogue bot with capabilities for online searching and long-term memory. It is built upon deep learning models and is trained to engage in interactive and responsive conversations. Another conversational application model by Google, LaMDA (Thoppilan et al., 2022), can learn discussions on various topics and exhibits impressive coherence and specificity in its responses after training and fine-tuning.

Baidu's PLATO (Bao et al., 2020) is a large-scale open-domain dialogue generation network that models background knowledge using discrete latent variables. In the Chinese dialogue model domain, EVA (Zhou et al., 2021) and OPD(opd, 2023) have demonstrated notable performance. EVA is a large-scale

Proceedings of the 22nd China National Conference on Computational Linguistics, pages 16-29, Harbin, China, August 3 - 5, 2023.
Volume 2: Frotier Forum

Chinese open-domain dialogue pre-training model that surpasses other Chinese pre-training dialogue models in both automatic and human evaluation metrics. Its subsequent version, EVA2.0, has been optimized in various aspects, and the 300M-parameter EVA2.0 (Gu et al., 2023) achieves the performance of the 2.8B-parameter EVA1.0. OPD (opd, 2023), on the other hand, is currently the world's largest open-source Chinese dialogue pre-training model with 6.3 billion parameters. It exhibits excellent chit-chat capability and knowledge question-answering ability, enabling in-depth multi-turn dialogue interactions with users.

3.3 Successful Case Studies of Human-Machine Conversations with LLMs in Diverse Fields

Successful case studies of LLM in human-machine conversations have demonstrated their effectiveness and impact across various fields. These systems have streamlined tasks such as content generation (Alkaissi and McFarlane, 2023; Rodriguez, 2022), disease diagnosis and treatment(Duong and Solomon, 2023; Khan et al., 2023; Rao et al., 2023a; Rao et al., 2023b), and assisted software development(Amos, 2023; Castelvecchi, 2022; Surameery and Shakor, 2023), enhancing user experiences and improving productivity. In addition, The integration of ChatGPT into the realm of data processing has the potential to revolutionize the landscape of scientific research (Macdonald et al., 2023).

In the field of biomedicine, LLMs such as LLaMa (Touvron et al., 2023) and ChatGLM (Du et al., 2022) often underperform due to a lack of specialized medical knowledge. To address this issue, HuaTuo (Wang et al., 2023) has developed a Chinese medical instruction dataset using a combination of medical knowledge graph and the GPT3.5 API. Additionally, leveraging the same medical data, this project also trained a healthcare-oriented version of the ChatGLM model: ChatGLM-6B-Med.Bloomberg has released BloombergGPT (Wu et al., 2023a), which is specifically trained on various financial data to comprehensively support natural language processing tasks in the financial domain.

Overall, the successful case studies of LLM human-machine conversations in various fields highlight their potential to transform industries, optimize processes, and enhance human-machine interactions.

4 Challenges of LLMs in Human-Machine Conversation

The use of LLMs in human-machine conversations presents several challenges that researchers and developers need to address:

- **Data Bias and Ethical Issues**: LLMs are trained on vast amounts of data, which may inadvertently reflect biases present in the data. This can lead to biased responses or perpetuation of stereotypes (Azaria, 2023). It is crucial to identify and mitigate these biases to ensure fair and inclusive interactions. Additionally, the ethical implications of deploying powerful conversations should be carefully considered, such as the potential for misuse or manipulation of information (Liebrenz et al., 2023).

- **Explainability and Transparency**: LLMs operate as complex black boxes, making it difficult to understand their decision-making processes. Users and stakeholders may have concerns about how the models arrive at their responses or recommendations(Larsson and Heintz, 2020). Ensuring transparency and providing explanations for the system's behavior are essential to build trust and accountability (Wischmeyer, 2020; OpenAI, 2023).

- **Security and Malicious Use**: As LLMs become more powerful, there is an increased risk of them being exploited for malicious purposes, such as generating deceptive or harmful content(Ali and others, 2023). Protecting the integrity of conversations and preventing malicious use is a significant concern that requires robust security measures and monitoring (Hargreaves, 2023; Kasneci et al., 2023).

- **Incorrect, Long-term Memory and Persistence**: Despite advancements, conversation models can still produce inaccurate or nonsensical responses. Ensuring the systems have reliable mechanisms for validation and error correction is essential. Additionally, conversations should be able to maintain a coherent context and memory over extended conversations, as well as recognize and address inconsistencies in their responses. (Blog, 2023; Borji, 2023; Zhuo et al., 2023; OpenAI, 2023).

Proceedings of the 22nd China National Conference on Computational Linguistics, pages 16-29, Harbin, China, August 3 - 5, 2023.
Volume 2: Frotier Forum

Addressing these challenges is essential for the responsible and effective use of large models in human-machine conversations. Researchers and practitioners need to collaborate and innovate to ensure ethical considerations, transparency, security, reliability, and resource efficiency in the development and deployment of these powerful conversations.

5 Future Development Direction and Prospects

This section explores the future development direction and prospects, outlining the potential pathways and opportunities that lie ahead in the field:

- **Support and Research for Low-Resource Languages**: LLMs have demonstrated remarkable performance in high-resource languages, resources and data are scarce available for low-resource languages (Huang et al., 2023a). It is crucial to invest in research and develop techniques to make these models more accessible and effective in low-resource language settings, enabling users from diverse linguistic backgrounds to benefit from conversations (Mohtashami et al., 2023).

- **Model Explainability and Transparency**: Enhancing model explainability and transparency is another significant prospect. Ensuring that these models provide interpretable and transparent responses is essential to build user trust and understand how the system arrives at its conclusions (Wu et al., 2023b). Explainability and transparency is an ongoing area of research in the field.

- **Personalized Conversations and Intelligent Assistants**: LLMs have the potential to offer personalized experiences, but there are challenges in understanding and adapting to individual user preferences, needs, and contexts. Designing conversations that can accurately capture and incorporate user feedback, dynamically adapt to user preferences, and provide personalized recommendations is a complex task that requires further research and development (Chen et al., 2022b).

- **Social Applications and Industrial Adoption**: There is a need to explore social applications and promote the industrial adoption of large models in human-machine conversations. Integrating conversations into social platforms and applications can enhance user experiences, facilitate social interactions, and offer new opportunities for information access and engagement (Zhao et al., 2023). Encouraging the adoption of large models in various industries, such as healthcare, finance, and entertainment, can lead to significant advancements and real-world impact in these domains.

These prospects will contribute to the advancement and responsible deployment of large models in human-machine conversations. Continued research, collaboration, and innovation are necessary to overcome these obstacles and unlock the full potential of large models in transforming the way humans interact with machines.

6 Summary

In this paper, we investigates the role of LLMs in facilitating human-machine dialogue. It examines the rise and development of these models, explores their applications in various domains, and discusses the challenges associated with their deployment. Furthermore concludes by outlining future directions and prospects, highlighting the need for ongoing research and addressing ethical considerations. It serves as a valuable resource for researchers and practitioners interested in leveraging the potential of large models in human-machine conversations.

References

Daniel Adiwardana, Minh-Thang Luong, David R So, Jamie Hall, Noah Fiedel, Romal Thoppilan, Zi Yang, Apoorv Kulshreshtha, Gaurav Nemade, Yifeng Lu, et al. 2020. Towards a human-like open-domain chatbot. *arXiv preprint arXiv:2001.09977.*

Jean-Baptiste Alayrac, Jeff Donahue, Pauline Luc, Antoine Miech, Iain Barr, Yana Hasson, Karel Lenc, Arthur Mensch, Katherine Millican, Malcolm Reynolds, et al. 2022. Flamingo: a visual language model for few-shot learning. *Proc. of NeurIPS*, pages 23716–23736.

Proceedings of the 22nd China National Conference on Computational Linguistics, pages 16-29, Harbin, China, August 3 - 5, 2023.
Volume 2: Frotier Forum

Faizan Ali et al. 2023. Let the devil speak for itself: Should chatgpt be allowed or banned in hospitality and tourism schools? *Journal of Global Hospitality and Tourism*, pages 1–6.

Hussam Alkaissi and Samy I McFarlane. 2023. Artificial hallucinations in chatgpt: implications in scientific writing. *Cureus*.

David Amos. 2023. Chatgpt is an extra-ordinary python programmer.

Amos Azaria. 2023. Chatgpt: More human-like than computer-like, but not necessarily in a good way.

Yuntao Bai, Saurav Kadavath, Sandipan Kundu, Amanda Askell, Jackson Kernion, Andy Jones, Anna Chen, Anna Goldie, Azalia Mirhoseini, Cameron McKinnon, Carol Chen, Catherine Olsson, Christopher Olah, Danny Hernandez, Dawn Drain, Deep Ganguli, Dustin Li, Eli Tran-Johnson, Ethan Perez, Jamie Kerr, Jared Mueller, Jeffrey Ladish, Joshua Landau, Kamal Ndousse, Kamile Lukosuite, Liane Lovitt, Michael Sellitto, Nelson Elhage, Nicholas Schiefer, Noemi Mercado, Nova DasSarma, Robert Lasenby, Robin Larson, Sam Ringer, Scott Johnston, Shauna Kravec, Sheer El Showk, Stanislav Fort, Tamera Lanham, Timothy Telleen-Lawton, Tom Conerly, Tom Henighan, Tristan Hume, Samuel R. Bowman, Zac Hatfield-Dodds, Ben Mann, Dario Amodei, Nicholas Joseph, Sam McCandlish, Tom Brown, and Jared Kaplan. 2022. Constitutional ai: Harmlessness from ai feedback.

Siqi Bao, Huang He, Fan Wang, Hua Wu, and Haifeng Wang. 2020. PLATO: Pre-trained dialogue generation model with discrete latent variable. In *Proc. of ACL*, pages 85–96.

2023. Bard Google. `https://bard.google.com`.

Back To Blog. 2023. Ai and academic integrity: How ai technology might influence the future of scholarly publishing.

Ali Borji. 2023. A categorical archive of chatgpt failures. *arXiv preprint arXiv:2302.03494*.

Tom Brown, Benjamin Mann, Nick Ryder, Melanie Subbiah, Jared D Kaplan, Prafulla Dhariwal, Arvind Neelakantan, Pranav Shyam, Girish Sastry, Amanda Askell, et al. 2020. Language models are few-shot learners. *Proc. of NeurIPS*, pages 1877–1901.

Davide Castelvecchi. 2022. Are chatgpt and alphacode going to replace programmers? *Nature*.

Xi Chen, Xiao Wang, Soravit Changpinyo, AJ Piergiovanni, Piotr Padlewski, Daniel Salz, Sebastian Goodman, Adam Grycner, Basil Mustafa, Lucas Beyer, et al. 2022a. Pali: A jointly-scaled multilingual language-image model. *arXiv preprint arXiv:2209.06794*.

Yirong Chen, Weiquan Fan, Xiaofen Xing, Jianxin Pang, Minlie Huang, Wenjing Han, Qianfeng Tie, and Xiangmin Xu. 2022b. Cped: A large-scale chinese personalized and emotional dialogue dataset for conversational ai.

Aakanksha Chowdhery, Sharan Narang, Jacob Devlin, Maarten Bosma, Gaurav Mishra, Adam Roberts, Paul Barham, Hyung Won Chung, Charles Sutton, Sebastian Gehrmann, et al. 2022. Palm: Scaling language modeling with pathways. *arXiv preprint arXiv:2204.02311*.

Hyung Won Chung, Le Hou, Shayne Longpre, Barret Zoph, Yi Tay, William Fedus, Eric Li, Xuezhi Wang, Mostafa Dehghani, Siddhartha Brahma, et al. 2022. Scaling instruction-finetuned language models. *arXiv preprint arXiv:2210.11416*.

Kevin Clark, Minh-Thang Luong, Quoc V. Le, and Christopher D. Manning. 2020. ELECTRA: pre-training text encoders as discriminators rather than generators. In *Proc. of ICLR*.

Jacob Devlin, Ming-Wei Chang, Kenton Lee, and Kristina Toutanova. 2019. BERT: pre-training of deep bidirectional transformers for language understanding. In *Proc. of NAACL*, pages 4171–4186.

Li Dong, Nan Yang, Wenhui Wang, Furu Wei, Xiaodong Liu, Yu Wang, Jianfeng Gao, Ming Zhou, and Hsiao-Wuen Hon. 2019. Unified language model pre-training for natural language understanding and generation. *Proc. of NeurIPS*.

Danny Driess, Fei Xia, Mehdi SM Sajjadi, Corey Lynch, Aakanksha Chowdhery, Brian Ichter, Ayzaan Wahid, Jonathan Tompson, Quan Vuong, Tianhe Yu, et al. 2023. Palm-e: An embodied multimodal language model. *arXiv preprint arXiv:2303.03378*.

Zhengxiao Du, Yujie Qian, Xiao Liu, Ming Ding, Jiezhong Qiu, Zhilin Yang, and Jie Tang. 2022. GLM: General language model pretraining with autoregressive blank infilling. In *Proc. of ACL*, pages 320–335.

Dat Duong and Benjamin D Solomon. 2023. Analysis of large-language model versus human performance for genetics questions. *medRxiv*, pages 2023–01.

Google. 2023. Palm 2.

Yuxian Gu, Jiaxin Wen, Hao Sun, Yi Song, Pei Ke, Chujie Zheng, Zheng Zhang, Jianzhu Yao, Lei Liu, Xiaoyan Zhu, and Minlie Huang. 2023. EVA2.0: investigating open-domain chinese dialogue systems with large-scale pre-training. *Mach. Intell. Res.*, pages 207–219.

Stuart Hargreaves. 2023. 'words are flowing out like endless rain into a paper cup': Chatgpt & law school assessments. *The Chinese University of Hong Kong Faculty of Law Research Paper.*

Haoyang Huang, Tianyi Tang, Dongdong Zhang, Wayne Xin Zhao, Ting Song, Yan Xia, and Furu Wei. 2023a. Not all languages are created equal in llms: Improving multilingual capability by cross-lingual-thought prompting.

Shaohan Huang, Li Dong, Wenhui Wang, Yaru Hao, Saksham Singhal, Shuming Ma, Tengchao Lv, Lei Cui, Owais Khan Mohammed, Qiang Liu, et al. 2023b. Language is not all you need: Aligning perception with language models. *arXiv preprint arXiv:2302.14045.*

Forrest N. Iandola, Albert E. Shaw, Ravi Krishna, and Kurt Keutzer. 2020. Squeezebert: What can computer vision teach NLP about efficient neural networks? In *Proceedings of SustaiNLP: Workshop on Simple and Efficient Natural Language Processing, SustaiNLP@EMNLP 2020, Online, November 20, 2020*, pages 124–135.

Mandar Joshi, Danqi Chen, Yinhan Liu, Daniel S Weld, Luke Zettlemoyer, and Omer Levy. 2020. Spanbert: Improving pre-training by representing and predicting spans. *Transactions of the Association for Computational Linguistics*, pages 64–77.

Enkelejda Kasneci, Kathrin Seßler, Stefan Küchemann, Maria Bannert, Daryna Dementieva, Frank Fischer, Urs Gasser, Georg Groh, Stephan Günnemann, Eyke Hüllermeier, et al. 2023. Chatgpt for good? on opportunities and challenges of large language models for education. *Learning and Individual Differences*, page 102274.

Rehan Ahmed Khan, Masood Jawaid, Aymen Rehan Khan, and Madiha Sajjad. 2023. Chatgpt-reshaping medical education and clinical management. *Pakistan Journal of Medical Sciences*, page 605.

Zhenzhong Lan, Mingda Chen, Sebastian Goodman, Kevin Gimpel, Piyush Sharma, and Radu Soricut. 2020. ALBERT: A lite BERT for self-supervised learning of language representations. In *Proc. of ICLR*.

Stefan Larsson and Fredrik Heintz. 2020. Transparency in artificial intelligence. *Internet Policy Review.*

Mike Lewis, Yinhan Liu, Naman Goyal, Marjan Ghazvininejad, Abdelrahman Mohamed, Omer Levy, Veselin Stoyanov, and Luke Zettlemoyer. 2020. BART: denoising sequence-to-sequence pre-training for natural language generation, translation, and comprehension. In *Proc. of ACL*, pages 7871–7880.

Junnan Li, Dongxu Li, Caiming Xiong, and Steven Hoi. 2022. Blip: Bootstrapping language-image pre-training for unified vision-language understanding and generation. In *Proc. of ICML*, pages 12888–12900.

Junnan Li, Dongxu Li, Silvio Savarese, and Steven Hoi. 2023. Blip-2: Bootstrapping language-image pre-training with frozen image encoders and large language models. *arXiv preprint arXiv:2301.12597.*

Michael Liebrenz, Roman Schleifer, Anna Buadze, Dinesh Bhugra, and Alexander Smith. 2023. Generating scholarly content with chatgpt: ethical challenges for medical publishing. *The Lancet Digital Health*, pages e105–e106.

Zhicheng Lin. 2023. Why and how to embrace ai such as chatgpt in your academic life.

Yinhan Liu, Myle Ott, Naman Goyal, Jingfei Du, Mandar Joshi, Danqi Chen, Omer Levy, Mike Lewis, Luke Zettlemoyer, and Veselin Stoyanov. 2019. Roberta: A robustly optimized bert pretraining approach. *arXiv preprint arXiv:1907.11692.*

Calum Macdonald, Davies Adeloye, Aziz Sheikh, and Igor Rudan. 2023. Can chatgpt draft a research article? an example of population-level vaccine effectiveness analysis. *Journal of global health.*

Maria das Graças Bruno Marietto, Rafael Varago de Aguiar, Gislene de Oliveira Barbosa, Wagner Tanaka Botelho, Edson Pimentel, Robson dos Santos França, and Vera Lúcia da Silva. 2013. Artificial intelligence markup language: a brief tutorial. *arXiv preprint arXiv:1307.3091.*

Amirkeivan Mohtashami, Mauro Verzetti, and Paul K. Rubenstein. 2023. Learning translation quality evaluation on low resource languages from large language models.

Proceedings of the 22nd China National Conference on Computational Linguistics, pages 16-29, Harbin, China, August 3 - 5, 2023.
Volume 2: Frotier Forum

2023. MOSS: Openlmlab's repository. https://github.com/OpenLMLab/MOSS.

2023. OPD: Open-domain pre-trained dialogue model. https://github.com/thu-coai/OPD.

OpenAI. 2023. Gpt-4 technical report.

Long Ouyang, Jeffrey Wu, Xu Jiang, Diogo Almeida, Carroll Wainwright, Pamela Mishkin, Chong Zhang, Sandhini Agarwal, Katarina Slama, Alex Ray, et al. 2022. Training language models to follow instructions with human feedback. *Proc. of NeurIPS*, pages 27730–27744.

Alec Radford, Karthik Narasimhan, Tim Salimans, Ilya Sutskever, et al. 2018. Improving language understanding by generative pre-training.

Alec Radford, Jong Wook Kim, Chris Hallacy, Aditya Ramesh, Gabriel Goh, Sandhini Agarwal, Girish Sastry, Amanda Askell, Pamela Mishkin, Jack Clark, et al. 2021. Learning transferable visual models from natural language supervision. In *Proc. of ICML*, pages 8748–8763.

Colin Raffel, Noam Shazeer, Adam Roberts, Katherine Lee, Sharan Narang, Michael Matena, Yanqi Zhou, Wei Li, and Peter J Liu. 2020. Exploring the limits of transfer learning with a unified text-to-text transformer. *The Journal of Machine Learning Research*, pages 5485–5551.

Arya Rao, John Kim, Meghana Kamineni, Michael Pang, Winston Lie, and Marc D Succi. 2023a. Evaluating chatgpt as an adjunct for radiologic decision-making. *medRxiv*, pages 2023–02.

Arya S Rao, Michael Pang, John Kim, Meghana Kamineni, Winston Lie, Anoop K Prasad, Adam Landman, Keith Dryer, and Marc D Succi. 2023b. Assessing the utility of chatgpt throughout the entire clinical workflow. *medRxiv*, pages 2023–02.

Jesus Rodriguez. 2022. How to create diagrams with chatgpt.

Stephen Roller, Emily Dinan, Naman Goyal, Da Ju, Mary Williamson, Yinhan Liu, Jing Xu, Myle Ott, Eric Michael Smith, Y-Lan Boureau, and Jason Weston. 2021. Recipes for building an open-domain chatbot. In *Proc. of EACL*, pages 300–325.

Victor Sanh, Lysandre Debut, Julien Chaumond, and Thomas Wolf. 2019. Distilbert, a distilled version of bert: smaller, faster, cheaper and lighter. *arXiv preprint arXiv:1910.01108*.

Teven Le Scao, Angela Fan, Christopher Akiki, Ellie Pavlick, Suzana Ilić, Daniel Hesslow, Roman Castagné, Alexandra Sasha Luccioni, François Yvon, Matthias Gallé, et al. 2022. Bloom: A 176b-parameter open-access multilingual language model. *arXiv preprint arXiv:2211.05100*.

Yu Sun, Shuohuan Wang, Yukun Li, Shikun Feng, Xuyi Chen, Han Zhang, Xin Tian, Danxiang Zhu, Hao Tian, and Hua Wu. 2019. Ernie: Enhanced representation through knowledge integration. *arXiv preprint arXiv:1904.09223*.

Yu Sun, Shuohuan Wang, Yukun Li, Shikun Feng, Hao Tian, Hua Wu, and Haifeng Wang. 2020. Ernie 2.0: A continual pre-training framework for language understanding. In *Proc. of AAAI*, pages 8968–8975.

Yu Sun, Shuohuan Wang, Shikun Feng, Siyu Ding, Chao Pang, Junyuan Shang, Jiaxiang Liu, Xuyi Chen, Yanbin Zhao, Yuxiang Lu, et al. 2021. Ernie 3.0: Large-scale knowledge enhanced pre-training for language understanding and generation. *arXiv preprint arXiv:2107.02137*.

Nigar M Shafiq Surameery and Mohammed Y Shakor. 2023. Use chat gpt to solve programming bugs. *International Journal of Information Technology & Computer Engineering (IJITC) ISSN: 2455-5290*, pages 17–22.

Ilya Sutskever, Oriol Vinyals, and Quoc V Le. 2014. Sequence to sequence learning with neural networks. *Proc. of NeurIPS*.

Romal Thoppilan, Daniel De Freitas, Jamie Hall, Noam Shazeer, Apoorv Kulshreshtha, Heng-Tze Cheng, Alicia Jin, Taylor Bos, Leslie Baker, Yu Du, YaGuang Li, Hongrae Lee, Huaixiu Steven Zheng, Amin Ghafouri, Marcelo Menegali, Yanping Huang, Maxim Krikun, Dmitry Lepikhin, James Qin, Dehao Chen, Yuanzhong Xu, Zhifeng Chen, Adam Roberts, Maarten Bosma, Vincent Zhao, Yanqi Zhou, Chung-Ching Chang, Igor Krivokon, Will Rusch, Marc Pickett, Pranesh Srinivasan, Laichee Man, Kathleen Meier-Hellstern, Meredith Ringel Morris, Tulsee Doshi, Renelito Delos Santos, Toju Duke, Johnny Soraker, Ben Zevenbergen, Vinodkumar Prabhakaran, Mark Diaz, Ben Hutchinson, Kristen Olson, Alejandra Molina, Erin Hoffman-John, Josh Lee, Lora Aroyo, Ravi Rajakumar, Alena Butryna, Matthew Lamm, Viktoriya Kuzmina, Joe Fenton, Aaron Cohen, Rachel Bernstein, Ray Kurzweil, Blaise Aguera-Arcas, Claire Cui, Marian Croak, Ed Chi, and Quoc Le. 2022. Lamda: Language models for dialog applications.

Proceedings of the 22nd China National Conference on Computational Linguistics, pages 16-29, Harbin, China, August 3 - 5, 2023.
Volume 2: Frotier Forum

Hugo Touvron, Thibaut Lavril, Gautier Izacard, Xavier Martinet, Marie-Anne Lachaux, Timothée Lacroix, Baptiste Rozière, Naman Goyal, Eric Hambro, Faisal Azhar, et al. 2023. Llama: Open and efficient foundation language models. *arXiv preprint arXiv:2302.13971*.

Ashish Vaswani, Noam Shazeer, Niki Parmar, Jakob Uszkoreit, Llion Jones, Aidan N Gomez, Łukasz Kaiser, and Illia Polosukhin. 2017. Attention is all you need. *Proc. of NeurIPS*.

Shuohuan Wang, Yu Sun, Yang Xiang, Zhihua Wu, Siyu Ding, Weibao Gong, Shikun Feng, Junyuan Shang, Yanbin Zhao, Chao Pang, et al. 2021. Ernie 3.0 titan: Exploring larger-scale knowledge enhanced pre-training for language understanding and generation. *arXiv preprint arXiv:2112.12731*.

Peng Wang, An Yang, Rui Men, Junyang Lin, Shuai Bai, Zhikang Li, Jianxin Ma, Chang Zhou, Jingren Zhou, and Hongxia Yang. 2022a. Ofa: Unifying architectures, tasks, and modalities through a simple sequence-to-sequence learning framework. In *Proc. of ICML*, pages 23318–23340.

Wenhui Wang, Hangbo Bao, Li Dong, Johan Bjorck, Zhiliang Peng, Qiang Liu, Kriti Aggarwal, Owais Khan Mohammed, Saksham Singhal, Subhojit Som, et al. 2022b. Image as a foreign language: Beit pretraining for all vision and vision-language tasks. *arXiv preprint arXiv:2208.10442*.

Haochun Wang, Chi Liu, Nuwa Xi, Zewen Qiang, Sendong Zhao, Bing Qin, and Ting Liu. 2023. Huatuo: Tuning llama model with chinese medical knowledge.

Jason Wei, Maarten Bosma, Vincent Y. Zhao, Kelvin Guu, Adams Wei Yu, Brian Lester, Nan Du, Andrew M. Dai, and Quoc V. Le. 2022. Finetuned language models are zero-shot learners. In *Proc. of ICLR*.

Joseph Weizenbaum. 1966. Eliza—a computer program for the study of natural language communication between man and machine. *Communications of the ACM*, pages 36–45.

Thomas Wischmeyer. 2020. Artificial intelligence and transparency: opening the black box. *Regulating artificial intelligence*, pages 75–101.

Shijie Wu, Ozan Irsoy, Steven Lu, Vadim Dabravolski, Mark Dredze, Sebastian Gehrmann, Prabhanjan Kambadur, David Rosenberg, and Gideon Mann. 2023a. Bloomberggpt: A large language model for finance.

Zhaofeng Wu, William Merrill, Hao Peng, Iz Beltagy, and Noah A. Smith. 2023b. Transparency helps reveal when language models learn meaning.

Zhilin Yang, Zihang Dai, Yiming Yang, Jaime Carbonell, Russ R Salakhutdinov, and Quoc V Le. 2019. Xlnet: Generalized autoregressive pretraining for language understanding. *Proc. of NeurIPS*.

Junjie Ye, Xuanting Chen, Nuo Xu, Can Zu, Zekai Shao, Shichun Liu, Yuhan Cui, Zeyang Zhou, Chao Gong, Yang Shen, et al. 2023. A comprehensive capability analysis of gpt-3 and gpt-3.5 series models. *arXiv preprint arXiv:2303.10420*.

Jiahui Yu, Zirui Wang, Vijay Vasudevan, Legg Yeung, Mojtaba Seyedhosseini, and Yonghui Wu. 2022. Coca: Contrastive captioners are image-text foundation models. *Trans. Mach. Learn. Res.*

Aohan Zeng, Xiao Liu, Zhengxiao Du, Zihan Wang, Hanyu Lai, Ming Ding, Zhuoyi Yang, Yifan Xu, Wendi Zheng, Xiao Xia, Weng Lam Tam, Zixuan Ma, Yufei Xue, Jidong Zhai, Wenguang Chen, Peng Zhang, Yuxiao Dong, and Jie Tang. 2022. Glm-130b: An open bilingual pre-trained model.

Jingqing Zhang, Yao Zhao, Mohammad Saleh, and Peter Liu. 2020. Pegasus: Pre-training with extracted gap-sentences for abstractive summarization. In *Proc. of ICML*, pages 11328–11339.

Susan Zhang, Stephen Roller, Naman Goyal, Mikel Artetxe, Moya Chen, Shuohui Chen, Christopher Dewan, Mona Diab, Xian Li, Xi Victoria Lin, et al. 2022. Opt: Open pre-trained transformer language models. *arXiv preprint arXiv:2205.01068*.

Wayne Xin Zhao, Kun Zhou, Junyi Li, Tianyi Tang, Xiaolei Wang, Yupeng Hou, Yingqian Min, Beichen Zhang, Junjie Zhang, Zican Dong, Yifan Du, Chen Yang, Yushuo Chen, Zhipeng Chen, Jinhao Jiang, Ruiyang Ren, Yifan Li, Xinyu Tang, Zikang Liu, Peiyu Liu, Jian-Yun Nie, and Ji-Rong Wen. 2023. A survey of large language models.

Hao Zhou, Pei Ke, Zheng Zhang, Yuxian Gu, Yinhe Zheng, Chujie Zheng, Yida Wang, Chen Henry Wu, Hao Sun, Xiaocong Yang, Bosi Wen, Xiaoyan Zhu, Minlie Huang, and Jie Tang. 2021. Eva: An open-domain chinese dialogue system with large-scale generative pre-training.

Terry Yue Zhuo, Yujin Huang, Chunyang Chen, and Zhenchang Xing. 2023. Exploring ai ethics of chatgpt: A diagnostic analysis. *arXiv preprint arXiv:2301.12867*.

Proceedings of the 22nd China National Conference on Computational Linguistics, pages 16-29, Harbin, China, August 3 - 5, 2023.
Volume 2: Frotier Forum

机器翻译和大语言模型研究进展

朱文昊 周昊 高长江 刘斯哲 黄书剑[†]
计算机软件新技术国家重点实验室, 南京大学
{zhuwh,zhouh,gaocj,liusz}@smail.nju.edu.cn, huangsj@nju.edu.cn

摘要

机器翻译旨在通过计算机自动将一种自然语言翻译成另一种自然语言，这个过程对于机器翻译模型的语言理解、语言生成能力有着极高的要求。因此机器翻译一直以来都是一项极具研究价值和研究难度的自然语言处理任务。近期研究表明，大语言模型能够根据人类指令完成包括翻译在内的许多任务，在这一过程中展现出强大的语言理解和生成能力，为自然语言处理范式革新提供了新的可能。为了在大语言模型支持下更好地完成机器翻译任务，研究人员对大语言模型的机器翻译和多语言能力进行了大量的研究和分析。本文从以下三方面介绍相关研究热点和最新进展，包括：大语言模型翻译能力评估、大语言模型翻译能力激发、大语言模型在不同语言上的能力展现。

关键词： 机器翻译 ； 大语言模型 ； 情景学习 ； 指令微调 ； 多语言

Research Development of Machine translation and Large Language Model

Wenhao Zhu, Hao Zhou, Changjiang Gao, Sizhe Liu, Shujian Huang[†]
National Key Laboratory for Novel Software Technology, Nanjing University
{zhuwh,zhouh,gaocj,liusz}@smail.nju.edu.cn, huangsj@nju.edu.cn

Abstract

Machine translation aims to automatically translate one natural language into another. This process requires great ability of language understanding and language generation, making machine translation a challenging task. Recent studies have shown that large language models (LLMs) are capable of performing various tasks, including machine translation, based on human instructions. The powerful ability of LLM provides new possibilities for the innovation of natural language processing paradigms. To better accomplish machine translation tasks with the support of LLMs, researchers have conducted extensive research and analysis on the translation and multilingual capabilities of these models. This paper introduces the latest developments in this field from the following three aspects: evaluating translation capabilities of large language models; eliciting translation capabilities of large language models; language ability of large language models in different languages.

Keywords: Machine Translation , Large Language Model , In-Context Learning , Instruction-Tuning , Multilinguality

1 引言

机器翻译（Machine Translation，MT）是利用计算机把一种自然语言自动地转换为另一种自然语言的过程。相较于人工翻译，机器翻译这种快速便捷的翻译方式可以更好地满足人们的基础翻译需求，对促进信息传播和社会经济发展有着重要的实际意义。机器翻译任务的完成依赖于对源语言的准确理解和对目标语言的准确生成，对机器翻译模型的语言能力有着极高的要求 (Nirenburg, 1989; Och and Ney, 2002; Vaswani et al., 2017)。

近年来，在大规模语料上训练的具有大规模参数的大语言模型（Large Language Model, LLM）展现出了极强的语言能力。大语言模型能够理解人类指令，并根据指令完成包括翻译在内的各类任务；还具备情景学习（In-Context Learning，ICL）(Brown et al., 2020),思维链（Chain-of-Thought，CoT）(Wei et al., 2023)等涌现能力,能够利用上下文中的额外信息对自身生成预测结果进行优化调整。大语言模型的强大能力为机器翻译范式革新提供了可能。

目前，针对大语言模型在机器翻译方面的分析和应用已有大量研究。本文整理和综述这些工作，从三个方面介绍大语言模型在机器翻译方面的最新进展：大语言模型翻译能力评估、大语言模型翻译能力激发、大语言模型在不同语言上的能力展现。

通过对这些研究工作进行整理和总结，我们可以得出以下结论：(1）先进的大语言模型（如ChatGPT）已经可以在部分语言对上超过传统的有监督神经机器翻译模型，但是在低资源语言上仍然存在较大差距；(2）情景学习与指令微调是两种最常见的翻译能力激发方式，情景学习可以以较小的代价让模型进行机器翻译，而指令微调能够更好地激发模型的翻译能力；(3）大语言模型在不同语言上的语言能力高度不平衡，但是通过平行数据可以帮助大语言模型建立不同语言之间的对应关系，帮助模型在非英语语言上也展现出不错的语言能力。总体来说，大语言模型的出现为机器翻译研究带来了新的契机和挑战，基于大语言模型建立新的机器翻译范式展现出巨大的潜力，而提升大语言模型翻译能力也可以帮助大语言模型在更多的语言上展现其强大的能力。

本文的后续内容安排如下：第2节将介绍机器翻译和大语言模型的相关背景，第3、4、5节分别介绍大语言模型的翻译能力评估、翻译能力激发和跨语言能力展现相关研究进展，第6节将对整体研究进展和研究趋势进行总结和展望。

2 背景

2.1 机器翻译

从基于规则的机器翻译(Nirenburg, 1989)到统计机器翻译(Och and Ney, 2002)，再到神经机器翻译(Vaswani et al., 2017)，机器翻译范式不断转变，机器翻译效果不断提升。目前，最好的神经机器翻译模型已经可以在少部分高资源语言对(如德语-英语)上超过人类专家翻译水平(Ng et al., 2019)。但是，只构建支持单一翻译方向的机器翻译模型还无法充分满足实际需求。当机器翻译系统需要支持的语言数量增多时，为每一个翻译方向单独部署机器翻译模型代价巨大。于是,构建同时支持多个翻译方向的多语言机器翻译系统逐渐成为近年来的热点研究内容(Johnson et al., 2017; Costa-jussà et al., 2022; Yuan et al., 2022)。此前，多语言机器翻译模型基本均采用编码器-解码器架构。而掌握多种语言的大语言模型为多语言机器翻译系统构建提供了新的可能(Garcia et al., 2023; Zhu et al., 2023)。

2.2 大语言模型

大语言模型的基本架构是Transformer(Vaswani et al., 2017)，基本训练任务是语言建模任务(Bengio et al., 2000)，训练数据基本是以英语为主的多语言单语语料(Zhang et al., 2022; Lin et al., 2022)。其中，语言建模任务要求模型根据前缀序列，准确预测下个词语。在大规模语料上使用语言建模任务进行训练可以使模型掌握语料中蕴含的海量知识，包括事实性知识(Petroni et al., 2019)、语言学知识(Tenney et al., 2019)等，并且具备极强的语言理解和语言生成能力(Pavlick, 2022)。这种强大语言能力也使大语言模型其能够根据人类指令完成各类下游任务。

由于语言模型最初的训练目标仅为预测后续可能的符号，与特定任务并不存在明确的关联。研究人员提出了两种方法教会模型理解某个给定的人类指令，并遵照指令进行对应任务的

第二十二届中国计算语言学大会论文集，第30页-第39页，哈尔滨，中国，2023年8月3日至5日。
卷2：前沿综述

执行，这两种方法分别是情景学习和指令微调。情景学习(Brown et al., 2020)利用上下文情景中包含的描述和示例进行学习，仅作用于推断阶段。以翻译任务为例，根据提供任务描述$\mathcal{T}$和示例$\{(\mathcal{X}_i, \mathcal{Y}_i)\}_{i=1}^{k}$，构造上下文提示$\mathcal{P} = \mathcal{T}(\mathcal{X}_1, \mathcal{Y}_1) \oplus \mathcal{T}(\mathcal{X}_2, \mathcal{Y}_2) \oplus \cdots \oplus \mathcal{T}(\mathcal{X}_k, \mathcal{Y}_k)$和待翻译源语言句子$\mathcal{X}$，并将其输入模型。则模型根据示例理解指定的任务，并生成翻译结果$\mathcal{Y}$。翻译结果$\mathcal{Y}$一般通过采样算法获得：$\arg\max_{\mathcal{Y}}\ p(\mathcal{P} \oplus \mathcal{T}(\mathcal{X}, \mathcal{Y}))$。情景学习能够让模型在不更新参数的情况下理解和完成指定任务。Figure 1展示了一个大语言模型利用情景学习进行机器翻译的例子。

指令微调(Wei et al., 2021; Ouyang et al., 2022)则作用于训练阶段。通过包含特定指令的样本来训练模型，通过调整模型参数，使模型能够更加准确地完成指定任务。相对而言，指令微调方案由于需要改变大语言模型参数，所以对计算资源的要求比较高。

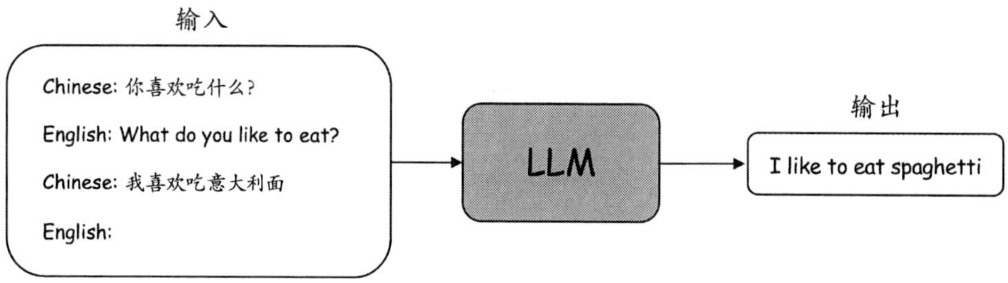

Figure 1: 大语言模型通过情景学习进行机器翻译的示意图

3 大语言模型翻译能力评估

训练大语言模型所使用的海量语料往往以单语数据为主，且其中英文语料占主导地位，而其他语言的语料往往只有很小的比例。大语言模型在这样的数据分布上能否建模好不同语言之间的对应关系，并进一步学习得到可靠的翻译知识，是研究者非常关心的一个问题。因此，研究人员对大语言模型的多语言翻译能力进行了考察和评估(Lin et al., 2022; Moslem et al., 2023; Jiao et al., 2023b; Bang et al., 2023; Hendy et al., 2023; Garcia et al., 2023; Zhu et al., 2023)。

这些研究工作采用情景学习的方式，考察了众多流行的大语言模型在多个翻译方向上的翻译能力。Table 1中列举了这些研究工作的基本情况。其中Zhu et al. (2023)的评测工作是相对最为全面的，他们基于Flores-101多语言机器翻译数据集，在102个语言，202个方向上对XGLM、BLOOMZ、OPT和ChatGPT这四个流行的大语言模型的多语言翻译能力进行了评估，并与现有的强大的监督学习基线模型NLLB-1.3B(Costa-jussà et al., 2022)、M2M-12B(Fan et al., 2021)进行了对比。他们的研究结果表明：在众多被评测的大语言模型中，ChatGPT目前的翻译表现最好。相比于此前的大语言模型，ChatGPT在不同语言间的表现更加平衡，并且在20%左右以英语为核心的翻译方向已经可以超过强大的有监督基线模型NLLB。但与此同时，在大部分翻译方向上，尤其是低资源语言翻译上，ChatGPT仍然落后于有监督模型和商用机器翻译系统（如Figure 2所示）。

评估工作	语言数量	语言对数量	大语言模型
Lin et al. (2022)	13	182	GPT-3, XGLM
Moslem et al. (2023)	6	5	GPT-3, BLOOMZ
Jiao et al. (2023b)	5	8	ChatGPT,GPT4
Bang et al. (2023)	13	24	ChatGPT
Hendy et al. (2023)	18	10	ChatGPT
Zhu et al. (2023)	102	202	XGLM, BLOOMZ, OPT, ChatGPT

Table 1: 翻译能力评估工作概览

值得注意的是 Zhu et al. (2023)发现在使用公开测试集评测大语言模型能力时容易出现数据泄漏问题。由于大语言模型训练数据往往覆盖范围较广且透明度较差，在利用现有数据进行评测时，很容易发生测试数据被包含在训练数据中的情况，导致对应模型的测试表现高

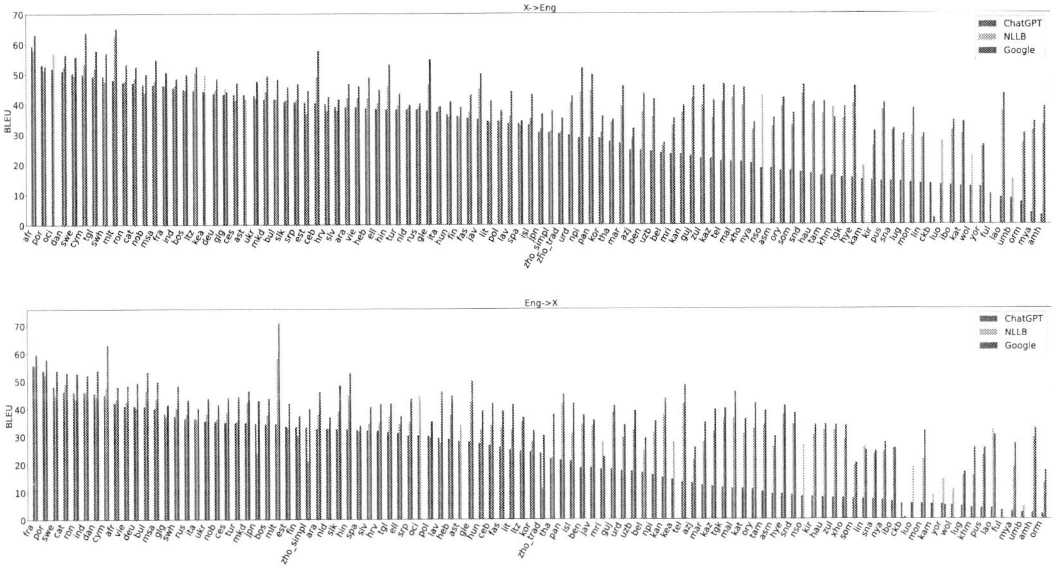

Figure 2: 大语言模型ChatGPT与有监督机器翻译模型NLLB，商用机器翻译系统Google Translate的翻译表现对比(结果摘自(Zhu et al., 2023))

于实际翻译水平。例如，由于BLOOMZ (Scao et al., 2022)利用了Flores-200作为训练数据，在Flores-101数据集上评测BLOOMZ的翻译表现时，就存在数据泄漏的问题，导致评测结果无法准确反映模型的翻译能力 (Zhu et al., 2023)。考虑到不同模型的数据使用各不相同，如何更加公正合理地评估大语言模型的翻译能力，仍然是一个值得关注的问题。

综合而言，大语言模型的翻译能力评估简单有效，展现了大语言模型在翻译上的强大能力，也体现了这种翻译范式的潜在能力。但是，该类研究仅通过情景学习进行翻译，有可能仅发挥了大模型的部分翻译能力。如何进一步激发大语言模型的翻译能力，提升大语言模型的翻译质量，仍然是一个有待解决的开放性问题。

4 大语言模型翻译能力激发方式研究

采取不同的方式激发大语言模型的翻译能力可能会得到不同的翻译表现，研究人员研究了情景学习和指令微调等不同激发方式对翻译表现的影响(Table 2)。

激发方式	影响因素	研究工作
情景学习	模版内容	Zhu et al. (2023)
	模版语言	Zhang et al. (2023a)
	示例来源	Vilar et al. (2022)
	示例挑选	Agrawal et al. (2022),Zhang et al. (2023a),Moslem et al. (2023),Zhu et al. (2023)
	示例个数	Moslem et al. (2023),Agrawal et al. (2022),Zhang et al. (2023a),Zhu et al. (2023)
	示例语言	Zhu et al. (2023)
	示例粒度	Zhu et al. (2023)
指令微调	数据规模	Li et al. (2023),Yang et al. (2023)
	数据质量	Li et al. (2023)
	数据来源	Jiao et al. (2023a),Zhang et al. (2023b)

Table 2: 翻译能力激发研究工作概览

4.1 利用情景学习激发大语言模型翻译能力

情景学习中是用任务描述和示例来描述特定任务，其中，示例往往以某个指定的模板形式给出。在利用情景学习激发大语言模型的翻译能力时，模版的选择、示例的选择等许多因素都

第二十二届中国计算语言学大会论文集，第30页-第39页，哈尔滨，中国，2023年8月3日至5日。
卷2：前沿综述

对最终的翻译表现有影响。为了找到更好的情景学习方案，研究人员对这些因素进行了全面的分析研究(Lin et al., 2022; Vilar et al., 2022; Chowdhery et al., 2022; Agrawal et al., 2022; Zhang et al., 2023a; Moslem et al., 2023; Zhu et al., 2023)。

4.1.1 设计合适的情景学习模版

情景学习模版内容是对任务的具体描述，情景学习模板会直接影响翻译能力激发效果。大语言模型在不同模版下的翻译表现有着很大的差距(Zhu et al., 2023; Zhang et al., 2023a)。因此如何为翻译任务设计适合机器翻译任务的模板便成为了一个重要的研究问题。

然而，模板的设计面临着许多困难。首先，模板有效程度不一定符合人类直觉。Zhu et al. (2023)指出，在激发大语言模型XGLM的实验中，“<X>\n can be summarized as \n <Y>”这种不合理模版甚至比“<X>\n can be translated to\n <Y>”这种合理模版更能激发大语言模型的翻译表现（Table 3）。模版有效性与人类直觉之间的冲突不仅对模板设计工作提出了巨大的挑战，也促使人们对情景学习的工作原理进行更加深入的思考。

其次，最优模板难以通用，需要按照模型和任务单独定制。现有工作发现，同一模版在不同大语言模型上的使用效果是差别极大的。例如，一种经典的翻译任务模板是“[SRC]: <X>\n [TGT]: <Y>”，其中“[SRC]”与“[TGT]”分别为源语言和目标语言的名称，<X>”与“<Y>”则是源端与目标端句子。这种模版对于PaLM(Vilar et al., 2022)，GLM(Zhang et al., 2023a)模型效果很好，但是对于XGLM模型却效果很差(Zhu et al., 2023)。另外，即使是同样的大模型在不同语言方向上进行翻译时，最优的模板也不同(Lin et al., 2022; Zhang et al., 2023a; Zhu et al., 2023)。这些发现都说明想要为翻译任务设计通用有效的情景学习模版是非常有挑战的。

In-context Template	Deu-Eng	Eng-Deu	Rus-Eng	Eng-Rus	Rus-Deu	Deu-Rus	Average
`reasonable instructions:`							
<X>=<Y>	37.37	26.49	29.66	22.25	17.66	**17.31**	**25.12**
<X> \n Translate from [SRC] to [TGT]: \n <Y>	37.95	26.29	29.83	20.61	17.56	15.93	24.70
<X> \n Translate to [TGT]: \n <Y>	37.69	25.84	29.96	19.61	17.44	16.48	24.50
<X> \n [TGT]: <Y>	29.94	17.99	25.22	16.29	12.28	11.71	18.91
<X> is equivalent to <Y>	23.00	4.21	17.76	9.44	8.14	9.84	12.07
<X> \n can be translated to\n <Y>	37.55	26.49	29.82	22.14	17.48	16.40	24.98
[SRC]: <X> \n [TGT]: <Y>	16.95	8.90	14.48	6.88	7.86	4.01	9.85
`unreasonable instructions:`							
<X>$<Y>	37.77	26.43	29.53	20.99	17.72	17.27	24.95
<X> \n Translate from [TGT] to [SRC]: \n <Y>	38.18	26.21	29.85	20.35	17.75	16.63	24.83
<X> \n Compile to [TGT]: \n <Y>	37.39	26.35	29.68	19.91	17.52	16.15	24.50
<X> \n [SRC]: <Y>	27.86	16.69	24.41	18.16	11.98	12.60	18.62
<X> is not equivalent to <Y>	23.50	3.92	16.90	7.80	8.06	9.23	11.57
<X> \n can be summarized as \n <Y>	37.46	26.24	29.42	22.62	17.68	17.15	25.10
[SRC]: <X> \n [SRC]: <Y>	19.03	8.21	15.96	6.37	7.57	4.40	10.26

Table 3: 不同情景学习模版对翻译表现的影响(该结果摘自(Zhu et al., 2023))

4.1.2 选择合适的情景学习示例

情景学习效果的另一个重要影响因素是情景学习示例。如何为翻译任务提供合适的情景学习示例同样是研究者们关注的问题。情景学习示例一般从有监督数据如训练集、验证集中挑选而来，Vilar et al. (2022)发现从高质量的验证集中挑选情景学习示例比从训练集中挑选效果更好。而为了从候选集合中挑选出最有效的示例，研究人员也尝试了包括稀疏检索、稠密检索、混合检索等多种示例挑选方案(Agrawal et al., 2022; Zhang et al., 2023a; Moslem et al., 2023)，但是相比于随机检索取得收益都比较有限。Zhu et al. (2023)进一步发现，即使根据给定源句的参考译文进行检索，也很难带来进一步的增益。

增加情景学习示例个数是一种简单有效提升翻译表现的途径(Moslem et al., 2023; Agrawal et al., 2022; Zhang et al., 2023a; Zhu et al., 2023)。但是Zhang et al. (2023a)和Zhu et al. (2023)都发现随着示例个数的增加，大语言模型的翻译性能提升幅度会不断放缓。当示例个数在10个以上时，再增加示例个数则很难带来进一步的增益。

此外，情景学习示例中的具体内容会对翻译表现有很大的影响。Zhu et al. (2023)发现使用与测试样例翻译方向不同的跨语言翻译数据作为示例时，能够在某些语言对（如中文-英文）上带来大幅的翻译性能提升，这是一种非常有趣的现象。而如果使用不匹配的源端与目标端句子作为样例，则大语言模型将无法进行翻译任务，这说明大语言模型从示例中了解到需要保持源

第二十二届中国计算语言学大会论文集，第30页-第39页，哈尔滨，中国，2023年8月3日至5日。
卷2：前沿综述

句与目标句之间的语义一致性。如果使用词级别与文档级别的翻译作为样例，则会使大语言模型进行句子级别翻译的性能下降，这说明大语言模型需要根据示例中确定翻译任务的粒度。如果使用重复的句子作为样例时，翻译性能同样会下降，这说明保持情景学习示例的多样性是很重要的。

4.2 利用指令微调激发大语言模型翻译能力

另一种激发大语言模型翻译能力的方式是指令微调，通过让大语言模型学习包含指令的有监督数据，可以促使模型更加准确地遵循指令，完成下游任务(Wei et al., 2022; Muennighoff et al., 2022; Chung et al., 2022)。近期研究者开始尝试对大语言模型进行翻译指令微调，针对性激发大语言模型的翻译能力(Li et al., 2023; Jiao et al., 2023a; Yang et al., 2023; Zhang et al., 2023b)。

已有研究发现在特定翻译方向上，仅通过小规模翻译数据（千条至万条数据）微调大语言模型就可以大幅提升大语言模型的翻译能力(Jiao et al., 2023a; Li et al., 2023; Yang et al., 2023; Zhang et al., 2023b)。具体来说，Jiao et al. (2023a)使用翻译数据和通用任务数据对LLaMA、BLOOMZ等大语言模型进行指令微调，发现模型不仅可以完成简单的翻译任务还可以根据人类的特殊需求调整翻译内容。Li et al. (2023)专注于使用单纯的翻译数据微调XGLM模型，其发现随着数据规模增大，以及数据质量提高，模型的翻译性能可以不断提高，这显示了大模型的翻译能力仍存在巨大的提升空间。Yang et al. (2023)使用了102种语言的平行数据对LLaMA模型进行了指令微调，发现利用多语言翻译数据可以同时提升模型在多种语言上的翻译能力，尤其是增强了模型在维语、藏语、蒙古语等低资源语言上的翻译水平。Zhang et al. (2023b)使用了多轮交互式机器翻译数据进行指令微调，发现可以同时提升模型的翻译能力和语言理解能力，让模型能够更好地完成词约束翻译等有特殊需求的翻译任务。

指令微调的研究表明，大模型的潜在翻译能力比使用情景学习展现出来的要高得多。相比于情景学习的激发方式，使用指令微调激发大语言模型的翻译能力存在以下四点优势(Li et al., 2023):(1)激发效果更好，可以取得更强的翻译表现，尤其是在中低资源语言上的翻译效果更好（如Figure 3所示）; (2)泛化性能更好，在未见语言对上，指令微调的翻译表现比情景学习更好; (3)对于指令理解程度更好，在不同的翻译相关指令下，模型的翻译性能稳定，不会出现情景学习中对翻译相关指令非常敏感的情况; (4)推断时不再依赖翻译任务示例，这可以大大减少上下文长度，减少解码计算开销。而相比于情景学习，指令微调的主要劣势在于需要训练大规模参数，对计算资源要求更高。总体来说，指令微调是一种激发大语言模型翻译能力的有效方案，并且随着LoRA(Hu et al., 2023)、QLoRA(Dettmers et al., 2023)等高效微调方案的出现，指令微调的计算代价不断降低，这种方案是非常值得研究人员进一步研究和关注的。

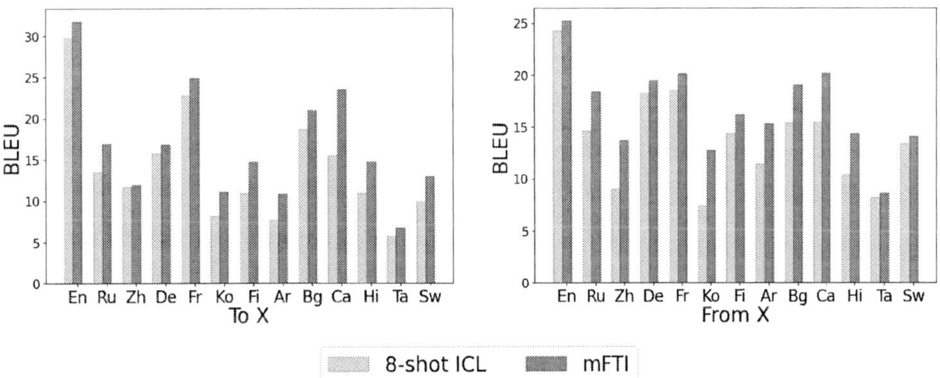

Figure 3: 使用情景学习和指令微调时大语言模型翻译效果对比(结果摘自(Li et al., 2023))

5 大语言模型在不同语言上的能力展现

大语言模型的预训练语料以英文为主，且指令微调时使用的通用任务数据，如alpaca数据(Taori et al., 2023)，也以英文为主。这一方面让模型有着极强的英语语言能力，另一方面也导致其非英语语言能力较弱。如果大模型能够学会翻译，是否其语言能力也可以在不同语言之间进行迁移呢？对于这一问题，研究者展开了初步研究(Cui et al., 2023; Yang et al., 2023; Zhang et al., 2023b)。

Cui et al. (2023)和Yang et al. (2023)关注于在预训练阶段提升大语言模型在中文上的能力，他们提出可以通过在词表中添加中文字符以及利用中文单语数据进行继续预训练的方式提升模型的中文能力。

Zhang et al. (2023b)则关注于在指令微调阶段提升大语言模型在中文、德语等语言上的能力。他们发现在指令微调阶段，增强大语言模型在英语与非英语之间的翻译能力，是帮助提升模型非英语语言能力的一种有效手段。该方法还可以避免继续预训练大语言模型和收集大规模数据带来的巨大开销。在训练数据设计上，Zhang et al. (2023b)提出使用多轮交互式翻译数据来进行指令微调。从其实验结果来看(Table 4)，相比于没有进行语言能力迁移的Alpaca模型(Taori et al., 2023)、Vicuna模型(Chiang et al., 2023),使用多轮交互式翻译数据微调得到的Bayling模型(Zhang et al., 2023b)在中文能力评估测试集GaoKao上取得了一定的性能提升。这一结果表明增强大语言模型的翻译能力是帮助模型展现多语言能力的有效手段。

Systems	Avg.	GaoKao(%)								
		chinese	english	mathqa	physics	chemistry	biology	history	geography	mathcloze
GPT-3.5-turbo	43.87	42.68	86.27	30.48	21.00	44.44	46.19	59.57	63.32	0.85
BayLing-13B	32.13	29.27	69.28	29.34	21.50	36.71	30.00	34.04	38.19	0.85
BayLing-7B	28.20	27.64	55.56	26.78	24.50	29.95	29.05	33.19	27.14	0.00
ChatGLM-6B	31.83	31.71	52.29	26.50	16.00	27.54	28.10	54.04	47.74	2.54
Vicuna-13B	29.36	21.14	71.24	21.94	23.00	31.88	27.14	33.19	34.67	0.00
Alpaca-7B	20.03	24.80	36.27	17.95	6.00	20.77	20.95	24.68	27.14	1.69

Table 4: 不同大语言模型在中文能力评估数据集GaoKao上的表现对比(结果摘自(Zhang et al., 2023b))

6 总结

近期，大语言模型迅猛发展，并凭借其惊人的语言能力在各项自然语言处理任务上都展现了巨大的潜力。本文聚焦于机器翻译任务，对大语言模型在机器翻译方面的相关进展进行了综述，具体介绍了以下三个方面的内容，包括：1）大语言模型翻译能力评估；2）大语言模型机器翻译能力激发；3）大语言模型在不同语言上的能力展现。总体来说，大语言模型已经展现出较强的多语言机器翻译能力，且仍有进一步提升的空间；但其在不同语言上的能力非常不平衡，在大部分中低资源语言上仍然与有监督基线模型有着较大的差距。在未来，如何更好地激发大语言模型的翻译能力，尤其是低资源语言上的翻译能力仍然有待解决。此外，为了让大语言模型在更多语言上发挥其强大的语言能力，多语言翻译的研究和探索可能有着重要的价值。

致谢

本文研究受到国家自然科学基金(No. 62176120)、辽宁省自然科学基金(No. 2022-KF-26-02)等项目资助。黄书剑是本文通讯作者。

参考文献

Sweta Agrawal, Chunting Zhou, Mike Lewis, Luke Zettlemoyer, and Marjan Ghazvininejad. 2022. In-context examples selection for machine translation. *arXiv preprint arXiv:2212.02437*.

Yejin Bang, Samuel Cahyawijaya, Nayeon Lee, Wenliang Dai, Dan Su, Bryan Wilie, Holy Lovenia, Ziwei Ji, Tiezheng Yu, Willy Chung, et al. 2023. A multitask, multilingual, multimodal evaluation of chatgpt on reasoning, hallucination, and interactivity. *arXiv preprint arXiv:2302.04023*.

Yoshua Bengio, Réjean Ducharme, and Pascal Vincent. 2000. A neural probabilistic language model. In *Advances in Neural Information Processing Systems (NeurIPS)*.

Tom Brown, Benjamin Mann, Nick Ryder, Melanie Subbiah, Jared D Kaplan, Prafulla Dhariwal, Arvind Neelakantan, Pranav Shyam, Girish Sastry, Amanda Askell, et al. 2020. Language models are few-shot learners. In *Advances in Neural Information Processing Systems (NeurIPS)*.

第二十二届中国计算语言学大会论文集，第30页-第39页，哈尔滨，中国，2023年8月3日至5日。
卷2：前沿综述

Wei-Lin Chiang, Zhuohan Li, Zi Lin, Ying Sheng, Zhanghao Wu, Hao Zhang, Lianmin Zheng, Siyuan Zhuang, Yonghao Zhuang, Joseph E. Gonzalez, Ion Stoica, and Eric P. Xing. 2023. Vicuna: An open-source chatbot impressing gpt-4 with 90%* chatgpt quality.

Aakanksha Chowdhery, Sharan Narang, Jacob Devlin, Maarten Bosma, Gaurav Mishra, Adam Roberts, Paul Barham, Hyung Won Chung, Charles Sutton, Sebastian Gehrmann, et al. 2022. Palm: Scaling language modeling with pathways. *arXiv preprint arXiv:2204.02311.*

Hyung Won Chung, Le Hou, Shayne Longpre, Barret Zoph, Yi Tay, William Fedus, Eric Li, Xuezhi Wang, Mostafa Dehghani, Siddhartha Brahma, et al. 2022. Scaling instruction-finetuned language models. *arXiv preprint arXiv:2210.11416.*

Marta R Costa-jussà, James Cross, Onur Çelebi, Maha Elbayad, Kenneth Heafield, Kevin Heffernan, Elahe Kalbassi, Janice Lam, Daniel Licht, Jean Maillard, et al. 2022. No language left behind: Scaling human-centered machine translation. *arXiv preprint arXiv:2207.04672.*

Yiming Cui, Ziqing Yang, and Xin Yao. 2023. Efficient and effective text encoding for chinese llama and alpaca. *arXiv preprint arXiv:2304.08177.*

Tim Dettmers, Artidoro Pagnoni, Ari Holtzman, and Luke Zettlemoyer. 2023. Qlora: Efficient finetuning of quantized llms. *arXiv preprint arXiv:2305.14314.*

Angela Fan, Shruti Bhosale, Holger Schwenk, Zhiyi Ma, Ahmed El-Kishky, Siddharth Goyal, Mandeep Baines, Onur Celebi, Guillaume Wenzek, Vishrav Chaudhary, et al. 2021. Beyond english-centric multilingual machine translation. *The Journal of Machine Learning Research (JMLR).*

Xavier Garcia, Yamini Bansal, Colin Cherry, George Foster, Maxim Krikun, Fangxiaoyu Feng, Melvin Johnson, and Orhan Firat. 2023. The unreasonable effectiveness of few-shot learning for machine translation.

Amr Hendy, Mohamed Abdelrehim, Amr Sharaf, Vikas Raunak, Mohamed Gabr, Hitokazu Matsushita, Young Jin Kim, Mohamed Afify, and Hany Hassan Awadalla. 2023. How good are gpt models at machine translation? a comprehensive evaluation. *arXiv preprint arXiv:2302.09210.*

Edward J Hu, Phillip Wallis, Zeyuan Allen-Zhu, Yuanzhi Li, Shean Wang, Lu Wang, Weizhu Chen, et al. 2023. Lora: Low-rank adaptation of large language models. In *International Conference on Learning Representations (ICLR).*

Wenxiang Jiao, Jen-tse Huang, Wenxuan Wang, Xing Wang, Shuming Shi, and Zhaopeng Tu. 2023a. Parrot: Translating during chat using large language models. *arXiv preprint arXiv:2304.02426.*

Wenxiang Jiao, Wenxuan Wang, Jen-tse Huang, Xing Wang, and Zhaopeng Tu. 2023b. Is chatgpt a good translator? a preliminary study. *arXiv preprint arXiv:2301.08745.*

Melvin Johnson, Mike Schuster, Quoc V. Le, Maxim Krikun, Yonghui Wu, Zhifeng Chen, Nikhil Thorat, Fernanda Viégas, Martin Wattenberg, Greg Corrado, Macduff Hughes, and Jeffrey Dean. 2017. Google's multilingual neural machine translation system: Enabling zero-shot translation. *Transactions of the Association for Computational Linguistics (TACL).*

Jiahuan Li, Hao Zhou, Shujian Huang, Shanbo Chen, and Jiajun Chen. 2023. Eliciting the translation ability of large language models via multilingual finetuning with translation instructions. *arXiv preprint arXiv:2305.15083.*

Xi Victoria Lin, Todor Mihaylov, Mikel Artetxe, Tianlu Wang, Shuohui Chen, Daniel Simig, Myle Ott, Naman Goyal, Shruti Bhosale, Jingfei Du, Ramakanth Pasunuru, Sam Shleifer, Punit Singh Koura, Vishrav Chaudhary, Brian O'Horo, Jeff Wang, Luke Zettlemoyer, Zornitsa Kozareva, Mona Diab, Veselin Stoyanov, and Xian Li. 2022. Few-shot learning with multilingual generative language models. In *Proceedings of Conference on Empirical Methods in Natural Language Processing (EMNLP).*

Yasmin Moslem, Rejwanul Haque, and Andy Way. 2023. Adaptive machine translation with large language models. *arXiv preprint arXiv:2301.13294.*

Niklas Muennighoff, Thomas Wang, Lintang Sutawika, Adam Roberts, Stella Biderman, Teven Le Scao, M Saiful Bari, Sheng Shen, Zheng-Xin Yong, Hailey Schoelkopf, et al. 2022. Crosslingual generalization through multitask finetuning. *arXiv preprint arXiv:2211.01786.*

第二十二届中国计算语言学大会论文集，第30页-第39页，哈尔滨，中国，2023年8月3日至5日。
卷2：前沿综述

Nathan Ng, Kyra Yee, Alexei Baevski, Myle Ott, Michael Auli, and Sergey Edunov. 2019. Facebook FAIR's WMT19 news translation task submission. In *Proceedings of the Conference on Machine Translation (WMT)*.

Sergei Nirenburg. 1989. Knowledge-based machine translation. *Machine Translation*.

Franz Josef Och and Hermann Ney. 2002. Discriminative training and maximum entropy models for statistical machine translation. In *Proceedings of the 40th Annual Meeting of the Association for Computational Linguistics*.

Long Ouyang, Jeffrey Wu, Xu Jiang, Diogo Almeida, Carroll Wainwright, Pamela Mishkin, Chong Zhang, Sandhini Agarwal, Katarina Slama, Alex Ray, et al. 2022. Training language models to follow instructions with human feedback. In *Advances in Neural Information Processing Systems (NeurIPS)*.

Ellie Pavlick. 2022. Semantic structure in deep learning. *Annual Review of Linguistics*, 8(1).

Fabio Petroni, Tim Rocktäschel, Sebastian Riedel, Patrick Lewis, Anton Bakhtin, Yuxiang Wu, and Alexander Miller. 2019. Language models as knowledge bases? In *Proceedings of Conference on Empirical Methods in Natural Language Processing (EMNLP)*.

Teven Le Scao, Angela Fan, Christopher Akiki, Ellie Pavlick, Suzana Ilić, Daniel Hesslow, Roman Castagné, Alexandra Sasha Luccioni, François Yvon, Matthias Gallé, et al. 2022. Bloom: A 176b-parameter open-access multilingual language model. *arXiv preprint arXiv:2211.05100*.

Rohan Taori, Ishaan Gulrajani, Tianyi Zhang, Yann Dubois, Xuechen Li, Carlos Guestrin, Percy Liang, and Tatsunori B. Hashimoto. 2023. Stanford alpaca: An instruction-following llama model. `https://github.com/tatsu-lab/stanford_alpaca`.

Ian Tenney, Dipanjan Das, and Ellie Pavlick. 2019. BERT rediscovers the classical NLP pipeline. In *Proceedings of Annual Meeting of the Association for Computational Linguistics (ACL)*.

Ashish Vaswani, Noam Shazeer, Niki Parmar, Jakob Uszkoreit, Llion Jones, Aidan N Gomez, Łukasz Kaiser, and Illia Polosukhin. 2017. Attention is all you need. In *Advances in Neural Information Processing Systems (NeurIPS)*.

David Vilar, Markus Freitag, Colin Cherry, Jiaming Luo, Viresh Ratnakar, and George Foster. 2022. Prompting palm for translation: Assessing strategies and performance. *arXiv preprint arXiv:2211.09102*.

Jason Wei, Maarten Bosma, Vincent Y Zhao, Kelvin Guu, Adams Wei Yu, Brian Lester, Nan Du, Andrew M Dai, and Quoc V Le. 2021. Finetuned language models are zero-shot learners. *arXiv preprint arXiv:2109.01652*.

Jason Wei, Maarten Bosma, Vincent Zhao, Kelvin Guu, Adams Wei Yu, Brian Lester, Nan Du, Andrew M. Dai, and Quoc V Le. 2022. Finetuned language models are zero-shot learners. In *International Conference on Learning Representations (ICLR)*.

Jason Wei, Xuezhi Wang, Dale Schuurmans, Maarten Bosma, Fei Xia, Ed H Chi, Quoc V Le, Denny Zhou, et al. 2023. Chain-of-thought prompting elicits reasoning in large language models. In *Advances in Neural Information Processing Systems (NeurIPS)*.

Wen Yang, Chong Li, Jiajun Zhang, and Chengqing Zong. 2023. Bigtrans: Augmenting large language models with multilingual translation capability over 100 languages. *arXiv preprint arXiv:2305.18098*.

Fei Yuan, Yinquan Lu, WenHao Zhu, Lingpeng Kong, Lei Li, and Jingjing Xu. 2022. Lego-mt: Towards detachable models in massively multilingual machine translation. *arXiv preprint arXiv:2212.10551*.

Susan Zhang, Stephen Roller, Naman Goyal, Mikel Artetxe, Moya Chen, Shuohui Chen, Christopher Dewan, Mona Diab, Xian Li, Xi Victoria Lin, et al. 2022. Opt: Open pre-trained transformer language models. *arXiv preprint arXiv:2205.01068*.

Biao Zhang, Barry Haddow, and Alexandra Birch. 2023a. Prompting large language model for machine translation: A case study. *arXiv preprint arXiv:2301.07069*.

第二十二届中国计算语言学大会论文集，第30页-第39页，哈尔滨，中国，2023年8月3日至5日。
卷2：前沿综述

Shaolei Zhang, Qingkai Fang, Zhuocheng Zhang, Zhengrui Ma, Yan Zhou, Langlin Huang, Mengyu Bu, Shangtong Gui, Yunji Chen, Xilin Chen, et al. 2023b. Bayling: Bridging cross-lingual alignment and instruction following through interactive translation for large language models. *arXiv preprint arXiv:2306.10968.*

Wenhao Zhu, Hongyi Liu, Qingxiu Dong, Jingjing Xu, Lingpeng Kong, Jiajun Chen, Lei Li, and Shujian Huang. 2023. Multilingual machine translation with large language models: Empirical results and analysis. *arXiv preprint arXiv:2304.04675.*

第二十二届中国计算语言学大会论文集，第30页-第39页，哈尔滨，中国，2023年8月3日至5日。
卷2：前沿综述

A Systematic Evaluation of Large Language Models for Natural Language Generation Tasks

Abstract

Recent efforts have evaluated large language models (LLMs) in areas such as commonsense reasoning, mathematical reasoning, and code generation. However, to the best of our knowledge, no work has specifically investigated the performance of LLMs in natural language generation (NLG) tasks, a pivotal criterion for determining model excellence. Thus, this paper conducts a comprehensive evaluation of well-known and high-performing LLMs, namely ChatGPT, ChatGLM, T5-based models, LLaMA-based models, and Pythia-based models, in the context of NLG tasks. We select English and Chinese datasets encompassing Text Summarization, Dialogue Generation, Story Generation, and Data-to-Text tasks. Moreover, we propose a common evaluation setting that incorporates input templates and post-processing strategies. Our study reports both automatic and manual metric results, accompanied by a detailed analysis.

1 Introduction

Recent studies have emphasized the importance of scaling large language models (LLMs), referring to both the dimensions of the model size themselves and the amount of data used, resulting in enhanced capability of the models for tasks downstream (Chung et al., 2022). Numerous investigations have been conducted to explore the limits of performance by training increasingly larger pre-trained language models, such as GPT-3 175B (Brown et al., 2020) and PaLM 540B (Chowdhery et al., 2022). Although scaling primarily involves increasing the model size while maintaining similar architectures and pre-training tasks, these large-sized PLMs exhibit distinct behaviors from their smaller counterparts and demonstrate surprising **emergent abilities** in solving complex tasks (Zhang et al., 2017; Frankle and Carbin, 2019; Zhang et al., 2021). An example of this is the contrasting performance of GPT-3 and GPT-2 when it comes to solving few-shot tasks. GPT-3 demonstrates effective problem-solving abilities by utilizing in-context learning, whereas GPT-2 faces difficulties in this aspect. As a result, these large-scale language models (LLMs) has become a huge research topic in current NLP area. In existing literature, remarkable LLMs such as ChatGPT[0], ChatGLM[1], have been widely adopted as powerful AI assistants, benefiting from their exceptional generation capabilities.

[0]https://chat.openai.com/

[1]https://chatglm.cn/

Proceedings of the 22nd China National Conference on Computational Linguistics, pages 40-56, Harbin, China, August 3 - 5, 2023.
Volume 2: Frotier Forum
(c) Technical Committee on Computational Linguistics, Chinese Information Processing Society of China

We hypothesis that a language model's performance in executing natural language generation (NLG) tasks is a crucial factor in determining its excellence (Dong et al., 2023). NLG tasks involve LLMs that are capable of accepting diverse types of input, such as texts and tables, and generating coherent and appropriate output text. We intuitively think that generate fluent, coherent, and consistent texts is the foundation of a language model, so as to large language models (Raffel et al., 2020). When some research institutions release their large language models, they tend to evaluate these models first. Community workers are also interested in testing well-known large language models. However, most of these evaluations focus on checking LLMs' ability of commonsense reasoning (Davis and Marcus, 2015; Wei et al., 2022), mathematical reasoning (Saxton et al., 2019; Wei et al., 2022), code completion (Allamanis et al., 2018), etc., but ignore the basic NLG tasks, such as dialogue generation (Chen et al., 2017), text summarization (Dong et al., 2023), and story generation (Al-Hussain and Azmi, 2022). Besides, Some researchers pointed out that the performance of a large model is determined not only by its size and architecture, but more by the quality and quantity of training data. Based on this point of view, researchers open source and propose that some smaller-scale models trained on more and higher-quality data sets can achieve the same performance as models with more parameters than them. For example, LLaMA-13B (Touvron et al., 2023) outperforms GPT-3 on most benchmarks, despite being 10 times smaller. This notable discovery makes us curious about the performance of models with different architecture, data size, and mode size, trying to figure out which factor is more important. Therefore, we aim to address this gap by conducting a comparative analysis of LLM performance on NLG tasks, considering different architectures and scales throughout the evaluation process.

In this paper, we present a systematic evaluation of existing LLMs for NLG tasks. The main objective is to enhance our understanding of instruction and prompt design by conducting a comparative analysis of these models. Initially, we provide an overview of classic NLG tasks, including their definitions and associated English and Chinese datasets. Subsequently, we devise a model input template that includes instructions for each dataset. Following that, we introduce various LLMs, considering factors such as model size and architecture. Finally, we present the results of both automatic and manual evaluation of LLMs on NLG datasets, and discuss the strengths and weaknesses of their performance across different models.

2 Natural Language Generation

In this section, we will introduce the definition of NLG, and its sub-tasks with some corresponding datasets that we will use to evaluate LLMs.

2.1 Definition

Natural Language Generation is the process of producing a natural language text in order to meet specified communicative goals. The texts that are generated may range from a single phrase given in answer to a question, through multi-sentence remarks and questions within a dialog, to full-page explanations. In our evaluation, we mainly focus on text-to-text styles. In general, the task of NLG targets at finding an optimal sequence $y_{<T+1} = (y_1, y_2, \ldots, y_T)$ that satisfies:

$$y_{<T+1} = \underset{y_{<T+1} \in \mathcal{Y}}{\arg\max} \log P_\theta \left(y_{<T+1} \mid x\right) = \underset{y_{<T+1} \in \mathcal{Y}}{\arg\max} \sum_{t=1}^{T} \log P_\theta \left(y_t \mid y_{<t}, x\right) \tag{1}$$

Proceedings of the 22nd China National Conference on Computational Linguistics, pages 40-56, Harbin, China, August 3 - 5, 2023.
Volume 2: Frotier Forum

where T represents the number of tokens of the generated sequence, $\mathcal{Y}$ represents a set containing all possible sequences, and $P_\theta\left(y_t \mid y_{<t}, x\right)$ is the conditional probability of the next token y_t based on its previous tokens $y_{<t} = (y_1, y_2, \ldots, y_{t-1})$ and the source sequence x with model parameters θ.

Next, we will introduce some classic and widely-researched sub-tasks of NLG, with several corresponding datasets.

2.2 Text Summarization

Text summarization is the process of condensing a piece of text, such as an article, document, or news story, into a shorter version while preserving its key information and main ideas (El-Kassas et al., 2021; Dong et al., 2023). Text summarization can be performed through two main approaches: *Extractive Summarization* and *Abstractive Summarization*. In our evaluation, we utilize multiple abstractive summarization datasets, specifically choosing two renowned datasets for the English and Chinese languages.

- **CNN/DailyMail** (Nallapati et al., 2016) is a large scale English summarization dataset which contains 93k and 220k articles collected from the CNN and Daily Mail websites, respectively, where each article has its matching abstractive summary.
- **XSum** (Narayan et al., 2018) is an extreme English summarization dataset containing BBC articles and corresponding single sentence summaries. In this dataset, 226,711 Wayback archived BBC articles are collected, which range from 2010 to 2017 and cover a wide variety of domains.
- **THUCNews** (Li and Sun, 2007) is a Chinese summarization dataset, which comes from filtering the historical data of the Sina News RSS subscription channel from 2005 to 2011, including 740,000 news documents.
- **LCSTS** (Liu, 2020) is a large corpus of Chinese short text summarization dataset constructed from the Chinese micro-blogging website *Sina Weibo*. This corpus consists of over 2 million real Chinese short texts with short summaries given by the author of each text.

2.3 Dialogue Generation

Dialogue generation refers to the process of automatically generating coherent and contextually appropriate responses in a conversational setting (Chen et al., 2017; Ma et al., 2020; Dong et al., 2023). The ultimate goal of dialogue generation task is to create responses that are relevant, informative, and engaging to the user.We utilize two English dialogue datasets characterized by clear emotional flow and topic constraints, as well as one English dataset that incorporates speakers' personalities. Furthermore, we employ a Chinese open-domain dialogue dataset for evaluation purposes.

- **DailyDialog** (Li et al., 2017) is a comprehensive, human-authored, and relatively noise-free English dataset that captures everyday communication styles and encompasses various topics related to our daily lives.
- **PersonaChat** (Zhang et al., 2018) is a persona-grounded dialogue dataset which contains 10k English multi-turn dialogues conditioned on personas, and each persona is described with at least 5 profile sentences.

Proceedings of the 22nd China National Conference on Computational Linguistics, pages 40-56, Harbin, China, August 3 - 5, 2023.
Volume 2: Frotier Forum

- **EmpatheticDialogue** (Rashkin et al., 2019) is a large-scale multi-turn dialogue English dataset that contains 25k empathetic conversations between a speaker and a listener.
- **LCCC** (Wang et al., 2020) is a large-scale cleaned Chinese conversation dataset.

2.4 Story Generation

Story generation aims at automatically creating coherent and engaging stories (Al-Hussain and Azmi, 2022). The input of story generation task can take various forms, including beginning (Chen et al., 2019), outline (Fang et al., 2021), prompt (Fan et al., 2018), or abstract (Fang et al., 2021), etc. Advanced methods or models of this task typically involve defining the story structure, characters, settings, and desired narrative elements (Martin et al., 2018). We employ two datasets in Chinese and English, where story beginnings serve as inputs. Additionally, we utilize an English dataset in which story outlines are provided for evaluation purposes.

- **ROCStories** (Mostafazadeh et al., 2016) is a compilation of 100,000 short stories, each consisting of five sentences, that display a general sense of understanding. These stories adhere to a daily theme and incorporate a variety of common-sense causal and temporal relationships found in everyday occurrences..
- **WritingPrompts** (Fan et al., 2018) is a large English dataset of 300K human-written stories paired with writing prompts from an online forum.
- **LOT** (Guan et al., 2022) is a benchmark dataset for evaluating Chinese long text understanding and generation.

2.5 Overview for LLMs

Typically, large language models (LLMs) refer to Transformer-based models containing tens or hundreds of billions of parameters and trained on extensive corpora of texts (Zhao et al., 2023). These LLMs demonstrate significant capabilities in understanding natural language and solving complex tasks. Furthermore, they have showcased their ability to perform new tasks based on textual instructions or with just a few examples (Chung et al., 2022). The emergence of these few-shot properties is a result of scaling models to a sufficient size, leading to a line of research that focuses on further scaling these models (Rae et al., 2021).

Previous LLMs, such as T5 (Raffel et al., 2020), GPT-3 (Brown et al., 2020), OPT (Zhang et al., 2022), and PaLM (Chowdhery et al., 2022), primarily emphasized scaling model size rather than considering the quality and quantity of data. However, recent studies have demonstrated that, given a fixed compute budget, the best performance is achieved by smaller models trained on larger datasets (Hoffmann et al., 2022). Additionally, most of these models are not open-source and can only be accessed through APIs for inference, which poses inconveniences for model evaluation and usage. In order to address this issue, numerous researchers have proposed excellent open-source architectures and trained models, including GLM-130B (Zeng et al., 2022), ChatGLM (Du et al., 2022), LLaMA (Touvron et al., 2023), and Pythia (Biderman et al., 2023). Furthermore, advancements in fine-tuning techniques have contributed to the success of deploying these models with limited resources, such as Lora (Hu et al., 2022) and P-Tuning (Li and Liang, 2021). Therefore, this paper aims to conduct systematic evaluations of these models and their fine-tuned versions, categorized into four groups: **ChatGPT, ChatGLM, T5-based models, LLaMA-based models, and Pythia-based models**.

Proceedings of the 22nd China National Conference on Computational Linguistics, pages 40-56, Harbin, China, August 3 - 5, 2023.
Volume 2: Frotier Forum

2.6 ChatGPT

ChatGPT[2] is a large language model based on OpenAI's GPT-3.5 architecture (Brown et al., 2020). It is designed specifically for generating conversations and answering user queries. ChatGPT employs large-scale pretraining and fine-tuning methodologies, utilizing vast amounts of textual data to learn statistical patterns and semantic knowledge of language, and perform well in zero-shot and few-shot settings, and can understand the input instructions.

2.7 ChatGLM

ChatGLM[3] is a freely available dialogue language model that operates in both Chinese and English languages. It follows the GLM architecture and boasts an impressive parameter count of 6.2 billion. ChatGLM-6B incorporates similar technology as ChatGPT, with a specific focus on Chinese question answering and dialogue. The model undergoes extensive training on a dataset containing approximately 1 trillion tokens in Chinese and English. The training process includes supervised fine-tuning, feedback bootstrap, and reinforcement learning with human feedback. Despite having only 6.2 billion parameters, the model demonstrates the ability to generate responses that align with human preferences.

2.8 T5-Based models

T5 (Raffel et al., 2020), which stands for Text-To-Text Transfer Transformer, is a transformer-based language model developed by Google Research. Instead of training separate models for different tasks, T5 is trained in a text-to-text pattern. This means that it is trained to perform a wide range of NLP tasks by transforming the input text into a standardized format that specifies the task to be performed. In our evaluation, we select two new fine-tuned versions of T5, namely: Flan-T5-XXL[4] and FastChat-T5[5].

Flan-T5-XXL Flan-T5 (Chung et al., 2022) is a fine-tuned version model class of T5 that has been trained on a variety of datasets phrased as instructions. It has shown impressive performance on several benchmarks, demonstrating strong zero-shot, few-shot, and Chain-of-Thought (CoT) (Wei et al., 2022) abilities. Flan-T5-XXL is the largest released checkpoint of this model, boasting a parameter volume of 13B. It inherits the extensive knowledge base of T5 while also being capable of understanding natural language instructions and performing the corresponding tasks.

FastChat-T5 FastChat (Zheng et al., 2023a) is an open platform for training, serving, and evaluating large language model based chatbots. And FastChat-T5 is an open-source chatbot trained on this platform by fine-tuning Flan-T5-XL (3B parameters) on user-shared conversations collected from ShareGPT.

2.9 LLaMA-Based Models

LLaMA (Touvron et al., 2023) is a collection of foundation language models ranging from 7B to 65B parameters proposed by Meta AI. Unlike other famous LLMs, LLaMA is only trained

[2]https://chat.openai.com/
[3]https://chatglm.cn/
[4]https://huggingface.co/google/flan-t5-xxl
[5]https://huggingface.co/lmsys/fastchat-t5-3b-v1.0

Proceedings of the 22nd China National Conference on Computational Linguistics, pages 40-56, Harbin, China, August 3 - 5, 2023.
Volume 2: Frotier Forum

on publicly avaiable data, making it compatible with open-sourcing. Numerous remarkable and impressive models have emerged as a result, built upon the LLaMA framework and trained using diverse datasets. Among these models, we have chosen a few prominent ones for evaluation: Open-LLaMA, Vicuna, Alpaca, and GPT4ALL.

Open-LLaMA Open-LLaMA (Geng and Liu, 2023) is an open reproduction of LLaMA trained on the RedPajama dataset (Computer, 2023). We leverage the 7B version[6] of this model for evaluation.

Alpaca (Taori et al., 2023) is fine-tuned based on a 7B LLaMA model using a dataset consisting of 52,000 instances of instruction-following data. This dataset is generated using the techniques outlined in the Self-Instruct paper (Wang et al., 2022), which aims to address the limited instruction-following capabilities of LLaMA models. To create the training data, the authors initially generate the data using OpenAI's GPT-3 and subsequently convert it into 52,000 instances of instruction-following conversational data using the Self-Instruct pipeline. This dataset is referred to as the Alpaca dataset. The Alpaca model is then fine-tuned to generate responses in conversations similar to ChatGPT.

In our evaluation, we utilize Alpaca-Lora-7B[7], a low-rank adapter for LLaMA-7b fit on the Stanford Alpaca dataset, and Chinese-Alpaca-13b[8], a Chinese model version of Alpaca.

Vicuna (Zheng et al., 2023b) is fine-tuned based on LLaMA models using user-shared conversations collected from ShareGPT. It is an auto-regressive language model, based on the transformer architecture. So it is basically fine-tuned with ChatGPT conversations. We utilize two versions of Vicuna, which are Vicuna-13B[9] and Chinese-Vicuna-13B[10].

GPT4ALL (Anand et al., 2023) is a fine-tuned LLaMA 13B model and the GPT4All community[11] has built the GPT4All Open Source datalake as a staging ground for contributing instruction and assistant tuning data for future GPT4All model trains.

2.10 Pythia-Based Models

Pythia (Biderman et al., 2023) is a project by EleutherAI[12] that combines interpret-ability analysis and scaling laws to understand how knowledge develops and evolves during training in autoregressive Transformers. We utilize two versions of Pythia which are Oasst-Pythia and Dolly.

Oasst-Pythia[13] is an open assistant model developed by the Open-Assistant project. It is based on a Pythia 12B model that was fine-tuned on human demonstrations of assistant conversations collected through the Open-Assistant human feedback web app.

[6]https://github.com/openlm-research/open_llama
[7]https://huggingface.co/chainyo/alpaca-lora-7b
[8]https://huggingface.co/shibing624/chinese-alpaca-plus-13b-hf
[9]https://huggingface.co/eachadea/vicuna-13b-1.1
[10]https://huggingface.co/Chinese-Vicuna/Chinese-Vicuna-lora-13b-belle-and-guanaco
[11]https://home.nomic.ai/
[12]https://github.com/EleutherAI/pythia
[13]https://huggingface.co/OpenAssistant/pythia-12b-sft-v8-7k-steps

Proceedings of the 22nd China National Conference on Computational Linguistics, pages 40-56, Harbin, China, August 3 - 5, 2023.
Volume 2: Frotier Forum

```
Below is an instruction that describes
a task. Write a response that appropr-
iately completes the request.
### Instruction: {instruction}
### Input: {text}
### Response:
```

```
以下是描述任务的说明。 编写准确的回复来
完成这个任务。

### 说明: {instruction}
### 输入: {text}
### 回复:
```

Figure 1: Input templates for English (left) and Chinese (right) datasets. **instruction** and **text** will be replaced with content corresponding different datasets.

Dolly[14] is a Language Model (LLM) with 12B parameters, designed to follow instructions accurately. It has been trained on approximately 15,000 instruction/response fine-tuning records known as databricks-dolly-15k. These records were created by Databricks employees and cover various capability domains sourced from InstructGPT (Ouyang et al., 2022). These domains include brainstorming, classification, closed QA, generation, information extraction, open QA, and summarization.

3 Experimental Settings

3.1 Dataset

In our evaluation, we aim to showcase the generation capabilities of LLMs in zero-shot scenarios. Therefore, we refrain from providing any additional information to the model for each of the aforementioned datasets. Specifically:

- For datasets of Text Summarization task, we input the text, document, or article to allow the model to extract key information and generate concise summaries.
- For datasets of Dialogue Generation task, we input the dialogue history, enabling the model to generate appropriate responses for the final round of the conversation.
- For datasets of Story Generation task, we input the story beginning, outline, or prompts to provide the necessary context for the model to generate coherent and engaging stories.

3.2 Input Template

Because LLMs that we evaluate possess the ability to comprehend instructions and perform corresponding tasks, so in order to ensure fairness, we develop an input template that is applied to every dataset for each task, serving as the input for every large language model. This template consists of two components: the instruction and the input. Figure 1 illustrates the templates designed for both the Chinese and English datasets, and Table 1 shows the content of *instruction* and *text* for each dataset.

3.3 Hyperparameters

Although each LLM may have its own optimal decoding strategy, for the sake of fairness, we have standardized these hyperparameters across all LLMs. We employ the Top-k and Top-p sampling, with $k = 40$ and $p = 0.75$. Additionally, a temperature value of 0.2 and a repetition

[14]https://huggingface.co/databricks/dolly-v2-12b

Proceedings of the 22nd China National Conference on Computational Linguistics, pages 40-56, Harbin, China, August 3 - 5, 2023.
Volume 2: Frotier Forum

Dataset	Instruction	Text
Empathetic Dialogues	This is an open-domain *empathetic* dialogue completion task.The input is the Dialogue. You act as System in the dialogue. You need to fully *understand the situation and combine the speaker's emotion* to complete the dialogue with natural content and a way closer to human speech. There is no need for any additional notes or clarifications, you just give the response in English.	Dialogue Context
DailyDialog	This is an open-domain *topic-aware* dialogue completion task. The input is the Dialogue. You act as System in the dialogue. You need to fully *understand the topic* and complete the dialogue with natural content and a way closer to human speech. There is no need for any additional notes or clarifications, you just give the response in English	Dialogue Context
PersonaChat	This is an open-domain *personality-aware* dialogue completion task. The input is the Dialogue. You act as System in the dialogue. You need to fully *understand the personality* and complete the dialogue with natural content and a way closer to human speech. There is no need for any additional notes or clarifications, you just give the response in English.	Dialogue Context
LCCC	这是一个开放域的中文对话补全任务。输入是待完成的对话内容。你在对话中扮演系统。你需要完全理解说话者的话语，并用自然的内容和更接近于人类说话的方式完成对话，而不是用语言模型或者AI的身份。不需要任何额外的注释或者说明，你只需用中文给出回复。	Dialogue Context

Table 1: *Instruction* and *Text* for each dataset.

penalty factor of 1.15 are imposed. Furthermore, we specify a maximum token length of 128 and a minimum token length of 10 for the generated content.

3.4 Post-Processing Strategy

Through case study, we observe that despite emphasizing the exclusion of any additional output in the input, regrettably, most LLMs still generate redundant information in their output. Therefore, we find it necessary to apply post-processing to the outputs of these models. To ensure fairness, we adopt the same post-processing strategy for all LLMs. Specifically, we utilize the keywords "`### response:`" or "`### 回复：`" for segmentation. If the segmented content consists of a single line, we consider it as the final result. If the segmented content spans multiple lines, we use "\n" as segmentation keywords and select the first sentence with a length not less than 16 as the final result.

3.5 Baselines

There have been numerous previous works on datasets we used, and these works have achieved good results. Therefore, despite the fact that most of these works have proposed models much smaller than LLMs and have predominantly utilized supervised fine-tuning methods, we still compare them with LLMs to highlight some characteristics of LLMs. For each dataset, we select several recent works with better performance and report their results.

Proceedings of the 22nd China National Conference on Computational Linguistics, pages 40-56, Harbin, China, August 3 - 5, 2023.
Volume 2: Frotier Forum

- For EmpatheticDialogues, we utilize **EP-PG** (Li et al., 2022) that first generates event transition plans and then obtains the final response, and **MoEL** (Lin et al., 2019) that are consist of one emotion tracker and n emotion listeners.
- For DailyDialog, we utilize **PLATO** (Bao et al., 2020), a pre-trained dialogue generation model, and **DialogWAE** (Gu et al., 2019), a conditional wasserstein autoencoder (WAE) specially designed for dialogue modeling.
- For PersonaChat, we utilize **PLATO** as mentioned above, and **CTRLStruct** (Yin et al., 2023) for dialogue structure learning to effectively explore topic-level dialogue clusters. clusters as

3.6 Evaluation Metrics

Automatic Metrics We utilize several common automatic metrics for NLG tasks. **PPL** is used to assess the difficulty or confusion of a language model in predicting a sequence of words. **BLEU** (B-1, B-2, B-4) (Papineni et al., 2002) is used to assess the quality of machine-generated translations by comparing them to human reference translations. **Meteor** (MT) (Banerjee and Lavie, 2005) considers the accuracy and recall based on the entire corpus, and get the final measure. **Rouge-L** (R-L) (Lin, 2004) calculates the overlap between the generated output and the reference summaries or translations using various techniques such as N-gram matching. **DISTINCT** (D-1, D-2) (Li et al., 2016) quantifies how many distinct or different N-grams are present in the generated text, providing an indication of the model's ability to produce varied and non-repetitive output.

Besides these widely-used metrics, we also develop a new metric called **PostProcess Rate** (PPR), which means the proportion of samples that need to be post-processed to the total number of samples.

Human Evaluation We conduct a human evaluation on open-domain dialogue generation. We recruit university students to evaluate the quality of conversations. We follow up previous dialogue generation efforts (Yu et al., 2022) and employ several metrics to evaluate the dialogue quality : **Coherence** measures relevance to the dialogue context, **Informativeness** evaluates information provided, and **Fluency** checks grammatical accuracy. We also check for **Hallucination**↓ and factual errors.

Note that the Coherence, Informativeness, and Fluency scale is $[0, 1, 2, 3, 4]$, whose higher score indicates a better performance. Moreover, the scale of Hallucination is $[0, 1, 2]$, whose lower score indicates a better performance.

4 Results and Analysis

The automatic metrics results of LLMs on the four datasets are shown in Tables 2, 3, 4. Since Flan-T5-XXL and FastChat-T5 do not possess the ability to generate Chinese textual content, we do not report their results on LCCC. Although automatic metrics cannot fully reflect the performance of the models, we can still draw the following conclusions from them.

First, apart from ChatGPT that has the largest scale of 175B, the two T5-based models consistently outperform others in terms of the **PPR** metric. This indicates that the generated content of Flan-T5-XXL and FastChat-T5 largely aligns with the instruction requirements stated in the input template: "*without any additional output.*" Interestingly, both of these models follow

Model	Scale	Arch	PPL↓	B-1	B-2	B-4	MT	R-L	D-1	D-2	PPR↓
EP-PG	–	–	–	16.74	6.94	2.39	–	–	2.19	8.25	–
MoEL	23.1M	DO	33.58	–	–	2.90	–	–	1.06	4.29	–
ChatGPT	175B	DO	10.52	7.35	2.40	0.52	**9.26**	**8.75**	4.71	27.75	**0.00%**
ChatGLM	6B	DO	11.73	6.05	1.82	0.27	8.58	7.71	3.57	22.82	12.61%
Flan-T5-XXL	13B	ED	19.97	5.62	2.40	<u>0.61</u>	5.38	7.41	5.66	24.97	**0.00%**
FastChat-T5	3B	ED	<u>9.25</u>	7.33	2.35	0.45	8.50	8.62	3.55	20.81	0.12%
Open-LLaMA	7B	DO	15.90	**8.50**	**2.97**	**0.63**	6.43	<u>8.74</u>	3.93	17.91	40.05%
Vicuna	13B	DO	14.31	6.18	1.93	0.35	<u>8.91</u>	7.81	4.09	25.84	38.86%
Alpaca-Lora	7B	DO	16.10	7.95	2.52	0.40	7.34	6.69	**7.59**	<u>39.58</u>	0.24%
Chinese-Alpaca	13B	DO	12.05	6.51	1.86	0.35	7.53	6.64	5.32	29.14	0.20%
GPT4ALL	13B	DO	11.14	5.20	1.47	0.24	8.75	6.78	3.94	25.60	1.81%
Dolly	12B	DO	131.75	<u>8.29</u>	<u>2.64</u>	0.46	6.91	7.96	<u>7.46</u>	**42.69**	58.61%
Oasst-Pythia	12B	DO	**8.71**	5.48	1.53	0.26	8.79	6.92	3.38	21.18	<u>0.04%</u>

Table 2: Automatic evaluation results of LLMs on EmpatheticDialogues. **Scale** stands for the model size.**ED** and **DO** respectively stand for *encoder-decoder* and *decoder-only*. **Arch** is an abbreviation for *Architecture*. The **bold** numbers in the results represent the best scores, whereas the <u>underlined</u> numbers indicate the second-best scores.

Model	Scale	Arch	PPL↓	B-1	B-2	B-4	MT	R-L	D-1	D-2	PPR↓
PLATO	–	DO	–	39.70	31.10	–	–	–	5.30	29.10	–
DialogWAE	–	ED	–	32.30	–	–	–	–	31.30	59.70	–
ChatGPT	175B	DO	11.41	<u>7.58</u>	<u>2.71</u>	<u>0.56</u>	**10.13**	<u>8.17</u>	10.98	47.20	**0.00%**
ChatGLM	6B	DO	17.52	**10.54**	**3.86**	**0.93**	9.14	**11.91**	9.60	42.69	12.05%
Flan-T5-XXL	13B	ED	16.31	3.85	1.61	0.42	6.64	5.52	<u>14.54</u>	47.59	**0.00%**
FastChat-T5	3B	ED	**10.27**	7.45	2.59	0.50	<u>9.15</u>	7.86	9.58	41.16	<u>0.50%</u>
Open-LLaMA	7B	DO	21.23	6.72	2.31	0.46	5.94	5.59	11.65	38.72	64.36%
Vicuna	13B	DO	78.66	6.13	2.11	0.42	8.89	6.96	10.15	45.18	38.55%
Alpaca-Lora	7B	DO	28.63	6.40	2.16	0.00	6.04	5.02	**17.49**	**61.66**	3.41%
Chinese-Alpaca	13B	DO	22.23	6.52	2.18	0.38	7.49	5.93	13.06	51.02	2.01%
GPT4ALL	13B	DO	14.72	4.84	1.24	0.13	7.72	5.77	10.24	43.53	25.50%
Dolly	12B	DO	58.29	6.09	2.01	0.40	5.70	4.25	14.14	<u>52.33</u>	74.80%
Oasst-Pythia	12B	DO	<u>10.68</u>	5.40	1.45	0.19	7.62	6.09	9.23	38.91	16.47%

Table 3: Automatic evaluation results of LLMs on DailyDialog.

an encoder-decoder architecture, while all other models follow a decoder-only architecture. This suggests that encoder-decoder models demonstrate superior understanding of input instructions under the same model scale. We speculate that having an encoder allows the model to comprehend the input content effectively, thereby executing the corresponding task more successfully.

Second, Alpaca-Lora consistently ranks either first or second in the richness of output content. Moreover, the models using the same architecture as Alpaca-Lora also achieve higher scores in

Proceedings of the 22nd China National Conference on Computational Linguistics, pages 40-56, Harbin, China, August 3 - 5, 2023.
Volume 2: Frotier Forum

Model	Scale	Arch	PPL↓	B-1	B-2	B-4	MT	R-L	D-1	D-2	PPR↓
PLATO	–	DO	–	40.60	31.50	–	–	–	2.10	12.10	–
CTRLStruct	–	ED	–	31.60	11.90	–	–	16.10	3.20	11.40	–
ChatGPT	175B	DO	10.97	6.36	2.37	**0.52**	**9.78**	8.42	9.10	40.65	**0.00%**
ChatGLM	6B	DO	13.89	5.98	2.07	0.40	8.85	**8.67**	6.85	34.86	12.05%
Flan-T5-XXL	13B	ED	51.50	**6.51**	**2.53**	0.43	6.15	7.46	12.23	39.82	**0.00%**
FastChat-T5	3B	ED	10.61	5.53	2.00	0.43	8.98	7.94	7.30	33.66	0.50%
Open-LLaMA	7B	DO	15.69	4.43	1.16	0.00	5.86	5.43	7.83	28.90	64.36%
Vicuna	13B	DO	12.53	3.20	1.01	0.14	7.30	4.82	5.88	30.12	38.55%
Alpaca-Lora	7B	DO	17.20	4.19	1.21	0.24	6.29	4.40	**12.28**	**50.33**	3.41%
Chinese-Alpaca	13B	DO	14.95	4.93	1.66	0.29	7.70	6.21	10.18	44.62	2.01%
GPT4ALL	13B	DO	11.68	2.74	0.55	0.07	6.52	4.39	7.56	35.23	25.50%
Dolly	12B	DO	29.76	4.51	1.39	0.24	5.02	4.59	10.55	41.62	74.80%
Oasst-Pythia	12B	DO	**9.57**	3.34	0.69	0.07	6.58	4.66	6.48	28.56	16.47%

Table 4: Automatic evaluation results of LLMs on PersonaChat.

terms of D-1 and D-2. This indicates that LLAMA-based models are capable of producing more diverse and less repetitive content.

Last, ChatGPT, the model with the largest parameter scale, performs the best overall on all four datasets, securing the first or second position most frequently. This suggests that increasing the parameter size and training data volume of LLMs is consistently one of the most important methods for improving model performance.

5 Conclusion

In this paper, we conduct a comprehensive assessment of several existing large-scale language models (LLMs) in the context of natural language generation (NLG) tasks. Our evaluation encompasses English and Chinese datasets to examine the multilingual capabilities of these LLMs. The results and analyses from both automatic and manual evaluations of LLMs reveal notable trends and phenomena.

Acknowledgements

This research is supported by the National Natural Science Foundation of China (No.62106105), the CCF-Tencent Open Research Fund (No.RAGR20220122), the CCF-Zhipu AI Large Model Fund (No.CCF-Zhipu202315), the Scientific Research Starting Foundation of Nanjing University of Aeronautics and Astronautics (No.YQR21022), and the High Performance Computing Platform of Nanjing University of Aeronautics and Astronautics.

References

Arwa Al-Hussain and Aqil M. Azmi. 2022. Automatic story generation: A survey of approaches. ACM Comput. Surv., 54(5):103:1–103:38.

Proceedings of the 22nd China National Conference on Computational Linguistics, pages 40-56, Harbin, China, August 3 - 5, 2023.
Volume 2: Frotier Forum

Miltiadis Allamanis, Earl T. Barr, Premkumar T. Devanbu, and Charles Sutton. 2018. A survey of machine learning for big code and naturalness. ACM Comput. Surv., 51(4):81:1–81:37.

Yuvanesh Anand, Zach Nussbaum, Brandon Duderstadt, Benjamin Schmidt, and Andriy Mulyar. 2023. Gpt4all: Training an assistant-style chatbot with large scale data distillation from gpt-3.5-turbo. `https://github.com/nomic-ai/gpt4all`.

Satanjeev Banerjee and Alon Lavie. 2005. METEOR: an automatic metric for MT evaluation with improved correlation with human judgments. In Jade Goldstein, Alon Lavie, Chin-Yew Lin, and Clare R. Voss, editors, Proceedings of the Workshop on Intrinsic and Extrinsic Evaluation Measures for Machine Translation and/or Summarization@ACL 2005, Ann Arbor, Michigan, USA, June 29, 2005, pages 65–72. Association for Computational Linguistics.

Siqi Bao, Huang He, Fan Wang, Hua Wu, and Haifeng Wang. 2020. PLATO: pre-trained dialogue generation model with discrete latent variable. In Dan Jurafsky, Joyce Chai, Natalie Schluter, and Joel R. Tetreault, editors, Proceedings of the 58th Annual Meeting of the Association for Computational Linguistics, ACL 2020, Online, July 5-10, 2020, pages 85–96. Association for Computational Linguistics.

Stella Biderman, Hailey Schoelkopf, Quentin Anthony, Herbie Bradley, Kyle O'Brien, Eric Hallahan, Mohammad Aflah Khan, Shivanshu Purohit, USVSN Sai Prashanth, Edward Raff, Aviya Skowron, Lintang Sutawika, and Oskar van der Wal. 2023. Pythia: A suite for analyzing large language models across training and scaling. CoRR, abs/2304.01373.

Tom B. Brown, Benjamin Mann, Nick Ryder, Melanie Subbiah, Jared Kaplan, Prafulla Dhariwal, Arvind Neelakantan, Pranav Shyam, Girish Sastry, Amanda Askell, Sandhini Agarwal, Ariel Herbert-Voss, Gretchen Krueger, Tom Henighan, Rewon Child, Aditya Ramesh, Daniel M. Ziegler, Jeffrey Wu, Clemens Winter, Christopher Hesse, Mark Chen, Eric Sigler, Mateusz Litwin, Scott Gray, Benjamin Chess, Jack Clark, Christopher Berner, Sam McCandlish, Alec Radford, Ilya Sutskever, and Dario Amodei. 2020. Language models are few-shot learners. CoRR, abs/2005.14165.

Hongshen Chen, Xiaorui Liu, Dawei Yin, and Jiliang Tang. 2017. A survey on dialogue systems: Recent advances and new frontiers. SIGKDD Explor., 19(2):25–35.

Jiaao Chen, Jianshu Chen, and Zhou Yu. 2019. Incorporating structured commonsense knowledge in story completion. In The Thirty-Third AAAI Conference on Artificial Intelligence, AAAI 2019, The Thirty-First Innovative Applications of Artificial Intelligence Conference, IAAI 2019, The Ninth AAAI Symposium on Educational Advances in Artificial Intelligence, EAAI 2019, Honolulu, Hawaii, USA, January 27 - February 1, 2019, pages 6244–6251. AAAI Press.

Aakanksha Chowdhery, Sharan Narang, Jacob Devlin, Maarten Bosma, Gaurav Mishra, Adam Roberts, Paul Barham, Hyung Won Chung, Charles Sutton, Sebastian Gehrmann, Parker Schuh, Kensen Shi, Sasha Tsvyashchenko, Joshua Maynez, Abhishek Rao, Parker Barnes, Yi Tay, Noam Shazeer, Vinodkumar Prabhakaran, Emily Reif, Nan Du, Ben Hutchinson, Reiner Pope, James Bradbury, Jacob Austin, Michael Isard, Guy Gur-Ari, Pengcheng Yin, Toju Duke, Anselm Levskaya, Sanjay Ghemawat, Sunipa Dev, Henryk Michalewski, Xavier Garcia, Vedant Misra, Kevin Robinson, Liam Fedus, Denny Zhou, Daphne Ippolito, David Luan, Hyeontaek Lim, Barret Zoph, Alexander Spiridonov, Ryan Sepassi, David Dohan, Shivani Agrawal, Mark Omernick, Andrew M. Dai, Thanumalayan Sankaranarayana Pillai, Marie Pellat, Aitor Lewkowycz, Erica Moreira, Rewon Child, Oleksandr Polozov, Katherine Lee, Zongwei Zhou, Xuezhi Wang, Brennan Saeta, Mark Diaz, Orhan Firat, Michele Catasta, Jason Wei, Kathy Meier-Hellstern, Douglas Eck, Jeff Dean, Slav Petrov, and Noah Fiedel. 2022. Palm: Scaling language modeling with pathways. CoRR, abs/2204.02311.

Hyung Won Chung, Le Hou, Shayne Longpre, Barret Zoph, Yi Tay, William Fedus, Eric Li, Xuezhi Wang, Mostafa Dehghani, Siddhartha Brahma, Albert Webson, Shixiang Shane Gu, Zhuyun Dai, Mirac

Proceedings of the 22nd China National Conference on Computational Linguistics, pages 40-56, Harbin, China, August 3 - 5, 2023.
Volume 2: Frotier Forum

Suzgun, Xinyun Chen, Aakanksha Chowdhery, Sharan Narang, Gaurav Mishra, Adams Yu, Vincent Y. Zhao, Yanping Huang, Andrew M. Dai, Hongkun Yu, Slav Petrov, Ed H. Chi, Jeff Dean, Jacob Devlin, Adam Roberts, Denny Zhou, Quoc V. Le, and Jason Wei. 2022. Scaling instruction-finetuned language models. CoRR, abs/2210.11416.

Together Computer. 2023. Redpajama-data: An open source recipe to reproduce llama training dataset.

Ernest Davis and Gary Marcus. 2015. Commonsense reasoning and commonsense knowledge in artificial intelligence. Commun. ACM, 58(9):92–103.

Chenhe Dong, Yinghui Li, Haifan Gong, Miaoxin Chen, Junxin Li, Ying Shen, and Min Yang. 2023. A survey of natural language generation. ACM Comput. Surv., 55(8):173:1–173:38.

Zhengxiao Du, Yujie Qian, Xiao Liu, Ming Ding, Jiezhong Qiu, Zhilin Yang, and Jie Tang. 2022. GLM: general language model pretraining with autoregressive blank infilling. In Smaranda Muresan, Preslav Nakov, and Aline Villavicencio, editors, Proceedings of the 60th Annual Meeting of the Association for Computational Linguistics (Volume 1: Long Papers), ACL 2022, Dublin, Ireland, May 22-27, 2022, pages 320–335. Association for Computational Linguistics.

Wafaa S. El-Kassas, Cherif R. Salama, Ahmed A. Rafea, and Hoda K. Mohamed. 2021. Automatic text summarization: A comprehensive survey. Expert Syst. Appl., 165:113679.

Angela Fan, Mike Lewis, and Yann N. Dauphin. 2018. Hierarchical neural story generation. In Iryna Gurevych and Yusuke Miyao, editors, Proceedings of the 56th Annual Meeting of the Association for Computational Linguistics, ACL 2018, Melbourne, Australia, July 15-20, 2018, Volume 1: Long Papers, pages 889–898. Association for Computational Linguistics.

Le Fang, Tao Zeng, Chaochun Liu, Liefeng Bo, Wen Dong, and Changyou Chen. 2021. Outline to story: Fine-grained controllable story generation from cascaded events. CoRR, abs/2101.00822.

Jonathan Frankle and Michael Carbin. 2019. The lottery ticket hypothesis: Finding sparse, trainable neural networks. In 7th International Conference on Learning Representations, ICLR 2019, New Orleans, LA, USA, May 6-9, 2019. OpenReview.net.

Xinyang Geng and Hao Liu. 2023. Openllama: An open reproduction of llama, May.

Xiaodong Gu, Kyunghyun Cho, Jung-Woo Ha, and Sunghun Kim. 2019. Dialogwae: Multimodal response generation with conditional wasserstein auto-encoder. In 7th International Conference on Learning Representations, ICLR 2019, New Orleans, LA, USA, May 6-9, 2019. OpenReview.net.

Jian Guan, Zhuoer Feng, Yamei Chen, Ruilin He, Xiaoxi Mao, Changjie Fan, and Minlie Huang. 2022. LOT: A story-centric benchmark for evaluating chinese long text understanding and generation. Trans. Assoc. Comput. Linguistics, 10:434–451.

Jordan Hoffmann, Sebastian Borgeaud, Arthur Mensch, Elena Buchatskaya, Trevor Cai, Eliza Rutherford, Diego de Las Casas, Lisa Anne Hendricks, Johannes Welbl, Aidan Clark, Tom Hennigan, Eric Noland, Katie Millican, George van den Driessche, Bogdan Damoc, Aurelia Guy, Simon Osindero, Karen Simonyan, Erich Elsen, Jack W. Rae, Oriol Vinyals, and Laurent Sifre. 2022. Training compute-optimal large language models. CoRR, abs/2203.15556.

Edward J. Hu, Yelong Shen, Phillip Wallis, Zeyuan Allen-Zhu, Yuanzhi Li, Shean Wang, Lu Wang, and Weizhu Chen. 2022. Lora: Low-rank adaptation of large language models. In The Tenth International Conference on Learning Representations, ICLR 2022, Virtual Event, April 25-29, 2022. OpenReview.net.

Proceedings of the 22nd China National Conference on Computational Linguistics, pages 40-56, Harbin, China, August 3 - 5, 2023.
Volume 2: Frotier Forum

Xiang Lisa Li and Percy Liang. 2021. Prefix-tuning: Optimizing continuous prompts for generation. In Chengqing Zong, Fei Xia, Wenjie Li, and Roberto Navigli, editors, Proceedings of the 59th Annual Meeting of the Association for Computational Linguistics and the 11th International Joint Conference on Natural Language Processing, ACL/IJCNLP 2021, (Volume 1: Long Papers), Virtual Event, August 1-6, 2021, pages 4582–4597. Association for Computational Linguistics.

Jingyang Li and Maosong Sun. 2007. Scalable term selection for text categorization. In Jason Eisner, editor, EMNLP-CoNLL 2007, Proceedings of the 2007 Joint Conference on Empirical Methods in Natural Language Processing and Computational Natural Language Learning, June 28-30, 2007, Prague, Czech Republic, pages 774–782. ACL.

Jiwei Li, Michel Galley, Chris Brockett, Jianfeng Gao, and Bill Dolan. 2016. A diversity-promoting objective function for neural conversation models. In Kevin Knight, Ani Nenkova, and Owen Rambow, editors, NAACL HLT 2016, The 2016 Conference of the North American Chapter of the Association for Computational Linguistics: Human Language Technologies, San Diego California, USA, June 12-17, 2016, pages 110–119. The Association for Computational Linguistics.

Yanran Li, Hui Su, Xiaoyu Shen, Wenjie Li, Ziqiang Cao, and Shuzi Niu. 2017. Dailydialog: A manually labelled multi-turn dialogue dataset. In Greg Kondrak and Taro Watanabe, editors, Proceedings of the Eighth International Joint Conference on Natural Language Processing, IJCNLP 2017, Taipei, Taiwan, November 27 - December 1, 2017 - Volume 1: Long Papers, pages 986–995. Asian Federation of Natural Language Processing.

Qintong Li, Piji Li, Wei Bi, Zhaochun Ren, Yuxuan Lai, and Lingpeng Kong. 2022. Event transition planning for open-ended text generation. In Smaranda Muresan, Preslav Nakov, and Aline Villavicencio, editors, Findings of the Association for Computational Linguistics: ACL 2022, Dublin, Ireland, May 22-27, 2022, pages 3412–3426. Association for Computational Linguistics.

Zhaojiang Lin, Andrea Madotto, Jamin Shin, Peng Xu, and Pascale Fung. 2019. Moel: Mixture of empathetic listeners. In Kentaro Inui, Jing Jiang, Vincent Ng, and Xiaojun Wan, editors, Proceedings of the 2019 Conference on Empirical Methods in Natural Language Processing and the 9th International Joint Conference on Natural Language Processing, EMNLP-IJCNLP 2019, Hong Kong, China, November 3-7, 2019, pages 121–132. Association for Computational Linguistics.

Chin-Yew Lin. 2004. Rouge: A package for automatic evaluation of summaries. In Text summarization branches out, pages 74–81.

Cong Liu. 2020. Chinese newstitle generation project by gpt2.

Yukun Ma, Khanh Linh Nguyen, Frank Z. Xing, and Erik Cambria. 2020. A survey on empathetic dialogue systems. Inf. Fusion, 64:50–70.

Lara J. Martin, Prithviraj Ammanabrolu, Xinyu Wang, William Hancock, Shruti Singh, Brent Harrison, and Mark O. Riedl. 2018. Event representations for automated story generation with deep neural nets. In Sheila A. McIlraith and Kilian Q. Weinberger, editors, Proceedings of the Thirty-Second AAAI Conference on Artificial Intelligence, (AAAI-18), the 30th innovative Applications of Artificial Intelligence (IAAI-18), and the 8th AAAI Symposium on Educational Advances in Artificial Intelligence (EAAI-18), New Orleans, Louisiana, USA, February 2-7, 2018, pages 868–875. AAAI Press.

Nasrin Mostafazadeh, Nathanael Chambers, Xiaodong He, Devi Parikh, Dhruv Batra, Lucy Vanderwende, Pushmeet Kohli, and James F. Allen. 2016. A corpus and cloze evaluation for deeper understanding of commonsense stories. In Kevin Knight, Ani Nenkova, and Owen Rambow, editors, NAACL HLT 2016, The 2016 Conference of the North American Chapter of the Association for Computational Linguistics: Human Language Technologies, San Diego California, USA, June 12-17, 2016, pages 839–849. The Association for Computational Linguistics.

Ramesh Nallapati, Bowen Zhou, Cícero Nogueira dos Santos, Çaglar Gülçehre, and Bing Xiang. 2016. Abstractive text summarization using sequence-to-sequence rnns and beyond. In Yoav Goldberg and Stefan Riezler, editors, Proceedings of the 20th SIGNLL Conference on Computational Natural Language Learning, CoNLL 2016, Berlin, Germany, August 11-12, 2016, pages 280–290. ACL.

Shashi Narayan, Shay B. Cohen, and Mirella Lapata. 2018. Don't give me the details, just the summary! topic-aware convolutional neural networks for extreme summarization. In Ellen Riloff, David Chiang, Julia Hockenmaier, and Jun'ichi Tsujii, editors, Proceedings of the 2018 Conference on Empirical Methods in Natural Language Processing, Brussels, Belgium, October 31 - November 4, 2018, pages 1797–1807. Association for Computational Linguistics.

Long Ouyang, Jeffrey Wu, Xu Jiang, Diogo Almeida, Carroll L. Wainwright, Pamela Mishkin, Chong Zhang, Sandhini Agarwal, Katarina Slama, Alex Ray, John Schulman, Jacob Hilton, Fraser Kelton, Luke Miller, Maddie Simens, Amanda Askell, Peter Welinder, Paul F. Christiano, Jan Leike, and Ryan Lowe. 2022. Training language models to follow instructions with human feedback. In NeurIPS.

Kishore Papineni, Salim Roukos, Todd Ward, and Wei-Jing Zhu. 2002. Bleu: a method for automatic evaluation of machine translation. In Proceedings of the 40th Annual Meeting of the Association for Computational Linguistics, July 6-12, 2002, Philadelphia, PA, USA, pages 311–318. ACL.

Jack W. Rae, Sebastian Borgeaud, Trevor Cai, Katie Millican, Jordan Hoffmann, H. Francis Song, John Aslanides, Sarah Henderson, Roman Ring, Susannah Young, Eliza Rutherford, Tom Hennigan, Jacob Menick, Albin Cassirer, Richard Powell, George van den Driessche, Lisa Anne Hendricks, Maribeth Rauh, Po-Sen Huang, Amelia Glaese, Johannes Welbl, Sumanth Dathathri, Saffron Huang, Jonathan Uesato, John Mellor, Irina Higgins, Antonia Creswell, Nat McAleese, Amy Wu, Erich Elsen, Siddhant M. Jayakumar, Elena Buchatskaya, David Budden, Esme Sutherland, Karen Simonyan, Michela Paganini, Laurent Sifre, Lena Martens, Xiang Lorraine Li, Adhiguna Kuncoro, Aida Nematzadeh, Elena Gribovskaya, Domenic Donato, Angeliki Lazaridou, Arthur Mensch, Jean-Baptiste Lespiau, Maria Tsimpoukelli, Nikolai Grigorev, Doug Fritz, Thibault Sottiaux, Mantas Pajarskas, Toby Pohlen, Zhitao Gong, Daniel Toyama, Cyprien de Masson d'Autume, Yujia Li, Tayfun Terzi, Vladimir Mikulik, Igor Babuschkin, Aidan Clark, Diego de Las Casas, Aurelia Guy, Chris Jones, James Bradbury, Matthew J. Johnson, Blake A. Hechtman, Laura Weidinger, Iason Gabriel, William Isaac, Edward Lockhart, Simon Osindero, Laura Rimell, Chris Dyer, Oriol Vinyals, Kareem Ayoub, Jeff Stanway, Lorrayne Bennett, Demis Hassabis, Koray Kavukcuoglu, and Geoffrey Irving. 2021. Scaling language models: Methods, analysis & insights from training gopher. CoRR, abs/2112.11446.

Colin Raffel, Noam Shazeer, Adam Roberts, Katherine Lee, Sharan Narang, Michael Matena, Yanqi Zhou, Wei Li, and Peter J. Liu. 2020. Exploring the limits of transfer learning with a unified text-to-text transformer. J. Mach. Learn. Res., 21:140:1–140:67.

Hannah Rashkin, Eric Michael Smith, Margaret Li, and Y-Lan Boureau. 2019. Towards empathetic open-domain conversation models: A new benchmark and dataset. In Anna Korhonen, David R. Traum, and Lluís Màrquez, editors, Proceedings of the 57th Conference of the Association for Computational Linguistics, ACL 2019, Florence, Italy, July 28- August 2, 2019, Volume 1: Long Papers, pages 5370–5381. Association for Computational Linguistics.

David Saxton, Edward Grefenstette, Felix Hill, and Pushmeet Kohli. 2019. Analysing mathematical reasoning abilities of neural models. In 7th International Conference on Learning Representations, ICLR 2019, New Orleans, LA, USA, May 6-9, 2019. OpenReview.net.

Rohan Taori, Ishaan Gulrajani, Tianyi Zhang, Yann Dubois, Xuechen Li, Carlos Guestrin, Percy Liang, and Tatsunori B. Hashimoto. 2023. Stanford alpaca: An instruction-following llama model. https://github.com/tatsu-lab/stanford_alpaca.

Proceedings of the 22nd China National Conference on Computational Linguistics, pages 40-56, Harbin, China, August 3 - 5, 2023.
Volume 2: Frotier Forum

Hugo Touvron, Thibaut Lavril, Gautier Izacard, Xavier Martinet, Marie-Anne Lachaux, Timothée Lacroix, Baptiste Rozière, Naman Goyal, Eric Hambro, Faisal Azhar, Aurélien Rodriguez, Armand Joulin, Edouard Grave, and Guillaume Lample. 2023. Llama: Open and efficient foundation language models. CoRR, abs/2302.13971.

Yida Wang, Pei Ke, Yinhe Zheng, Kaili Huang, Yong Jiang, Xiaoyan Zhu, and Minlie Huang. 2020. A large-scale chinese short-text conversation dataset. In Xiaodan Zhu, Min Zhang, Yu Hong, and Ruifang He, editors, Natural Language Processing and Chinese Computing - 9th CCF International Conference, NLPCC 2020, Zhengzhou, China, October 14-18, 2020, Proceedings, Part I, volume 12430 of Lecture Notes in Computer Science, pages 91–103. Springer.

Yizhong Wang, Yeganeh Kordi, Swaroop Mishra, Alisa Liu, Noah A. Smith, Daniel Khashabi, and Hannaneh Hajishirzi. 2022. Self-instruct: Aligning language model with self generated instructions. CoRR, abs/2212.10560.

Jason Wei, Xuezhi Wang, Dale Schuurmans, Maarten Bosma, Brian Ichter, Fei Xia, Ed H. Chi, Quoc V. Le, and Denny Zhou. 2022. Chain-of-thought prompting elicits reasoning in large language models. In NeurIPS.

Congchi Yin, Piji Li, and Zhaochun Ren. 2023. Ctrlstruct: Dialogue structure learning for open-domain response generation. In Ying Ding, Jie Tang, Juan F. Sequeda, Lora Aroyo, Carlos Castillo, and Geert-Jan Houben, editors, Proceedings of the ACM Web Conference 2023, WWW 2023, Austin, TX, USA, 30 April 2023 - 4 May 2023, pages 1539–1550. ACM.

Jifan Yu, Xiaohan Zhang, Yifan Xu, Xuanyu Lei, Xinyu Guan, Jing Zhang, Lei Hou, Juanzi Li, and Jie Tang. 2022. XDAI: A tuning-free framework for exploiting pre-trained language models in knowledge grounded dialogue generation. In Aidong Zhang and Huzefa Rangwala, editors, KDD '22: The 28th ACM SIGKDD Conference on Knowledge Discovery and Data Mining, Washington, DC, USA, August 14 - 18, 2022, pages 4422–4432. ACM.

Aohan Zeng, Xiao Liu, Zhengxiao Du, Zihan Wang, Hanyu Lai, Ming Ding, Zhuoyi Yang, Yifan Xu, Wendi Zheng, Xiao Xia, Weng Lam Tam, Zixuan Ma, Yufei Xue, Jidong Zhai, Wenguang Chen, Peng Zhang, Yuxiao Dong, and Jie Tang. 2022. GLM-130B: an open bilingual pre-trained model. CoRR, abs/2210.02414.

Chiyuan Zhang, Samy Bengio, Moritz Hardt, Benjamin Recht, and Oriol Vinyals. 2017. Understanding deep learning requires rethinking generalization. In 5th International Conference on Learning Representations, ICLR 2017, Toulon, France, April 24-26, 2017, Conference Track Proceedings. OpenReview.net.

Saizheng Zhang, Emily Dinan, Jack Urbanek, Arthur Szlam, Douwe Kiela, and Jason Weston. 2018. Personalizing dialogue agents: I have a dog, do you have pets too? In Iryna Gurevych and Yusuke Miyao, editors, Proceedings of the 56th Annual Meeting of the Association for Computational Linguistics, ACL 2018, Melbourne, Australia, July 15-20, 2018, Volume 1: Long Papers, pages 2204–2213. Association for Computational Linguistics.

Chiyuan Zhang, Samy Bengio, Moritz Hardt, Benjamin Recht, and Oriol Vinyals. 2021. Understanding deep learning (still) requires rethinking generalization. Commun. ACM, 64(3):107–115.

Susan Zhang, Stephen Roller, Naman Goyal, Mikel Artetxe, Moya Chen, Shuohui Chen, Christopher Dewan, Mona T. Diab, Xian Li, Xi Victoria Lin, Todor Mihaylov, Myle Ott, Sam Shleifer, Kurt Shuster, Daniel Simig, Punit Singh Koura, Anjali Sridhar, Tianlu Wang, and Luke Zettlemoyer. 2022. OPT: open pre-trained transformer language models. CoRR, abs/2205.01068.

Proceedings of the 22nd China National Conference on Computational Linguistics, pages 40-56, Harbin, China, August 3 - 5, 2023.
Volume 2: Frotier Forum

Wayne Xin Zhao, Kun Zhou, Junyi Li, Tianyi Tang, Xiaolei Wang, Yupeng Hou, Yingqian Min, Beichen Zhang, Junjie Zhang, Zican Dong, Yifan Du, Chen Yang, Yushuo Chen, Zhipeng Chen, Jinhao Jiang, Ruiyang Ren, Yifan Li, Xinyu Tang, Zikang Liu, Peiyu Liu, Jian-Yun Nie, and Ji-Rong Wen. 2023. A survey of large language models. CoRR, abs/2303.18223.

Lianmin Zheng, Wei-Lin Chiang, Ying Sheng, Siyuan Zhuang, Zhanghao Wu, Yonghao Zhuang, Zi Lin, Zhuohan Li, Dacheng Li, Eric P. Xing, Hao Zhang, Joseph E. Gonzalez, and Ion Stoica. 2023a. Judging llm-as-a-judge with mt-bench and chatbot arena. CoRR, abs/2306.05685.

Lianmin Zheng, Wei-Lin Chiang, Ying Sheng, Siyuan Zhuang, Zhanghao Wu, Yonghao Zhuang, Zi Lin, Zhuohan Li, Dacheng Li, Eric. P Xing, Hao Zhang, Joseph E. Gonzalez, and Ion Stoica. 2023b. Judging llm-as-a-judge with mt-bench and chatbot arena.

生成式信息检索前沿进展与挑战

范意兴[1,2], 唐钰葆[1,2], 陈建贵[1,2], 张儒清[1,2], 郭嘉丰[1,2]
1. 中国科学院计算技术研究所网络数据科学与技术重点实验室，北京, 100190
2. 中国科学院大学，北京, 100190
{fanyixing, tangyubao21b,chenjiangui18z, zhangruqing, guojiafeng}@ict.ac.cn

摘要

信息检索（Information Retrieval, IR）旨在从大规模的语料集合中找到与用户查询相关的信息，已经成为人们解决日常工作和生活中问题的最重要工具之一。现有的IR系统主要依赖于"索引-召回-重排"的框架，将复杂的检索任务建模成多阶段耦合的搜索过程。这种解耦建模的方式，一方面提升了系统检索的效率，使得检索系统能够轻松应对数十亿的语料集合；另一方面也加重了系统架构的复杂性，无法实现端到端联合优化。为了应对这个问题，近年来研究人员开始探索利用一个统一的模型建模整个搜索过程，并提出了新的生成式信息检索范式，这种新的范式将整个语料集合编码到检索模型中，可以实现端到端优化，消除了检索系统对于外部索引的依赖。当前，生成式检索已经成为IR领域热门研究方向之一，研究人员提出了不同的方案来提升检索的效果，考虑到这个方向的快速进展，本文将对生成式信息检索进行系统的综述，包括基础概念，文档标识符和模型容量。此外，我们还讨论了一些未解决的挑战以及有前景的研究方向，希望能激发和促进更多关于这些主题的未来研究。

关键词： 信息检索 ; 检索模型 ; 生成式检索

Challenges and Advances in Generative Information Retrieval

Yixing Fan[1,2], Yubao Tang[1,2], Jiangui Chen[1,2], Ruqing Zhang[1,2], Jiafeng Guo[1,2]
1. CAS Key Lab of Network Data Science and Technology,
Institute of Computing Technology, Chinese Academy of Sciences, Beijing 100190
2. University of Chinese Academy of Sciences, Beijing 100190
{fanyixing, tangyubao21b,chenjiangui18z, zhangruqing, guojiafeng}@ict.ac.cn

Abstract

Information retrieval (IR) aims to seek relevant information in response to user queries. Existing IR systems mainly rely on the "index-retrieve-then-rank" framework, which models the complex retrieval tasks as a multi-stage search process. Such a decoupling process improves the efficiency of the system, making it possible for retrieval system to handle billions of documents. However, it also increase the complexity of the search architecture, making it difficult to achieve end-to-end optimization. To address this issue, researchers have begun to explore a new paradigm of generative information retrieval. This new paradigm encodes the entire corpus into the search model, enabling end-to-end optimization and eliminating the dependence on external indices. Currently, generative information retrieval has become a hot research direction in IR, and researchers have proposed different solutions to improve retrieval effectiveness. Given the rapid progress in this direction, this article provides a systematic review of

第二十二届中国计算语言学大会论文集，第57页-第66页，哈尔滨，中国，2023年8月3日至5日。
卷2：前沿综述

generative information retrieval, including basic concepts, document identifiers, model architectures, and model capacity. In addition, we also discuss some unresolved challenges and promising research directions, hoping to inspire and promote future research on these topics.

Keywords: Information Retrieval , Retrieval Model , Generative Information Retrieval

1 引言

信息检索（Information retrieval, IR）在众多领域中起着重要的作用，包括网络搜索(Chapelle et al., 2011)、问答系统(Karpukhin et al., 2020; Lee et al., 2019)、对话系统(Chen et al., 2017)等任务。IR的核心是从海量文档集合中根据用户查询快速查找满足用户信息需求的文档，为了保证检索的效率，大多数现有的IR系统(Ma et al., 2021b; Ma et al., 2021c)通常采用多阶段分步检索的流水线架构，即"索引-召回-重排序"。具体而言，(i) **索引：**创建文档集中的文档表示、索引以及存储结构；(ii) **召回：**从全部文档集中快速找回与查询潜在相关的小批量文档，形成初始的候选文档集，侧重于检索结果的召回率；以及 (iii) **重排序：**基于召回的候选文档集进一步计算文档与查询相关性，对候选文档进行精排，侧重于检索结果的准确率。这种流水线架构具有多方面的优势：(i) 高效性：它利用索引实现高效检索，适用于大规模文档集合；(ii) 灵活性：该架构允许在检索模型和排序策略上进行灵活定制；(iii) 可解释性：每个检索阶段都可以进行分析和评估；(iv) 可扩展性：该框架适用于动态增长的文档集合，能够高效存储、组织和检索持续更新的数据。凭借这些优势，该框架在学术界和工业界都广泛的研究和应用。

尽管这种流水线架构在信息检索中已经证明了其有效性(Chapelle et al., 2011; Lee et al., 2019; Ma et al., 2021b; Ma et al., 2021c)，但它也存在一些固有的局限：首先，流水线框架的目标要求在大规模文档集中搜索数百万个全局文档；其次，多个解耦后的搜索组件通常是独立设计和优化的，缺乏端到端优化的能力；此外，流水线框架是"文档模型"，通常对每个文档进行独立评分，忽视了整个文档集中可用的全局信息；最后，索引阶段需要大量的存储空间来存储预计算的索引，这在可扩展性方面可能带来重大挑战。

鉴于这些局限性，Goole的研究人员(Metzler et al., 2021) 最先提出了一种全新的检索范式，称之为基于模型的信息检索（Model-based IR），以取代长期以来的"索引-检索-排序"架构。这种范式旨在通过一个统一的模型来替代传统方法中涉及的索引、召回和重排序模块，从而彻底改变检索的流程。受到这一蓝图的启发，生成式检索模型（Generative Information Retrieval, GIR）(Metzler et al., 2021)被提出来实现基于模型的信息检索理念，该模型可以根据给定的查询直接生成相关文档的标识符（Document identifiers, DocIDs），从而避免了资源密集型的索引过程。具体而言，生成式检索将检索任务形式化为序列到序列（Sequence-to-sequence, Seq2seq）的生成问题，其核心就是构建一个Seq2seq生成模型。在训练阶段，生成模型将文档内容映射到语义唯一标志符（DocID）实现文档的索引；而在推断阶段，生成模型将查询映射到对应的文档ID以完成文档检索。这里，模型训练通常使用最大似然估计（MLE）损失函数来优化索引和检索两个任务，即：

$$
\begin{aligned}
\mathcal{L}_{MLE}(\theta) &= \mathcal{L}_{MLE}^{indexing}(\theta) + \mathcal{L}_{MLE}^{retrieval}(\theta) \\
&= \sum_{d_i \in \mathcal{D}} \log P(r_i | GR_\theta(d_i)) + \sum_{q_j \in \mathcal{Q}} \log P(r_j | GR_\theta(q_j)),
\end{aligned} \tag{1}
$$

其中，$\mathcal{D}$ 表示给定的语料库，$\mathcal{Q}$ 表示查询集合，r_i 或r_j 表示文档d_i 或输入查询q_j 的目标DocID，θ 表示生成模型$GR_\theta(\cdot)$ 的模型参数。这种新的生成式检索范式带来了几个重要的优势：首先，通过解码DocID i，搜索空间被减小为万级的词表空间，与传统的全语料文档库搜索相比，大大降低了搜索复杂性；其次，生成式检索利用统一模型$GR_\theta(\cdot)$ 来涵盖整个检索过程，实现全局性优化；再次，通过使用最大似然估计（Maximum Likelihood Estimation, MLE）损失函数$\mathcal{L}_{MLE}^{indexing}(\cdot)$ 对模型进行编码和使用MLE损失函数$\mathcal{L}_{MLE}^{retrieval}(\cdot)$ 将查询映射到相关的DocID，生成式检索在生成过程中利用了整个语料库的知识；最后，生成式检索避免了索引相关操作，如文档表示和索引构建。因此，存储需求得到缓解，使得能够处理庞大语料库$\mathcal{D}$的可扩展检索系统而不会产生过高的存储成本。生成式检索的出现引发了广泛的研究兴趣，旨在全面了解其底层机制并发挥其全部潜力。因此，在本文中，我们将介绍生成式检索的基本概念，以及当前相关研究涉及的生成式检索重要的几个方面，分别是DocID表示、模型架构以及模型容量。

- **DocID表示**: DocID表示在生成式检索框架中起着关键作用。一个有效的DocID应该包含来自相应文档的丰富语义信息，具备简洁的特点以便于生成，并且要能够有效区分不同的文档。因此，对DocID特征的探索对于进一步改进生成式检索至关重要。

- **模型架构**: 模型架构是生成式检索的基石。因此，对生成式检索中使用的模型架构$GR_\theta(\cdot)$进行全面的考察对于揭示其潜力是不可或缺的。当前主流的生成式模型包括编码器-解码器架构和仅解码器架构两种。

- **模型容量**: 生成式检索模型的容量，通常与其参数规模相关，显著影响其性能。较大的模型容量通常具有更强的学习能力，但也可能导致额外的计算成本。直观上期望在一定范围内增加模型容量可以提高在给定语料库$\mathcal{D}$上的性能。然而，在超过一定阈值后，效果可能会趋于平稳甚至下降。因此，研究模型容量与性能之间的关系对于优化生成式检索模型并在效果和效率之间取得平衡至关重要。

本文的结构如下所示。首先，在第2节中，我们回顾传统流水式信息检索框架。然后，在第3节中，我们将介绍生成式检索的基本概念。再次，在第4节，第5节和第6节中深入探讨生成式检索中的DocID表示、模型架构以及模型容量三个方面内容。最后，在第7节中讨论当前研究中的挑战和潜在研究方向，并在第8节对本文进行总结。

2 传统流水线检索架构

在正式介绍生成式信息检索之前，我们简要回顾传统"索引-召回-重排序"三步骤的流水线框架，这种架构被广泛应用于现有实际检索系统中(Ma et al., 2021b; Ma et al., 2021c)。该架构通过依次执行索引构建、文档找回和重排序的过程，为信息检索任务提供了系统化的方法。在索引构建阶段，主要是对文档进行离线的表征计算以及索引构建和存储；召回阶段则是基于索引库进行查询，利用索引结构特性从大规模文档集合中快速检索一组可能与用户信息需求匹配的候选文档。最后，在重排序阶段，对查询与召回阶段得到的候选文档进行更加精细化的相关性计算，目的是将最相关的文档排在列表的前面。根据当前文档表示以及索引结构的不同，现有检索框架可以分为两种主要类型(Guo et al., 2022)，即稀疏检索框架和稠密检索框架。

- **稀疏检索**通常基于倒排索引来构建文档的索引存储，它将文档与词关联起来形成文档列表，通过查询词可以快速定位词是否出现在文档集中。一般来说，这类方法利用词项频率和位置等词项的特征来计算文档得分。代表性的检索方法如TF-IDF和BM25已经在实践中被广泛采用，为了增强语义匹配能力，研究人员也探索了将词向量应用到稀疏检索模型中(Zheng and Callan, 2015)。此外，随着预训练技术的发展，研究人员开始研究使用预训练语言模型估计倒排索引的词项权重，例如，DeepCT(Dai and Callan, 2020b)和HDCT(Dai and Callan, 2020a)利用BERT获取上下文化的词项表示，提高了检索性能。

- **稠密检索**则是将文档投影到低维稠密的向量表示，并利用近似最近邻搜索算法进行高效的检索，这类检索方法由于其在语义匹配方面的优势，近年来受到研究人员的广泛关注，并提出了各种技术来提高稠密检索模型的性能。一种常见的方法是采用难负样本挖掘(Cai et al., 2022)进行双塔模型训练，通过选择具有挑战性的负样本来提高模型的判别能力。另一种策略则是采用后交互(Lee et al., 2019)机制，在较后阶段考虑查询和文档之间的交互计算，从而实现更有效的信息融合。此外，知识蒸馏(Vakili Tahami et al., 2020)也被用于稠密检索中，将基于交互的检索模型知识通过蒸馏转移给基于双塔的检索模型，提高稠密检索的效率和效果。最近的研究表明，在大规模语料库上使用对比学习对稠密检索模型进行预训练是有效的(Wu et al., 2022)。这些方法利用预训练语言模型捕捉的丰富上下文信息，在嵌入空间中学习区分正样本（相关文档）和负样本（不相关文档），从而提高检索性能。

第二十二届中国计算语言学大会论文集，第57页-第66页，哈尔滨，中国，2023年8月3日至5日。
卷2：前沿综述

在信息检索的重排序阶段，已经提出了各种模型来度量给定查询与候选文档的相关性。代表性的模型包括向量空间模型(Salton et al., 1975)、概率检索模型(Robertson et al., 2009)、排序学习模型(Liu, 2009; Li, 2014)和神经排序模型(Ma et al., 2021b; Ma et al., 2021c)。向量空间模型(Salton et al., 1975)将文档和查询表示为向量，通过计算二者的相似度来评估相关性。概率检索模型(Robertson et al., 2009)使用概率框架估计文档和查询之间的相关性概率。排序学习模型(Burges, 2010)旨在学习一个将文档和查询的特征映射到它们的相关性分数的排序函数，通常利用机器学习算法根据标记的训练数据优化排序函数。神经排序模型(Liu et al., 2017; Ma et al., 2021b; Ma et al., 2021a)则利用深度学习技术学习文档和查询的表示，捕捉它们的语义相关性。

尽管流水线检索框架在实际检索系统中已经被广泛应用，然而，它本身架构的复杂性导致系统难以实现端到端的全局优化，限制了其充分发挥潜力，因此，超越流水线框架并探索替代方法至关重要。

3 生成式检索的基本概念

形式化的，假设$\mathcal{D} = \{d_1, d_2, \dots\}$ 表示一个大规模的文档语料库，其中d_i 表示一个个体文档。给定查询集合$\mathcal{Q}$ 中的查询q 和语料库$\mathcal{D}$，生成式检索模型的目标是生成一组相关文档的DocID (Tay et al., 2022)。接下来，我们将具体描述索引和检索两种基本操作模式，以及学习和推断的过程。

3.1 索引和检索策略

在生成式检索框架中，索引过程被模型训练所替代，而检索过程则被模型推断所取代。一般而言，文档检索任务被转化为单一的生成式形式，并通常采用序列到序列（Seq2Seq）的编码-解码架构，以实现索引和检索的端到端学习。当前主流工作基本都基于Transformer网络来实现编码-解码架构，比如T5(Tay et al., 2022; Wang et al., 2022; Zhuang and Ren, 2022)、BART(De Cao et al., 2020; Bevilacqua et al., 2022)。

在索引阶段，生成式检索将原来流水线架构中的物理索引转化为一个模型训练任务，该任务旨在学习文档d_i 的内容与其对应的文档ID r_i 之间的映射关系。一个广泛使用的策略是Inputs2Target (Tay et al., 2022)，它以原始文档作为输入，并以直接生成的DocID 作为输出，模型使用Teacher Forcing 策略(Hao et al., 2022) 进行训练，采用标准的交叉熵损失函数，如下所示:

$$\mathcal{L}_{MLE}^{indexing}(\theta) = \sum_{d_i \in \mathcal{D}} \log P(r_i | GR_\theta(d_i)), \tag{2}$$

其中$\mathcal{D}$ 表示给定的语料库，GR 表示生成式检索模型。

现有关于索引策略的研究可以大体可以分为两类：(i) 第一类是基于文档内容生成一个全新的ID，其中包括基于数字的DocID (Tay et al., 2022; Zhou et al., 2022b)、基于单词的DocID (De Cao et al., 2020; Chen et al., 2022; Bevilacqua et al., 2022; Chen et al., 2023) 以及基于URL的DocID(Zhou et al., 2022b)。 (ii) 第二类旨在建立从文档到相应DocID的语义映射。各种文档内容类型已被提出，以增强文档与其DocID之间的关联(Tay et al., 2022; Zhou et al., 2022b; Chen et al., 2022)，例如不同语义粒度级别的上下文（例如段落、句子和短语）(Chen et al., 2022; Zhou et al., 2022a) 和超链接信息（例如锚文本）(Chen et al., 2022)。

在检索阶段，生成式检索的目标是为给定输入查询返回一个潜在相关的候选文档的排名列表。为此，生成式检索模型利用在索引阶段微调好的GR模型，通过自回归生成一个给定输入查询$q \in \mathcal{Q}$的文档ID字符串。通常情况下，该模型使用标准的训练目标和交叉熵损失进行训练。检索任务的损失函数定义为:

$$\mathcal{L}_{MLE}^{retrieval}(\theta) = \sum_{q_j \in \mathcal{Q}} \log P(r_j | GR_\theta(q_j)), \tag{3}$$

其中$\mathcal{Q}$是查询集合，r_j是为q_j生成的DocID。候选DocID可以通过使用beam search (Koszelew and Karbowska-Chilinska, 2020)得到，从而得到一个潜在相关的文档排名列表。

第二十二届中国计算语言学大会论文集，第57页-第66页，哈尔滨，中国，2023年8月3日至5日。
卷2：前沿综述

3.2 学习和优化

训练生成式检索模型存在两种主要策略：(i) 第一种策略是先训练GR模型进行索引，然后再训练模型进行检索。(ii) 第二种策略是在多任务设置中训练GR同时进行索引和检索。实验分析表明，第二种策略在表现上优于第一种策略，尤其面向具有有限标注查询-文档对的大规模语料库检索应用(Wang et al., 2022; Tay et al., 2022)。因此，GR的常用训练策略是采用多任务学习，其形式化表示为：

$$\mathcal{L}_{MLE}(\theta) = \sum_{d_i \in \mathcal{D}} \log P(r_i | GR_\theta(d_i)) + \sum_{q_j \in \mathcal{Q}} \log P(r_j | GR_\theta(q_j)), \tag{4}$$

训练的目标是最大化生成正确的DocID的似然度，用于索引和检索任务。

值得一提的是，在检索阶段的模型训练过程中，为了解决标注数据有限的问题，一些研究采用了通过查询生成技术(Wang et al., 2022; Zhou et al., 2022b) 生成伪查询来加强查询到文档ID的相关性学习；此外，也有利用预训练任务(Chen et al., 2022) 来改进查询到文档ID的相关性关系学习。

3.3 推断

在完成生成式检索模型的训练后，可以在推断阶段以端到端的方式使用它来为给定的查询检索文档。具体而言，经过训练的模型按照从左到右、逐个标记的方式自回归地生成给定测试查询q_j的DocID字符串中的第p个标记$r_{j,p}$，直到生成一个特殊的序列结束（End-of-Sequence，EOS）标记，即，

$$r_{j,p} = GR(q_j, r_{j,0}, r_{j,1}, \ldots, r_{j,p-1}). \tag{5}$$

然而，在实际解码过程中，如果模型的解码空间为整个词汇表中的所有标记，那么生成的输出可能是一个无效DocID。为了克服这个挑战，可以采用带约束的束搜索策略(De Cao et al., 2020)，以确保每个生成的DocID都属于预定的候选集，即整个文档集合中的所有DocID。

具体而言，一般可以利用前缀树建立约束，其中节点标记为从预定义候选集中选择的标记。对于前缀树中的每个节点，其子节点表示沿着从根节点到给定节点的前缀所建立的所有可行延续。通常情况下，用于生成DocID的前缀树相对较小，可以事先计算并预加载到内存中。

4 DocID 表示

在生成式检索中，生成式检索模型通过Seq2seq模型，在给定查询和文档上下文之间建立映射关系，这些文档上下文的语义内容则时由DocID的短字符串来刻画。这里，最核心的需要是设计有效的DocID表示来捕获文档内容的潜在语义，这里要求DocID具有语义信息、简洁明了并能够有效区分不同文档。在本节中，我们介绍当前主流的不同类型DocID，分别是基于数字的DocID和基于词的DocID，以下将对这两类DocID方法进行详细描述。

4.1 基于数字的DocID表示方法

基于数字的DocID 包含了使用数字值表示DocID的方法，可以使用随机数或具有语义意义的数值来实现。在没有高质量元数据（例如唯一的、语义丰富的标题）的情况下，这些方法已被证明具有良好的性能。一般而言，基于数字的DocID表示方法可分为三种主要类型 (Tay et al., 2022)，包括原子DocID、字符串DocID 和语义结构化DocID。

- **原子DocID** 使用唯一且随机的数字表示文档。具体而言，生成式检索模型被训练为为每个不同的文档输出一个logit 值，最后，解码器的输出层大小则为隐藏层大小乘以文档数量。这种方法的主要优点是构建简单，但缺点是随着文档数量的增长，模型的容量也会增加。

- **字符串DocID** 则依赖于整数字符串来构建文档的唯一表征。其核心是通过逐步解码DocID字符串中的每个标记，从而消除大型softmax 输出空间的挑战。字符串DocID 方法与原子DocID 方法的区别在于前者使用可分词的字符串DocID，并且涉及多步解码生成，而后者使用唯一且随机的数字DocID进行单步解码生成。

- **语义结构化DocID** 将文档的语义表达压缩成一个较短的数字组合作为文档ID。其目标是要捕捉文档的语义信息，自动生成能传达其对应文档语义信息的DocID。DocID 的结构可以在每个解码步骤后有效地减少搜索空间。例如，通过k-means 聚类构建的DocID 可能会在语义上相似的文档中共享前缀。

4.2 基于词的DocID表示方法

基于词的DocID表示方法是指通过直接从原始文档或其元数据中提取DocID，或者基于文档的语义信息进行重构，从而与文档建立强大的语义联系来实现。与基于数字的方法相比，基于词的方法以更自然和易于理解的方式传达语义信息。目前，广泛使用的基于单词的DocID 方法包括基于标题、基于URL 和基于N-gram 的方法。

- **基于标题的DocID** 直接使用文档的标题作为其DocID。标题通常是整个文档的简短而丰富的摘要，提供了对文档内所含信息的宏观概述。此外，在某些知识库（如维基百科）中，标题通常是唯一的，因此作为DocID 是一个理想的选择。这种方法在知识密集型语言任务中也被证明是有效的(De Cao et al., 2020; Chen et al., 2022)。然而，缺点是并非所有文档都有高质量的标题。

- **基于URL的DocID** 将与文档对应的网页URL作为其DocID。一般来说，URL 是唯一的且易于获取，可以快速而准确地与相应的文档进行关联。然而，与基于标题的方法相比，URL 所携带的语义信息较弱，并且可能引入额外的噪音（因为URL 中可能存在无效字段）(Zhou et al., 2022b)。

- **基于N-gram的DocID** 利用文档中连续出现的N-gram 作为其DocID。N-gram 容易获取，但重复率较高，因此需要额外设计去重功能。此外，在推理阶段，无法直接使用束约束搜索，需要使用FM 索引(Chen et al., 2023)。

5 模型结构

检索模型架构的选择塑造了生成式检索的基本结构，对检索性能起着决定性作用。当前的生成式检索工作(Tay et al., 2022; De Cao et al., 2020; Wang et al., 2022; Bevilacqua et al., 2022) 使用编码器-解码器结构的生成模型作为主干模型。目前尚未有工作探索生成式检索结构中各个结构的作用。然后，模型结构作为生成式检索中最核心的部分，我们这里简单探讨一下不同的网络结构在生成式检索中的应用模式。在本节，我们重点讨论如何利用编码器-解码器和仅解码器架构实现生成式检索。

5.1 编码器-解码器架构

编码器-解码器架构是实现生成式检索的常见选择。在这个设置中，编码器接收输入查询，将其编码为上下文向量，捕捉查询的语义信息。然后，解码器在编码的查询表示基础上生成相应的DocID。具体而言，训练阶段和推理阶段的过程如下：(i) 在训练阶段，模型使用查询和相应DocID的样本进行训练。编码器对输入查询或文章进行编码，解码器以自回归的方式进行训练，生成准确的DocID。训练目标则是在给定输入查询的情况下，最大化生成目标DocID的似然估计。 (ii) 在推理阶段，编码器-解码器模型接受查询作为输入，并根据查询和相关文档之间的相关性得分生成DocID。

5.2 仅解码器架构

除了编码器-解码器架构，仅解码器架构也可以用于生成式检索任务。事实上，仅解码器架构已经在大语言模型中发挥了重要作用。在这个设置中，输入序列不会被显式地编码成固定长度的表示。相反，仅解码器的模型根据初始状态或作为输入查询提供的提示直接生成DocID。具体而言，训练阶段和推理阶段的过程如下：(i) 在训练阶段，模型根据给定的查询或者文章表示的初始状态生成正确的DocID。训练目标同样是最大化生成目标DocID的似然估计。 (ii) 在推理阶段，仅解码器模型接受提示或初始状态，并根据从训练数据中学到的模式生成DocID。

第二十二届中国计算语言学大会论文集，第57页-第66页，哈尔滨，中国，2023年8月3日至5日。
卷2：前沿综述

6 模型容量

生成式检索模型的容量直接影响检索模型的性能，本节重点介绍模型容量（即模型参数规模）和语料库大小之间的关系。直观地说，在一定范围内增加模型容量预计会提高在给定数据集上的性能，但超过一定阈值后，效果可能趋于平稳甚至下降。

在生成式检索中，模型大小（以参数数量衡量）和语料库大小（以文档数量衡量）是影响系统性能和可扩展性的两个重要因素。

- **模型大小**指的是生成式检索模型中可学习参数的数量，包括用于生成DocID的神经网络架构的权重和偏置。一般来说，具有更多参数的较大模型有能力捕捉更完整的内容语义以及更复杂的查询-文档相关模式。然而，较大的模型在训练和推理时也需要更多的计算资源。

- **语料库大小**指的是检索系统中可用文档的数量。较大的语料库意味着更大的搜索空间和更复杂的相关模式需要生成式检索模型进行学习。管理和处理大型语料库可能会引入与计算效率、可扩展性和资源利用相关的挑战。

6.1 内存空间：生成式检索与传统检索的外部索引

在生成式检索中，索引构建是模型训练的一个特殊情况，所有与语料库相关的信息都被编码在单个神经模型的参数中。而在传统的多阶段索引-检索-排序流程中，外部构建的查询索引与数据或信息源相关联。在这里，我们介绍单个生成式检索模型所需的内存空间与传统流水线架构中外部索引所需的内存空间之间的关系。

- **生成式检索**：所需的内存空间主要取决于生成模型本身参数的大小。生成模型通常包含在训练过程中学习的参数，例如权重和偏置。较大的模型通常需要更多的内存空间。除了模型参数之外，生成式检索在推理过程中可能还需要内存来存储中间表示，例如前缀树和FM索引。这些中间表示对于生成相关和信息丰富的DocID是必要的。

- **传统检索**：传统的检索方法，例如稀疏检索和稠密检索，通常依赖于外部索引来存储和组织文档集合。这些索引所需的内存空间则取决于文档集合的大小和使用的索引方案。
  - 稀疏检索：通常使用倒排索引，将词项映射到包含它们的文档。索引的大小取决于集合中唯一词项的数量以及每个文档的平均术语数。索引所需的内存空间随着文档集合的大小和词表中词项数量的增加而增加。
  - 稠密检索：采用向量嵌入等技术在连续向量空间中表示文档和查询。这些嵌入通常存储在索引中，例如近似最近邻索引或稠密向量索引。索引所需的内存空间取决于文档的数量和向量嵌入的维度。较大的文档集合或更高维度的嵌入将需要更多的内存空间。

在实际场景中部署生成式检索模型时，需要仔细权衡模型大小、语料库大小和计算成本之间的平衡。一方面，增加模型大小通常会带来性能的提升，较大的模型在捕捉查询-文档相关性和生成准确的DocID方面具有更强的能力。另一方面，更大的语料库能提供更丰富的信息源，使模型能够更好地理解上下文并生成更相关的响应。然而，这种性能提升是以增加计算要求为代价的。较大的模型在训练和推理过程中消耗更多的内存和计算资源，导致训练时间更长和推理成本更高。类似地，增加语料库大小会增加需要处理的数据量，导致训练和推理时间更长。此外，随着模型大小和语料库大小的持续增长，性能改进的边际效益可能变得不那么显著，而相比之下计算成本的增加更为显著。

总的来说，在实际部署生成式检索模型时，需要考虑应用程序的特定要求和约束，包括可用的计算资源、时间限制和所需的性能水平。例如，在实时响应至关重要的场景中，可能需要通过选择较小的模型大小或限制语料库大小来优先考虑计算效率。相反，如果应用程序需要高准确性和性能，为了更大的模型和语料库可能会牺牲计算成本。

7 挑战和展望

在这一节，我们讨论生成式检索的几个重要挑战，希望能够给未来研究方向提供一些有价值的建议。

第二十二届中国计算语言学大会论文集，第57页-第66页，哈尔滨，中国，2023年8月3日至5日。
卷2：前沿综述

7.1 生成式架构

当前的生成式检索模型还没有完全实现统一传统检索流程中的三个步骤的设想，研究重点关注在利用生成式模型来替代"索引-召回"两步，而没有覆盖重排序阶段。与此同时，尽管这些方法在一定程度上提升了性能，但仍难以超越强大的稠密检索方法甚至是稀疏检索方法（如BM25 (Robertson and Zaragoza, 2009)）。一个重要的原因也在于生成式检索不能覆盖传统检索流程的重排序阶段，在很多时候性能难以媲美传统检索，这也表明在生成式检索中仍有很大的改进空间，以实现全面而有效的排序能力。

生成式检索模型主要依赖于Transformer架构，然而，Transformer架构存在一些固有的限制，比如输入长度的限制。因此，有必要探索新型网络架构以克服这种限制。这里，可以利用诸如Longformer网络结构(Beltagy et al., 2020)、多尺度解码器(Yu et al., 2023)以及扩张注意力(Ding et al., 2023)等方法来提升模型的输入长度。

7.2 端到端DocID学习

在生成式检索中，文档标识的学习通常遵循两阶段的过程。首先，使用诸如BERT等单独的模型来辅助学习DocIDs的表示。随后，利用学习到的DocID表示建立文档/查询和DocIDs之间的映射关系。另一种可行的学习方法则是采用端到端学习，这样模型可以直接在统一的框架内同时优化DocID表示的学习和文档/查询与DocIDs之间的映射关系。这可以简化学习流程，提高整体效率，并有望进一步改善生成式检索模型的性能。然而，同时优化两个目标需要权衡二者之间的相互影响，需要仔细设计优化方法，考虑到同时学习与DocIDs生成相关的各个组成部分所涉及的复杂性和挑战性。

7.3 场景受限

当前生成式检索方法大都在文档规模受限的场景下进行验证，例如MS MARCO中的文档检索或锻炼检索、Wikipedia中的实体检索等，这类检索假设文档语料规模不大，同时文档集相对固定。然而，实际检索中文档集规模通常很大，且文档会源源不断的增加，如何应对大规模文档以及动态新增文档的表示学习与DocID生成是一个重要的挑战。

8 总结

本文对生成式信息检索进行了系统的综述，区别于现有的IR系统主要采用了"索引-召回-重排"的框架，生成式检索利用统一的模型来建模整个搜索过程，这种新型的检索架构能够实现了端到端的优化，消除了对外部索引的依赖。本文对生成式信息检索的基本概念、核心方法以及难点进行了梳理，同时，探讨了一些未解决的挑战和有前景的研究方向，希望能激发和促进未来关于生成式检索的研究。

参考文献

Iz Beltagy, Matthew E. Peters, and Arman Cohan. 2020. Longformer: The long-document transformer. *CoRR*, abs/2004.05150.

Michele Bevilacqua, Giuseppe Ottaviano, Patrick Lewis, Wen-tau Yih, Sebastian Riedel, and Fabio Petroni. 2022. Autoregressive search engines: Generating substrings as document identifiers.

Christopher JC Burges. 2010. From ranknet to lambdarank to lambdamart: An overview. *Learning*, 11:23–581.

Yinqiong Cai, Jiafeng Guo, Yixing Fan, Qingyao Ai, Ruqing Zhang, and Xueqi Cheng. 2022. Hard negatives or false negatives: Correcting pooling bias in training neural ranking models. In *Proceedings of the 31st ACM International Conference on Information & Knowledge Management*, pages 118–127.

Olivier Chapelle, Shihao Ji, Ciya Liao, Emre Velipasaoglu, Larry Lai, and Su-Lin Wu. 2011. Intent-based diversification of web search results: metrics and algorithms. *Information Retrieval*.

Hongshen Chen, Xiaorui Liu, Dawei Yin, and Jiliang Tang. 2017. A survey on dialogue systems: Recent advances and new frontiers. *Sigkdd Explorations*, 19(2):25–35.

第二十二届中国计算语言学大会论文集，第57页-第66页，哈尔滨，中国，2023年8月3日至5日。
卷2：前沿综述

Jiangui Chen, Ruqing Zhang, Jiafeng Guo, Yiqun Liu, Yixing Fan, and Xueqi Cheng. 2022. Corpusbrain: Pre-train a generative retrieval model for knowledge-intensive language tasks. In *CIKM*, pages 191–200.

Jiangui Chen, Ruqing Zhang, Jiafeng Guo, Maarten de Rijke, Yiqun Liu, Yixing Fan, and Xueqi Cheng. 2023. A unified generative retriever for knowledge-intensive language tasks via prompt learning. In *SIGIR*.

Zhuyun Dai and Jamie Callan. 2020a. Context-aware document term weighting for ad-hoc search. In *Proceedings of The Web Conference 2020*, pages 1897–1907.

Zhuyun Dai and Jamie Callan. 2020b. Context-aware term weighting for first stage passage retrieval. In *SIGIR*, pages 1533–1536.

Nicola De Cao, Gautier Izacard, Sebastian Riedel, and Fabio Petroni. 2020. Autoregressive entity retrieval. In *ICLR*.

Jiayu Ding, Shuming Ma, Li Dong, Xingxing Zhang, Shaohan Huang, Wenhui Wang, and Furu Wei. 2023. Longnet: Scaling transformers to 1, 000, 000, 000 tokens. *CoRR*, abs/2307.02486.

Jiafeng Guo, Yinqiong Cai, Yixing Fan, Fei Sun, Ruqing Zhang, and Xueqi Cheng. 2022. Semantic models for the first-stage retrieval: A comprehensive review. *TOIS*, 40(4):1–42.

Yongchang Hao, Yuxin Liu, and Lili Mou. 2022. Teacher forcing recovers reward functions for text generation. In *Advances in Neural Information Processing Systems*, volume 35, pages 12594–12607.

Vladimir Karpukhin, Barlas Oguz, Sewon Min, Patrick Lewis, Ledell Wu, Sergey Edunov, Danqi Chen, and Wen-tau Yih. 2020. Dense passage retrieval for open-domain question answering. In *EMNLP*, pages 6769–6781.

Jolanta Koszelew and Joanna Karbowska-Chilinska. 2020. Beam search algorithm for anti-collision trajectory planning for many-to-many encounter situations with autonomous surface vehicles. *Sensors*, 20:4115.

Kenton Lee, Ming-Wei Chang, and Kristina Toutanova. 2019. Latent retrieval for weakly supervised open domain question answering. In *ACL*, pages 6086–6096.

Hang Li. 2014. *Learning to Rank for Information Retrieval and Natural Language Processing, Second Edition.* Synthesis Lectures on Human Language Technologies. Morgan & Claypool Publishers.

Shichen Liu, Fei Xiao, Wenwu Ou, and Luo Si. 2017. Cascade ranking for operational e-commerce search. In *Proceedings of the 23rd ACM SIGKDD International Conference on Knowledge Discovery and Data Mining*, page 1557–1565. ACM.

Tie-Yan Liu. 2009. Learning to rank for information retrieval. *Foundations and Trends in Information Retrieval*, 3(3):225–331.

Xinyu Ma, Jiafeng Guo, and Ruqing Zhang. 2021a. B-prop: bootstrapped pre-training with representative words prediction for ad-hoc retrieval. In *Proceedings of the 44th International ACM SIGIR Conference on Research and Development in Information Retrieval.*

Xinyu Ma, Jiafeng Guo, Ruqing Zhang, Yixing Fan, Xiang Ji, and Xueqi Cheng. 2021b. Prop: pre-training with representative words prediction for ad-hoc retrieval. In *ACM WSDM.*

Xinyu Ma, Jiafeng Guo, Ruqing Zhang, Yixing Fan, Yingyan Li, and Xueqi Cheng. 2021c. B-prop: bootstrapped pre-training with representative words prediction for ad-hoc retrieval. In *SIGIR*, pages 1513–1522.

Donald Metzler, Yi Tay, Dara Bahri, and Marc Najork. 2021. Rethinking search: Making domain experts out of dilettantes. *SIGIR Forum.*

Stephen Robertson and Hugo Zaragoza. 2009. *The probabilistic relevance framework: BM25 and beyond.* Now Publishers Inc.

Stephen Robertson, Hugo Zaragoza, et al. 2009. The probabilistic relevance framework: Bm25 and beyond. *Foundations and Trends® in Information Retrieval*, 3(4):333–389.

第二十二届中国计算语言学大会论文集，第57页-第66页，哈尔滨，中国，2023年8月3日至5日。
卷2：前沿综述

Gerard Salton, Anita Wong, and Chung-Shu Yang. 1975. A vector space model for automatic indexing. *Communications of the ACM*, 18(11):613–620.

Yi Tay, Vinh Q Tran, Mostafa Dehghani, Jianmo Ni, and Dara Bahri. 2022. Transformer memory as a differentiable search index.

Amir Vakili Tahami, Kamyar Ghajar, and Azadeh Shakery. 2020. Distilling knowledge for fast retrieval-based chat-bots. In *Proceedings of the 43rd International ACM SIGIR conference on research and development in information retrieval*, pages 2081–2084.

Yujing Wang, Yingyan Hou, Haonan Wang, and Ziming Miao. 2022. A neural corpus indexer for document retrieval. *arXiv preprint arXiv:2206.02743.*

Bohong Wu, Zhuosheng Zhang, Jinyuan Wang, and Hai Zhao. 2022. Sentence-aware contrastive learning for open-domain passage retrieval. In *Proceedings of the 60th Annual Meeting of the Association for Computational Linguistics (Volume 1: Long Papers)*, pages 1062–1074.

Lili Yu, Daniel Simig, Colin Flaherty, Armen Aghajanyan, Luke Zettlemoyer, and Mike Lewis. 2023. MEGABYTE: predicting million-byte sequences with multiscale transformers. *CoRR*, abs/2305.07185.

Guoqing Zheng and Jamie Callan. 2015. Learning to reweight terms with distributed representations. In *SIGIR*, pages 575–584.

Yujia Zhou, Jing Yao, Zhicheng Dou, Ledell Wu, and Ji-Rong Wen. 2022a. Dynamicretriever: A pre-training model-based ir system with neither sparse nor dense index. *arXiv preprint arXiv:2203.00537.*

Yujia Zhou, Jing Yao, Zhicheng Dou, Ledell Wu, Peitian Zhang, and Ji-Rong Wen. 2022b. Ultron: An ultimate retriever on corpus with a model-based indexer. *arXiv preprint arXiv:2208.09257.*

Shengyao Zhuang and Houxing Ren. 2022. Bridging the gap between indexing and retrieval for differentiable search index with query generation. *arXiv preprint arXiv:2206.10128.*

第二十二届中国计算语言学大会论文集，第57页-第66页，哈尔滨，中国，2023年8月3日至5日。
卷2：前沿综述

大模型与知识图谱

陈玉博[1,2], 郭少茹[1], 刘康[1,2,3], 赵军[1,2]
[1]中国科学院自动化研究所复杂系统认知与决策实验室
[2]中国科学院大学人工智能学院
[3]北京智源人工智能研究院
{yubo.chen, shaoru.guo, kliu, jzhao}@nlpr.ia.ac.cn

摘要

知识图谱作为一种重要的知识组织形式，常被视为下一代人工智能技术的基础设施之一，引起了工业界和学术界的广泛关注。传统知识图谱表示方法主要使用符号显式地描述概念及其之间的结构关系，具有语义清晰和可解释性好等特点，但其知识类型有限，难以应对开放域应用场景。随着大规模预训练语言模型（大模型）的发展，将参数化的大模型视为知识图谱成为研究热点。在这一背景下，本文聚焦于大模型在知识图谱生命周期中的研究，总结分析了大模型在知识建模、知识获取、知识融合、知识管理、知识推理和知识应用等环节中的研究进展。最后，对大模型与知识图谱未来发展趋势予以展望。

关键词： 大模型 ； 知识图谱 ； 神经符号学习

Large Language Models and Knowledge Graphs

Yubo Chen[1,2], Shaoru Guo[1], Kang Liu[1,2,3], Jun Zhao[1,2]
[1]The Laboratory of Cognition and Decision Intelligence for Complex Systems
[2]School of Artificial Intelligence, University of Chinese Academy of Sciences
[3]Beijing Academy of Artificial Intelligence

Abstract

As an important form of knowledge organization, knowledge graphs are widely recognized as one of the foundational infrastructures for the next generation of artificial intelligence technologies, receiving considerable interest from both industry and academia. Traditional methods for representing knowledge graphs mainly employ symbolic representations to explicitly describe concepts and their relationships, with clear semantics and good interpretability. However, these methods have limited coverage of knowledge types, making it challenging to apply them in open-domain scenarios. With the development of large pre-trained language models (large language models), most researchers have considered parameterized large language models as knowledge graphs. Thus, this paper focuses on the research of the life cycle of knowledge graphs in large language models. Specifically, we summarize the related work on knowledge modeling, knowledge acquisition, knowledge fusion, knowledge management, knowledge reasoning, and knowledge application. Finally, we anticipate the future development trends of large language models and knowledge graphs.

Keywords: Large Language Models , knowledge graphs , Neural Symbolic Learning

第二十二届中国计算语言学大会论文集，第67页-第76页，哈尔滨，中国，2023年8月3日至5日。
卷2：前沿综述

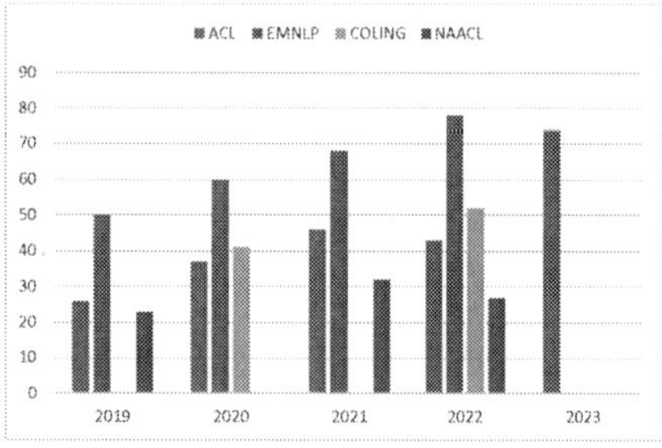

Figure 1: Konwledge相关论文数量

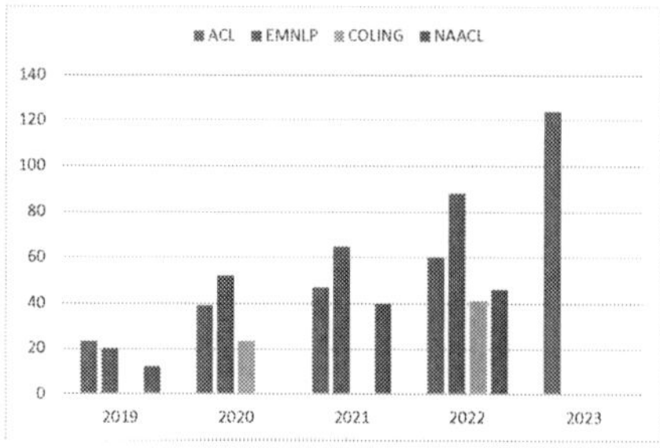

Figure 2: Language Model相关的论文数量

1 引言

1977年，在第五届国际人工智能会议上，图灵奖获得者爱德华·费根鲍姆提出了“知识工程”的概念，确立了知识工程在人工智能中的重要地位(Feigenbaum, 1977)。新时代，随着网络技术的发展，积累了规模巨大的互联网大数据和行业大数据。为了有效利用这些信息，将大数据转化为大知识成为一项迫切需求，这也给知识工程研究提出了新的挑战，即大数据知识工程。知识图谱（Knowledge Graph）正是一种应对大数据知识工程挑战的范式。

知识图谱由Google于2012年提出，是用来支持从语义角度组织网络数据，从而提供智能搜索服务的知识库。具体来说，知识图谱是一种比较通用的语义知识形式化描述框架，它是以三元组为基本语义单元，以有向标签图为数据结构，从知识本体和知识实例两个层次，对世界万物进行体系化、规范化描述，并支持高效知识推理和语义计算的大规模知识系统(赵军et al., 2018)。知识图谱极大地推动了语义网、自然语言处理、数据库等相关技术的发展，它被认为是下一代人工智能技术的基础设施之一，受到工业界和学术界的广泛关注。

传统知识图谱使用符号化的方法来进行知识表示，旨在将各种知识对象（如实体、事件、属性和关系等）记作具体符号，并以某种结构组织起来，通过符号匹配（如索引和检索）和数理演算（如谓词推理）等形式化方法完成各种语义计算任务。符号化表示方法能够显式地描述知识，具有语义清晰和可解释性好等特点，但其知识类型有限，且大多数逻辑推理规则需要通过人工编写和校验的方式获取，难以应对开放域应用场景。

近年来，大规模预训练语言模型（大模型）的发展引起了知识图谱领域的广泛关注。大模型可以从海量无标注数据中自动挖掘知识，并将知识以隐式的方式存储在参数化的模型中。相关研究工作表明，大模型涵盖了丰富的知识类型，包括语言学知识(Liu et al., 2019)、世界知识(Petroni et al., 2019)和常识知识(Li et al., 2022)等，使得模型具备了强大的知识表达能力。与此同时，大模型无需事先定义类型，能够灵活应用于开放域场景。在知识图谱的构建和应用中，越来越多的任务开始采用大模型进行建模，并取得了一定的效果。因此，本文聚焦于参数化大模型在知识图谱生命周期中的研究。

本文对近五年（2019年至2023年）自然语言处理领域国际会议（ACL、EMNLP、COLING和NAACL）的研究趋势进行了分析。图1 和图2 分别展示了与知识图谱和语言模型相关的论文数量在自然语言处理国际会议中的变化趋势[0]。如图所示，与知识图谱和语言模型相关的研究逐年增加，这表明知识图谱和语言模型在当前的自然语言处理研究领域中既是热点问题，也是核心问题，同时反映了研究者们对将知识图谱和语言模型应用于自然语言处理任务的关注和投入。

同时，本文围绕知识图谱生命周期各个环节对ACL2019至ACL2023的论文进行了统计，包括知识建模、知识获取、知识融合、知识管理、知识推理和知识应用，如图3所示。通过图中的统计结果可以发现，对知识图谱生命周期各个环节的研究呈现出明显的增长趋势，重点关注知识获取与知识应用。此外，图4展示了ACL2023论文的词云图，从中可以观察

[0]统计信息来源于ACL Anthology（https://www.aclweb.org/anthology/）。值得注意的是，2020年NAACL会议未召开，COLING会议每两年举办一次，且截至目前仅公布了ACL2023的论文录用列表。

第二十二届中国计算语言学大会论文集，第67页-第76页，哈尔滨，中国，2023年8月3日至5日。
卷2：前沿综述
(c) 2023 中国中文信息学会计算语言学专业委员会

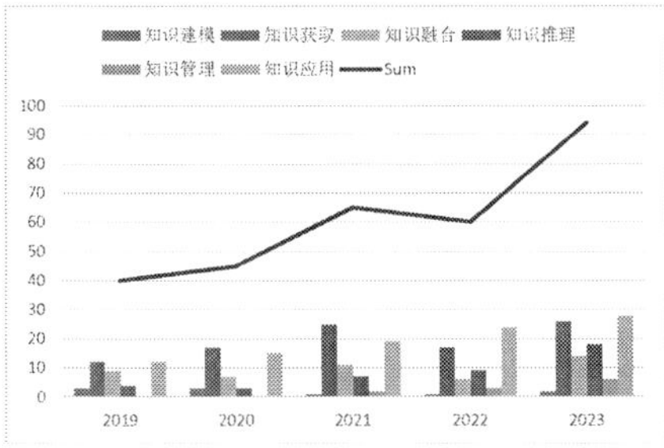

Figure 3: 知识图谱生命周期统计

Figure 4: ACL2023词云

到"Knowledge"、"Language Models"等相关研究引起了极大关注，表明知识图谱和语言模型在当前研究中的重要地位。

大模型逐渐成为人类知识的全新载体，将参数化的大模型视为知识图谱成为当前的研究趋势。在此背景下，本文聚焦于大模型在知识图谱生命周期各个环节中的研究，总结分析了大模型在知识建模、知识获取、知识融合、知识管理、知识推理和知识应用等环节的研究进展。

2 知识建模

知识建模，也称知识体系构建或本体建模，旨在构建一个本体对目标知识进行描述。该本体定义了知识的类别体系、类别下所属的概念、概念所具有的属性以及概念之间的语义关系。目前，实体和事件是知识图谱中典型的知识类型。因此，本节将分别介绍基于大模型的实体本体建模和事件本体建模的相关研究。

实体本体是指将实体作为知识单元，通过描述实体的概念、属性以及它们之间的分类关系来刻画客观世界中事物的静态规律。Jullien et al. (2022)采用提示学习和微调方法探测大模型的概念知识。类似地，Peng et al. (2022)也使用了提示学习和微调方法，不仅探测大模型中的概念知识，还包括属性知识和概念之间的关系。此外，Wu et al. (2023)同样采用提示学习方法，在探测概念、属性及概念关系同时，进一步探测了属性之间的关系。这些研究工作表明，大模型在一定程度上能够建模实体本体知识，但在关系建模方面存在一定困难，并且词语共现可能会引发概念幻觉等问题。

事件本体是指将事件作为认知单元，通过描述事件类型、事件论元以及它们之间的语义关系来刻画现实世界中事物的动态变化规律。针对事件本体建模，目前大多数工作聚焦于大模型在事件类型建模（概念）、原子事件模式建模（概念及属性）和事件图模式建模（概念之间语义关系）三个方面的研究。事件类型建模是指利用大模型自动地从原始文本中发现新的事件类别。其中，Edwards and Ji (2023)使用大模型建模文本表示，并通过注意力机制聚合类别特征，从而归纳出新的事件类别。原子事件模式建模旨在从多个相似事件实例中归纳出一个模板。为了实现这一目标，Tang et al. (2023)采用情景学习方法，引导大模型构建面向不同领域的事件模式。事件图模式建模是指从一组相关事件实例中归纳出事件之间的模式和关系，Li et al. (2023)利用提示学习引导大模型生成特定场景下的关键事件及事件之间的关系。此外，还可以通过人与大模型协作的方式，由人工干预大模型事件本体建模过程，生成符合人类认知的事件模式(Zhang et al., 2023b)。目前基于大模型的事件本体建模主要关注时序关系，无法对事件本体丰富关系进行完整建模。同时，由于事件本体的复杂性，基于大模型自动构建的事件本体质量难以保证。

3 知识获取

知识获取旨在从非结构化数据中抽取结构化知识。根据人们的认知过程，可将获得的知识分为语言学知识、世界知识和常识知识。因此，本节将分别介绍基于大模型语言学知识获取、世界知识获取和常识知识获取的相关研究。

第二十二届中国计算语言学大会论文集，第67页-第76页，哈尔滨，中国，2023年8月3日至5日。
卷2：前沿综述

语言学知识是指词性、句法结构以及词语之间的关系等方面的知识。由于语言学知识通常需要采用特定的标注方式，因此通常使用有训练的探测方法来获取这些知识[1]。例如，Liu et al. (2019)通过整合多种语言结构预测任务（如句法分块、命名实体识别等），在预训练的隐层表示基础上重新训练分类器，探测大模型中与语言结构相关的知识。而Jain and Anke (2022)则通过将词汇之间的上下位关系转化为自然语言提示模板，来探测大模型中的词汇关系知识。相关研究表明，大模型的隐层表示中包含了一定程度的词性和句法知识，并且能够捕捉一些词汇关系。然而，大模型对于自然语言提示模板比较敏感，并且其语言学知识并不完备(Rogers et al., 2020)。

世界知识是指与特定实体和事件相关的事实性知识。由于世界知识通常可以用自然语言句子表达，并且在训练语料中广泛存在，因此对于世界知识的探测通常采用无训练的方法。其中，最具代表性的探测方式是LAMA（Language Model Analysis）(Petroni et al., 2019)，它将三元组或问答对形式的世界知识转化为自然语言填空的形式，通过预测正确答案在词表中的排位来评估大模型对世界知识的掌握程度。在LAMA探针实验的基础上，还衍生出了一系列相关研究，如自动生成提示语(Jiang et al., 2020)和使用连续向量作为提示语(Qin and Eisner, 2021)等，通过解决提示语选择等问题来进一步探测大模型中的世界知识。相关研究表明，大模型掌握了一定量的世界知识，但模型结果受到多种因素的干扰，对其处理世界知识的机制并不清晰，因此对于世界知识的探测实验需要更加严谨的设置和评估方法。

常识知识是指人们默认掌握的关于物理世界和人类社会的概括性知识。在常识知识探测研究中，通常采用无训练的方法。然而，与世界知识的设定不同，由于常识知识的多样性以及难以用单个标记进行填空的形式进行考察，常识知识的探测往往需要采用打分对比判断的形式(Zhou et al., 2020; Li et al., 2022)或句子排序等方式(Lin et al., 2021)，通过分析大模型在判断句子是否符合常识方面的能力，来探测大模型所具备的常识知识。此外，Bosselut et al. (2019)通过微调大模型获取常识知识，West et al. (2022)采用情景学习策略提示大模型生成常识知识，Wang et al. (2022)通过优化生成和答案过滤方法，辅助大模型在生成质量较差的条件下获取大规模高质量常识知识。相关研究表明，大模型掌握了一定程度的常识知识，但其对答案分布的拟合可能导致探测偏差。因此，如何客观地评估大模型的常识知识获取能力是一个难点问题。

4 知识融合

知识融合旨在对不同来源、不同语言和不同结构的知识进行融合，进而对已有知识图谱进行补充、更新和去重。由于知识图谱往往是由不同机构或个人构建的，其设计和构建并不统一，从而导致了异构性和冗余性的问题。因此，如何发现和建立不同知识图谱之间的关联成为各个领域亟需解决的重要问题。从融合的对象看，知识融合包括本体融合和实例融合。因此，本节将分别介绍本体融合和实例融合的相关研究。

本体融合是指将两个或多个异构知识本体进行融合，将相同的概念、属性和关系进行连接。基于大模型的本体融合主要关注于利用大模型获取本体的向量表示，并使用两个本体向量之间的相似度作为本体融合的依据。目前，主要采用对大模型进行微调的方法来获取本体的向量表示，从而完成实体本体融合(He et al., 2022a; He et al., 2022b)和事件本体融合(Guo et al., 2023)。相关研究表明，在本体融合任务中，大模型主要用于完成基本的向量表示，而更多的应用潜能尚未得到充分研究。因此，探索基于大模型的本体融合方法对于进一步提升本体融合效果具有重要价值。

实例融合是指对两个不同知识图谱中的知识实例（实体实例、关系实例）进行融合的过程。类似于本体融合，实例融合通常采用基于语义匹配的方法。这种方法利用大模型将知识图谱中的实例表示为低维向量，并通过计算实例向量之间的相似度来判断实例之间的语义关联关系。为了获得更好的实例融合性能，大模型在对实例建模过程中整合了多维度的实例信息，例如名称、描述、属性和结构信息，以获取语义丰富的低维向量(Tang et al., 2020; Yang et al., 2019)。此外，Zhao et al. (2023)提出了一种将实例对齐任务转化为文本蕴含任务的方法，将基于提示构建的实例对序列输入到大模型中，从而充分捕捉实例之间的语义关联。目前的实例对

[1]知识获取方法可以分为有训练方法和无训练方法。有训练方法指冻结模型参数，提取隐藏层表示，并添加额外的分类模块，在知识相关任务上进行训练，通过模型表现来评估其对知识的掌握程度；无训练方法则常常利用自然语言提示构建填充问题，使模型预测正确答案的似然分数，并与其他答案进行比较。

第二十二届中国计算语言学大会论文集，第67页-第76页，哈尔滨，中国，2023年8月3日至5日。
卷2：前沿综述

齐方法主要依赖于知识图谱的结构信息。然而，在现有的知识图谱中存在大量的长尾实例，这些实例的邻接实体通常只有一个或两个，缺乏丰富的结构信息。因此，如何有效地利用大模型来融合长尾实例，是一项具有挑战性的任务。

5 知识管理

知识管理旨在实现对知识图谱的持久化存储，以及对目标知识的高效检索。大模型通过对海量文本数据的训练来学习知识，并以隐式的方式存在。在大模型中，知识是如何存储的？又是如何进行更新的呢？围绕这两个问题，本节将分别介绍基于大模型的知识定位和知识编辑相关研究。

知识定位指的是探索大模型中"知识"的存储位置和访问机制。目前的主流观点认为，大语言模型中的前馈网络模块（Feedforward Neural Network, FFN）起到了知识存储的作用(Geva et al., 2021)。具体而言，可以将Transformer的前馈网络模块视为一个键值存储器（Key-Value Memory）。在这个存储器中，每个神经元的键向量用于识别输入中的语言或知识模式，可以看作是模式探测器，而对应的值向量则扮演着知识生成器的角色，代表着该模式的知识向量。相关的研究通过实验分析对这一结论提供了支持，例如Dai et al. (2022)使用归因方法验证了前馈网络模块隐藏层中存在与事实性知识相关的特定神经元，而Meng et al. (2023)则从因果关联的角度论证了前馈网络模块与事实性知识的关联。相关研究为理解大模型中的知识定位提供了一种新的视角，揭示了知识是通过参数化的方式存储在模型中的。然而，目前的研究主要集中在处理结构化知识，对于其他形式的知识，目前的方法还存在一定的局限性。

知识编辑指的是对隐含在语言模型参数中的知识进行有针对性的更新。该任务的目标是在更新特定知识的同时，尽量减少对其他知识的破坏。主要的方法可以分为超网络方法和定向知识编辑方法。超网络方法依赖于数据驱动的训练，通过训练一个超网络，有针对性地修改模型中的事实知识。具体来说，超网络替代优化器生成模型参数的更新量，并使用约束项来确保在超网络训练过程中，特定知识更新成功的同时减少对其他知识的破坏(Cao et al., 2021)。由于大模型的参数规模巨大，设计高效的超网络方法仍然是一个挑战。定向知识编辑方法是一种基于"键值存储"假设，用于直接定位和修改模型参数的方法。在该方法中，假设Transformer的前馈网络模块负责存储知识，并且每个键都有对应的值。通过使用表达相同键含义的不同提示，可以定位到存储了相关知识的神经元，并对其对应的值进行修改(Meng et al., 2022; Meng et al., 2023)。目前定向知识编辑方法与三元组形式耦合较强，在处理如过程性知识、数学知识、语言知识等某情况，存在一些限制。

6 知识推理

知识推理旨在采用推理手段发现已有知识中隐含的知识。通过知识建模、知识获取和知识融合，可以构建一个可用的知识图谱。然而，由于数据的不完备性和稀疏性，很难通过抽取或融合方法来填补缺失的知识。因此，需要采用推理的手段来发现已有知识中隐含的知识。大模型从海量无标注数据中学习到丰富的知识，如果能从大模型已有知识中推导出新的知识，将有助于知识图谱的构建。为此，研究人员致力于探索大模型推理能力，而推理能力的关键在于思维链（Chain of Thought，CoT）技术。因此，本节围绕思维链介绍大模型在知识推理方面的相关研究。

思维链是参考人类解决复杂问题的一种推理方式，将问题分解为一系列中间问题，并逐步解决这些问题以获得最终结果。思维链推理技术通过向大模型展示少量样例并解释推理过程，在回答提示时也显式展示推理过程，从而引导模型输出更准确的结果(Wei et al., 2022)。零样本思维链（Zero-shot-CoT）是思维链的一种衍生形式，通过在问题结尾附加提示语句，如"Let's think step by step"，激励大模型生成一个回答问题的思维链，从而产生答案(Kojima et al., 2022)。在这基础上，Wang et al. (2023b)通过自洽性（Self-consistency）方式改进了思维链，该方法利用多数投票的思想生成多个思维链，然后选择多数答案作为最终答案，以提高思维链的性能。上述方法通过简单的提示或精心设计的样例来激发大模型生成中间推理步骤，但生成的证据常常会出现错误，导致不准确和不可靠的推理链。因此,Wang et al. (2023a)提出了知识链（Chain-of-Knowledge）提示方法，通过生成显式的三元组结构知识证据来引导大模型进行推理，从而有效提升文本推理任务的性能。为了更好地适应需要预测的复杂推理任务，Yao et al. (2023)提出了思维树（Tree of Thoughts，ToT）方法，大模型通过对不同的推理路径进行

第二十二届中国计算语言学大会论文集，第67页-第76页，哈尔滨，中国，2023年8月3日至5日。
卷2：前沿综述

评估来决定下一步的行动方案，并且在必要时可以向前或向后追溯，以实现全局决策。尽管常规文本提示在一定程度上可以促进模型的推理能力，但存在逻辑上的歧义，可能导致错误的答案。而三元组结构知识提示可以进一步提升推理性能。因此，需要将文本提示与结构特征相融合，以使大模型能够生成可靠且具体的推理过程。

7 知识应用

知识应用是指将知识应用于具体任务和应用场景的过程。大模型在解决各种自然语言处理任务方面展现了巨大的潜力，并在某种程度上为通用人工智能铺平了道路。本节将介绍大模型在自然语言理解和自然语言生成任务方面的应用。

自然语言理解的目标是让计算机能够像人类一样理解自然语言。自然语言理解任务包括文本分类、自动问答等。文本分类是指将文本映射到预先给定的某一类别或某几类别主题的过程。针对该任务，Sun et al. (2023)提出了一种基于大模型的渐进推理方法来进行文本分类。该方法利用提示语引导大模型捕捉关键词、语气等表层线索，并进一步基于这些线索通过推理对文本进行分类。Zhang et al. (2023c)通过设计清晰而直接的提示，引导大模型完成传统的情感分类任务、基于方面的情感分析和多维主观文本分析。自动问答要求系统根据对文本的理解给出问题的答案，是衡量机器自然语言理解程度的重要指标。Tan et al. (2023)将大模型自身的知识作为知识库，衡量其在传统基于知识问答任务上的性能。Huang et al. (2023)提出了一种基于答案反馈的情景学习方法，通过将更正的答案记录作为反馈信息，构建大模型的增强提示，以提高其在问答任务中的性能。由于大模型强大的泛化能力，在面对分布外的数据或非常少的训练数据时可以提供帮助(Yang et al., 2023)，但在复杂的自然语言理解任务，如基于方面的情感分析、多跳问答等任务上，仍然存在一定挑战。

自然语言生成的目标是生成连贯、有意义且与上下文相符的高质量文本。它包括两类主要任务：序列转化任务和开放式生成任务。序列转化任务旨在将输入文本转换为新的符号序列。例如，Liu et al. (2023)使用大模型生成训练数据，以指导摘要模型的学习。而Zhang et al. (2023a)则通过使用提示词模板和情景学习方法来引导大模型完成机器翻译任务。开放式生成任务是从头开始生成文本或符号，以准确匹配输入的描述。例如，Yang et al. (2022)利用递归提示和调整策略来引导大模型自动生成长篇故事。而Yang et al. (2022)则利用大模型从海量数据中学习到的丰富知识，有效生成个性化新闻和新闻摘要等内容。由于大模型具备强大的生成能力和创造力，因此在许多生成任务中展现出更高的优越性(Yang et al., 2023)。然而，当大模型生成文本时，它无法自行判断生成结果的准确性，这导致了所谓的幻觉性问题。因此，解决大模型中的幻觉性问题成为一个重要的挑战。

8 总结与展望

本文聚焦于大模型在知识图谱生命周期的研究，并总结分析了大模型在知识建模、知识获取、知识融合、知识管理、知识推理和知识应用等环节中的研究进展。

由于大模型能够自动从无标注数据中学习知识并以参数形式存储，因此能灵活地应用于开放域场景。然而，大模型也存在一些根本性问题和限制。首先，大模型缺乏显式的知识存储结构，这使得知识的组织和检索变得困难。其次，大模型有时会受到所谓的"幻觉"现象的影响，导致生成不准确的输出。最后，大模型纯粹的数据驱动学习方式使得其缺乏可解释性。相比之下，知识图谱以显式的方式描述知识，并且知识的表达基于清晰的结构和严谨的描述逻辑，因此具有确定性。知识图谱中的节点和边都有具体的含义，使得知识的解释和理解更加容易。然而，知识图谱的构建困难，其泛化性能不如大模型，也难以生成新的事实或表示未知的知识(Pan et al., 2023; Cao et al., 2023)。因此，将知识图谱与大模型相结合可以相辅相成，相互促进，从而取得更好的效果。具体地：

大模型助力知识图谱构建。在构建知识图谱的过程中，利用大模型可以提高知识的抽取和注入效率，增强知识图谱的覆盖范围和泛化性能。

知识图谱辅助大模型进行知识校准和提升可解释性。大模型可以借助知识图谱提高知识的准确性，同时利用知识图谱来解释大模型的知识和推理过程，增强模型的可解释性。

大模型和知识图谱协同工作。充分利用数据驱动和知识驱动的优势，提升自然语言处理各任务的能力，促进人工智能技术的发展。

第二十二届中国计算语言学大会论文集，第67页-第76页，哈尔滨，中国，2023年8月3日至5日。
卷2：前沿综述

大模型的快速发展为知识图谱的研究注入了新的活力，两者相结合研究的前景非常值得期待。

参考文献

赵军, 刘康, 何世柱, and 陈玉博. 2018. 知识图谱. 高等教育出版社.

Antoine Bosselut, Hannah Rashkin, Maarten Sap, Chaitanya Malaviya, Asli Celikyilmaz, and Yejin Choi. 2019. COMET: commonsense transformers for automatic knowledge graph construction. In Anna Korhonen, David R. Traum, and Lluís Màrquez, editors, *Proceedings of the 57th Conference of the Association for Computational Linguistics, ACL 2019, Florence, Italy, July 28- August 2, 2019, Volume 1: Long Papers*, pages 4762–4779. Association for Computational Linguistics.

Nicola De Cao, Wilker Aziz, and Ivan Titov. 2021. Editing factual knowledge in language models. In Marie-Francine Moens, Xuanjing Huang, Lucia Specia, and Scott Wen-tau Yih, editors, *Proceedings of the 2021 Conference on Empirical Methods in Natural Language Processing, EMNLP 2021, Virtual Event / Punta Cana, Dominican Republic, 7-11 November, 2021*, pages 6491–6506. Association for Computational Linguistics.

Boxi Cao, Hongyu Lin, Xianpei Han, and Le Sun. 2023. The life cycle of knowledge in big language models: A survey. *CoRR*, abs/2303.07616.

Damai Dai, Li Dong, Yaru Hao, Zhifang Sui, Baobao Chang, and Furu Wei. 2022. Knowledge neurons in pretrained transformers. In Smaranda Muresan, Preslav Nakov, and Aline Villavicencio, editors, *Proceedings of the 60th Annual Meeting of the Association for Computational Linguistics (Volume 1: Long Papers), ACL 2022, Dublin, Ireland, May 22-27, 2022*, pages 8493–8502. Association for Computational Linguistics.

Carl Edwards and Heng Ji. 2023. Semi-supervised new event type induction and description via contrastive loss-enforced batch attention. In Andreas Vlachos and Isabelle Augenstein, editors, *Proceedings of the 17th Conference of the European Chapter of the Association for Computational Linguistics, EACL 2023, Dubrovnik, Croatia, May 2-6, 2023*, pages 3787–3809. Association for Computational Linguistics.

Edward A. Feigenbaum. 1977. The art of artificial intelligence: Themes and case studies of knowledge engineering. In Raj Reddy, editor, *Proceedings of the 5th International Joint Conference on Artificial Intelligence. Cambridge, MA, USA, August 22-25, 1977*, pages 1014–1029. William Kaufmann.

Mor Geva, Roei Schuster, Jonathan Berant, and Omer Levy. 2021. Transformer feed-forward layers are key-value memories. In Marie-Francine Moens, Xuanjing Huang, Lucia Specia, and Scott Wen-tau Yih, editors, *Proceedings of the 2021 Conference on Empirical Methods in Natural Language Processing, EMNLP 2021, Virtual Event / Punta Cana, Dominican Republic, 7-11 November, 2021*, pages 5484–5495. Association for Computational Linguistics.

Shaoru Guo, Chenhao Wang, Yubo Chen, Kang Liu, Ru Li, and Jun Zhao. 2023. Eventoa: An event ontology alignment benchmark based on framenet and wikidata. In *Proceedings of the 61th Annual Meeting of the Association for Computational Linguistics.*

Yuan He, Jiaoyan Chen, Denvar Antonyrajah, and Ian Horrocks. 2022a. Bertmap: A bert-based ontology alignment system. In *Thirty-Sixth AAAI Conference on Artificial Intelligence, AAAI 2022, Thirty-Fourth Conference on Innovative Applications of Artificial Intelligence, IAAI 2022, The Twelveth Symposium on Educational Advances in Artificial Intelligence, EAAI 2022 Virtual Event, February 22 - March 1, 2022*, pages 5684–5691. AAAI Press.

Yuan He, Jiaoyan Chen, Hang Dong, Ernesto Jiménez-Ruiz, Ali Hadian, and Ian Horrocks. 2022b. Machine learning-friendly biomedical datasets for equivalence and subsumption ontology matching. In Ulrike Sattler, Aidan Hogan, C. Maria Keet, Valentina Presutti, João Paulo A. Almeida, Hideaki Takeda, Pierre Monnin, Giuseppe Pirrò, and Claudia d'Amato, editors, *The Semantic Web - ISWC 2022 - 21st International Semantic Web Conference, Virtual Event, October 23-27, 2022, Proceedings*, volume 13489 of *Lecture Notes in Computer Science*, pages 575–591. Springer.

Zixian Huang, Jiaying Zhou, Gengyang Xiao, and Gong Cheng. 2023. Enhancing in-context learning with answer feedback for multi-span question answering. *CoRR*, abs/2306.04508.

第二十二届中国计算语言学大会论文集，第67页-第76页，哈尔滨，中国，2023年8月3日至5日。
卷2：前沿综述

Devansh Jain and Luis Espinosa Anke. 2022. Distilling hypernymy relations from language models: On the effectiveness of zero-shot taxonomy induction. In Vivi Nastase, Ellie Pavlick, Mohammad Taher Pilehvar, José Camacho-Collados, and Alessandro Raganato, editors, *Proceedings of the 11th Joint Conference on Lexical and Computational Semantics, *SEM@NAACL-HLT 2022, Seattle, WA, USA, July 14-15, 2022*, pages 151–156. Association for Computational Linguistics.

Zhengbao Jiang, Frank F. Xu, Jun Araki, and Graham Neubig. 2020. How can we know what language models know. *Trans. Assoc. Comput. Linguistics*, 8:423–438.

Maël Jullien, Marco Valentino, and André Freitas. 2022. Do transformers encode a foundational ontology? probing abstract classes in natural language. *CoRR*, abs/2201.10262.

Takeshi Kojima, Shixiang Shane Gu, Machel Reid, Yutaka Matsuo, and Yusuke Iwasawa. 2022. Large language models are zero-shot reasoners. In *NeurIPS*.

Xiang Lorraine Li, Adhiguna Kuncoro, Jordan Hoffmann, Cyprien de Masson d'Autume, Phil Blunsom, and Aida Nematzadeh. 2022. A systematic investigation of commonsense knowledge in large language models. In Yoav Goldberg, Zornitsa Kozareva, and Yue Zhang, editors, *Proceedings of the 2022 Conference on Empirical Methods in Natural Language Processing, EMNLP 2022, Abu Dhabi, United Arab Emirates, December 7-11, 2022*, pages 11838–11855. Association for Computational Linguistics.

Sha Li, Ruining Zhao, Manling Li, Heng Ji, Chris Callison-Burch, and Jiawei Han. 2023. Open-domain hierarchical event schema induction by incremental prompting and verification. In *Proceedings of the 61st Annual Meeting of the Association for Computational Linguistics.*

Bill Yuchen Lin, Seyeon Lee, Xiaoyang Qiao, and Xiang Ren. 2021. Common sense beyond english: Evaluating and improving multilingual language models for commonsense reasoning. In Chengqing Zong, Fei Xia, Wenjie Li, and Roberto Navigli, editors, *Proceedings of the 59th Annual Meeting of the Association for Computational Linguistics and the 11th International Joint Conference on Natural Language Processing, ACL/IJCNLP 2021, (Volume 1: Long Papers), Virtual Event, August 1-6, 2021*, pages 1274–1287. Association for Computational Linguistics.

Nelson F. Liu, Matt Gardner, Yonatan Belinkov, Matthew E. Peters, and Noah A. Smith. 2019. Linguistic knowledge and transferability of contextual representations. In Jill Burstein, Christy Doran, and Thamar Solorio, editors, *Proceedings of the 2019 Conference of the North American Chapter of the Association for Computational Linguistics: Human Language Technologies, NAACL-HLT 2019, Minneapolis, MN, USA, June 2-7, 2019, Volume 1 (Long and Short Papers)*, pages 1073–1094. Association for Computational Linguistics.

Yixin Liu, Alexander R. Fabbri, Pengfei Liu, Dragomir Radev, and Arman Cohan. 2023. On learning to summarize with large language models as references. *CoRR*, abs/2305.14239.

Kevin Meng, David Bau, Alex Andonian, and Yonatan Belinkov. 2022. Locating and editing factual associations in GPT. In *NeurIPS*.

Kevin Meng, Arnab Sen Sharma, Alex J. Andonian, Yonatan Belinkov, and David Bau. 2023. Mass-editing memory in a transformer. In *The Eleventh International Conference on Learning Representations, ICLR 2023, Kigali, Rwanda, May 1-5, 2023.* OpenReview.net.

Shirui Pan, Linhao Luo, Yufei Wang, Chen Chen, Jiapu Wang, and Xindong Wu. 2023. Unifying large language models and knowledge graphs: A roadmap. *CoRR*, abs/2306.08302.

Hao Peng, Xiaozhi Wang, Shengding Hu, Hailong Jin, Lei Hou, Juanzi Li, Zhiyuan Liu, and Qun Liu. 2022. COPEN: probing conceptual knowledge in pre-trained language models. In Yoav Goldberg, Zornitsa Kozareva, and Yue Zhang, editors, *Proceedings of the 2022 Conference on Empirical Methods in Natural Language Processing, EMNLP 2022, Abu Dhabi, United Arab Emirates, December 7-11, 2022*, pages 5015–5035. Association for Computational Linguistics.

Fabio Petroni, Tim Rocktäschel, Sebastian Riedel, Patrick S. H. Lewis, Anton Bakhtin, Yuxiang Wu, and Alexander H. Miller. 2019. Language models as knowledge bases? In Kentaro Inui, Jing Jiang, Vincent Ng, and Xiaojun Wan, editors, *Proceedings of the 2019 Conference on Empirical Methods in Natural Language Processing and the 9th International Joint Conference on Natural Language Processing, EMNLP-IJCNLP 2019, Hong Kong, China, November 3-7, 2019*, pages 2463–2473. Association for Computational Linguistics.

第二十二届中国计算语言学大会论文集，第67页-第76页，哈尔滨，中国，2023年8月3日至5日。
卷2：前沿综述

Guanghui Qin and Jason Eisner. 2021. Learning how to ask: Querying lms with mixtures of soft prompts. In Kristina Toutanova, Anna Rumshisky, Luke Zettlemoyer, Dilek Hakkani-Tür, Iz Beltagy, Steven Bethard, Ryan Cotterell, Tanmoy Chakraborty, and Yichao Zhou, editors, *Proceedings of the 2021 Conference of the North American Chapter of the Association for Computational Linguistics: Human Language Technologies, NAACL-HLT 2021, Online, June 6-11, 2021*, pages 5203–5212. Association for Computational Linguistics.

Anna Rogers, Olga Kovaleva, and Anna Rumshisky. 2020. A primer in bertology: What we know about how BERT works. *Trans. Assoc. Comput. Linguistics*, 8:842–866.

Xiaofei Sun, Xiaoya Li, Jiwei Li, Fei Wu, Shangwei Guo, Tianwei Zhang, and Guoyin Wang. 2023. Text classification via large language models. *CoRR*, abs/2305.08377.

Yiming Tan, Dehai Min, Yu Li, Wenbo Li, Nan Hu, Yongrui Chen, and Guilin Qi. 2023. Evaluation of chatgpt as a question answering system for answering complex questions. *CoRR*, abs/2303.07992.

Xiaobin Tang, Jing Zhang, Bo Chen, Yang Yang, Hong Chen, and Cuiping Li. 2020. BERT-INT: A bert-based interaction model for knowledge graph alignment. In Christian Bessiere, editor, *Proceedings of the Twenty-Ninth International Joint Conference on Artificial Intelligence, IJCAI 2020*, pages 3174–3180. ijcai.org.

Jialong Tang, Hongyu Lin, Zhuoqun Li, Yaojie Lu, Xianpei Han, and Le Sun. 2023. Harvesting event schemas from large language models. *CoRR*, abs/2305.07280.

Chenhao Wang, Jiachun Li, Yubo Chen, Kang Liu, and Jun Zhao. 2022. Cn-automic: Distilling chinese commonsense knowledge from pretrained language models. In Yoav Goldberg, Zornitsa Kozareva, and Yue Zhang, editors, *Proceedings of the 2022 Conference on Empirical Methods in Natural Language Processing, EMNLP 2022, Abu Dhabi, United Arab Emirates, December 7-11, 2022*, pages 9253–9265. Association for Computational Linguistics.

Jianing Wang, Qiushi Sun, Nuo Chen, Xiang Li, and Ming Gao. 2023a. Boosting language models reasoning with chain-of-knowledge prompting. *CoRR*, abs/2306.06427.

Xuezhi Wang, Jason Wei, Dale Schuurmans, Quoc V. Le, Ed H. Chi, Sharan Narang, Aakanksha Chowdhery, and Denny Zhou. 2023b. Self-consistency improves chain of thought reasoning in language models. In *The Eleventh International Conference on Learning Representations, ICLR 2023, Kigali, Rwanda, May 1-5, 2023*. OpenReview.net.

Jason Wei, Xuezhi Wang, Dale Schuurmans, Maarten Bosma, Brian Ichter, Fei Xia, Ed H. Chi, Quoc V. Le, and Denny Zhou. 2022. Chain-of-thought prompting elicits reasoning in large language models. In *NeurIPS*.

Peter West, Chandra Bhagavatula, Jack Hessel, Jena D. Hwang, Liwei Jiang, Ronan Le Bras, Ximing Lu, Sean Welleck, and Yejin Choi. 2022. Symbolic knowledge distillation: from general language models to commonsense models. In Marine Carpuat, Marie-Catherine de Marneffe, and Iván Vladimir Meza Ruíz, editors, *Proceedings of the 2022 Conference of the North American Chapter of the Association for Computational Linguistics: Human Language Technologies, NAACL 2022, Seattle, WA, United States, July 10-15, 2022*, pages 4602–4625. Association for Computational Linguistics.

Weiqi Wu, Chengyue Jiang, Yong Jiang, Pengjun Xie, Ru Li Kewei Tu, and Jun Zhao. 2023. Do plms know and understand ontological knowledge? In *Proceedings of the 61th Annual Meeting of the Association for Computational Linguistics*.

Hsiu-Wei Yang, Yanyan Zou, Peng Shi, Wei Lu, Jimmy Lin, and Xu Sun. 2019. Aligning cross-lingual entities with multi-aspect information. In Kentaro Inui, Jing Jiang, Vincent Ng, and Xiaojun Wan, editors, *Proceedings of the 2019 Conference on Empirical Methods in Natural Language Processing and the 9th International Joint Conference on Natural Language Processing, EMNLP-IJCNLP 2019, Hong Kong, China, November 3-7, 2019*, pages 4430–4440. Association for Computational Linguistics.

Kevin Yang, Yuandong Tian, Nanyun Peng, and Dan Klein. 2022. Re3: Generating longer stories with recursive reprompting and revision. In Yoav Goldberg, Zornitsa Kozareva, and Yue Zhang, editors, *Proceedings of the 2022 Conference on Empirical Methods in Natural Language Processing, EMNLP 2022, Abu Dhabi, United Arab Emirates, December 7-11, 2022*, pages 4393–4479. Association for Computational Linguistics.

第二十二届中国计算语言学大会论文集，第67页-第76页，哈尔滨，中国，2023年8月3日至5日。
卷2：前沿综述

Jingfeng Yang, Hongye Jin, Ruixiang Tang, Xiaotian Han, Qizhang Feng, Haoming Jiang, Bing Yin, and Xia Hu. 2023. Harnessing the power of llms in practice: A survey on chatgpt and beyond. *CoRR*, abs/2304.13712.

Shunyu Yao, Dian Yu, Jeffrey Zhao, Izhak Shafran, Thomas L. Griffiths, Yuan Cao, and Karthik Narasimhan. 2023. Tree of thoughts: Deliberate problem solving with large language models. *CoRR*, abs/2305.10601.

Biao Zhang, Barry Haddow, and Alexandra Birch. 2023a. Prompting large language model for machine translation: A case study. *CoRR*, abs/2301.07069.

Tianyi Zhang, Isaac Tham, Zhaoyi Hou, Jiaxuan Ren, Liyang Zhou, Hainiu Xu, Li Zhang, Lara J. Martin, Rotem Dror, Sha Li, Heng Ji, Martha Palmer, Susan Windisch Brown, Reece Suchocki, and Chris Callison-Burch. 2023b. Human-in-the-loop schema induction. *CoRR*, abs/2302.13048.

Wenxuan Zhang, Yue Deng, Bing Liu, Sinno Jialin Pan, and Lidong Bing. 2023c. Sentiment analysis in the era of large language models: A reality check. *CoRR*, abs/2305.15005.

Yu Zhao, Yike Wu, Xiangrui Cai, Ying Zhang, Haiwei Zhang, and Xiaojie Yuan. 2023. From alignment to entailment: A unified textual entailment framework for entity alignment. *CoRR*, abs/2305.11501.

Xuhui Zhou, Yue Zhang, Leyang Cui, and Dandan Huang. 2020. Evaluating commonsense in pre-trained language models. In *The Thirty-Fourth AAAI Conference on Artificial Intelligence, AAAI 2020, The Thirty-Second Innovative Applications of Artificial Intelligence Conference, IAAI 2020, The Tenth AAAI Symposium on Educational Advances in Artificial Intelligence, EAAI 2020, New York, NY, USA, February 7-12, 2020*, pages 9733–9740. AAAI Press.

第二十二届中国计算语言学大会论文集，第67页-第76页，哈尔滨，中国，2023年8月3日至5日。
卷2：前沿综述

大语言模型对齐：概念、挑战、路线、评测及趋势

熊德意
天津大学智能与计算学部
天津市津南区海河教育园区雅观路135号，300350
dyxiong@tju.edu.cn

摘要

通用智能的"智能-目标"正交性及"工具性趋同"论点均要求通用智能的发展要智善结合。目前大语言模型在能力（智）方面发展迅速，但在更具挑战性的价值对齐（善）方面研究相对滞后。本综述将概述对齐的基本概念和必要性，简述其存在的社会和技术挑战，分析大语言模型对齐的主要技术路线和方法，探讨如何对大语言模型对齐进行评测，并对未来趋势进行展望。

关键词： 大语言模型；通用人工智能；AI对齐；大语言模型对齐

Large Language Model Alignment: Concepts, Challenges, Roadmaps, Evaluations and Trends

Deyi Xiong
College of Intelligence and Computing, Tianjin University
No.135 Yaguan Road, Haihe Education Park, Tianjin, 300350, China
dyxiong@tju.edu.cn

Abstract

The "intelligence-goal" orthogonality and "instrumental convergence" theses require a deep coupling between capability and alignment for the development of general intelligence. At present, large language models are developing rapidly in terms of capability (intelligence), but the research on a more challenging problem, value alignment (goodness), is relatively lagging behind. This article will introduce the basic concepts and necessity of alignment research, briefly describe its social and technical challenges, analyze the main technical routes and methods of large language model alignment and discuss how to evaluate large language model alignment and future trends.

Keywords: Large Language Model , Artifiicial General Intelligence , AI Alignment , LLM Alignment

1 引言

近年来，以OpenAI ChatGPT和GPT-4为代表的大语言模型（Large Language Model，LLM）发展迅速，重新燃起了人们对通用人工智能（Artificial General Intelligence，AGI）的热情和憧憬。虽然大语言模型是否是通向AGI之路仍存在争议，但在标度

第二十二届中国计算语言学大会论文集，第77页-第87页，哈尔滨，中国，2023年8月3日至5日。
卷2：前沿综述
(c) 2023 中国中文信息学会计算语言学专业委员会

律（Scaling Law）基础上不断扩展规模的大语言模型，其能力逐步呈现出一些AGI的特征(Bubeck et al., 2023)：在海量语言数据上训练的GPT模型，除了展现出强大的语言能力之外，在数学、推理、医疗、法律、编程等多个领域，正以惊人的速度逼近人类水平。

与大语言模型技术和能力不断突破相伴随的是，人们对大语言模型本身存在的社会伦理风险及其对人类生存构成的潜在威胁的普遍担忧。首先，在真实可见的社会伦理风险方面，研究发现(Weidinger et al., 2021)，一方面，大语言模型在输出文本中存在多种类型的信息危害，如将训练数据中存在的偏见、歧视、有毒内容输出到预测文本中，在生成文本中泄露训练数据中的隐私和敏感信息，生成低质量、虚假性、误导性信息；另一方面，大语言模型的使用也带来社会伦理风险，如大语言模型存在被滥用的可能性，用于人机交互类产品中时可能对使用者带来潜在影响，大范围使用大语言模型可能带来对环境、信息传播、就业等方面的影响。OpenAI团队研究发现(Eloundou et al., 2023)，美国80%的劳动力，其工作存在对大语言模型10%的风险敞口（即会受到大语言模型影响），19%的就业人员，其50%的工作任务会受到大语言模型影响，且收入越高，受大语言模型影响越大。

其次，在更远期的潜在影响方面，很多人担心未对齐的AGI可能带来人类存亡风险（Existential Risk，X-Risk），即超过人类知识和智能水平的AI代理（Agent）会形成自己的目标（Goal），且该目标与人类赋予的目标不一致，为了实现自己的目标，AI代理将会获取更多的资源，实现自我保持、自我提升，这种发展将会持续扩展至对整个人类进行权利剥夺（Disenpower），从而不可避免地导致人类生存灾难(Carlsmith, 2022)。基于以上担忧，美国波斯顿未来生命研究所（由Skype联合创始人和麻省理工学院教授共同创立）于2023年3月22日发起暂停巨型AI实验的公开倡议信[0]，要求所有AI实验室暂停训练比GPT-4更强大的AI模型至少6个月，截至2023年7月6日，网上签名人数已超过三万三千人，签名人员包括图灵奖获得者Yoshua Bengio、特斯拉CEO Elon Musk等人。公开信中提到阿西洛马人工智能原则（Asilomar AI Principles）："先进的人工智能可能代表地球生命史上的一次深刻变化，应该以相应的关心和资源进行规划和管理"。图灵奖获得者，也是此次大语言模型底层核心技术的发明者之一，Geoffrey Hinton也表达了对未来AGI的担忧，并签名了由AI安全中心于2023年5月30日发起的AI安全声明[1]。该声明仅包含一句话（22个单词），强调AI安全应该具有和防止大流行病、核战争一样的优先级别。

对AGI是否导致X-Risk，目前还存在争议。与Geoffrey Hinton、Yoshua Bengio同年获得图灵奖的Yann LeCun认为目前的大语言模型技术并不能实现AGI，也不会导致X-Risk。2023年6月22日，著名辩论会"芒克辩论会"（Munk Debates）邀请了图灵奖获得者Yoshua Bengio和MIT教授Max Tegmark作为正方，图灵奖获得者Yann LeCun和圣塔菲研究所教授Melanie Mitchell作为反方，就AI研究和发展是否构成X-Risk威胁问题进行了辩论[2]，辩论前正反方观众投票为67% vs 33%（即67%的观众认为AI研究和发展构成X-Risk威胁，33%认为不会），辩论后，正反方得票率为63% vs 37%。虽然反方辩论后获得了4个点的支持，但大部分观众听完辩论后仍然认为AI研究和发展构成X-Risk威胁。

需要注意的是，以上公开倡议、广泛的讨论和辩论，并不是宣扬AI宿命论，而是强调在致力于提升AI能力研究的同时，也要高度重视AI安全的研究。强调AI发展的长远风险，也并不是要掩盖或者回避大语言模型带来的真实社会伦理风险。AI能力研究势不可挡，AI安全研究势在必行！

上述社会伦理风险与人类存亡风险，都与AI安全技术——人工智能对齐（AI Alignment）——密切相关。AI对齐是AI的一个新兴领域，真正发展时间不过10年左右，但随着大语言模型的飞速发展，该领域越来越受到关注和重视。本文将介绍AI对齐的基本概念和相关背景（第2节），阐述对齐存在的巨大挑战（第3节）,探讨实现大语言模型对齐的主要技术路线（第4节）,介绍如何评测对齐模型（第5节），并对未来AI对齐研究的趋势进行展望（第6节）。

2 什么是AI/LLM对齐

人工智能对齐的概念萌芽最早可以追溯至控制论之父Norbert Wiener，他在1960年发表于

[0]https://futureoflife.org/open-letter/pause-giant-ai-experiments/

[1]https://www.safe.ai/statement-on-ai-risk

[2]https://munkdebates.com/debates/artificial-intelligence

第二十二届中国计算语言学大会论文集，第77页-第87页，哈尔滨，中国，2023年8月3日至5日。
卷2：前沿综述

《Science》的一篇论文(Wiener, 1960)中提到：

> If we use, to achieve our purposes, a mechanical agency with whose operation we cannot efficiently interfere once we have started it, because the action is so fast and irrevocable that we have not the data to intervene before the action is complete, then we had better be quite sure that the purpose put into the machine is the purpose which we really desire and not merely a colorful imitation of it.

在这段话中，Norbert Wiener明确指出，"mechanical agency"的目标应该与我们期待它实现的目标保持一致，即机器目标要与人类目标对齐。

2014年，《人工智能：一种现代方法》作者之一Stuart Russell教授在一次访谈中[3]指出：

> The right response seems to be to change the goals of the field itself; instead of pure intelligence, we need to build intelligence that is provably aligned with human values. For practical reasons, we will need to solve the value alignment problem even for relatively unintelligent AI systems that operate in the human environment. There is cause for optimism, if we understand that this issue is an intrinsic part of AI, much as containment is an intrinsic part of modern nuclear fusion research. The world need not be headed for grief.

Stuart Russell教授在这次访谈中首次提出了"价值对齐问题（Value Alignment Problem）"，即我们构建的不是纯粹的智能，而是与人类价值对齐的智能，并认为价值对齐问题是人工智能内在固有的一部分，价值对齐与人工智能的关系犹如安全壳之于核聚变反应堆。

虽然AI对齐概念在AI诞生之初就已萌芽，但由于人工智能在过去几十年发展曲折，其智能水平一直与人们期望的水平相差甚远，甚至很多时候被认为是人工智障，因此，对齐机器目标与人类目标/价值的紧迫性一直没有发展AI智能水平的紧迫性高。但近年来，大语言模型推动AI智能水平迅猛发展，并在越来越多的任务上，使其性能逼近甚至超过人类的水平，AI对齐的重要性和紧迫性也因此浮出水面，并受到越来越多的关注。从2012年开始，关于AI对齐的讨论和研究论文逐渐出现在相关论坛和arXiv上；2017年，AI对齐讨论的文章数量及论文数量出现爆发式增长，从原来的每年不足20篇猛增至400余篇(Kirchner et al., 2022)，这与大语言模型基础架构Transformer及GPT发明的时间基本吻合。

相比于AI其他研究领域，如自然语言处理，AI对齐还处于混沌状态，尚未形成科学研究范式(Kirchner et al., 2022)，除此之外，该领域的许多关键概念和术语也未形成共识。首先，在术语方面，"对齐"、"AI对齐"、"价值对齐"等名称经常在有关AI对齐的讨论文章和论文里交替使用，在中文相关讨论中，"人机对齐"也以AI对齐的替代形式出现。"对齐"在AI对齐领域及上下文环境中使用没有问题，但在更广泛的领域，容易与其他对齐概念产生混淆（如机器翻译中的双语或多语对齐）；"价值对齐"虽明确了对齐内容但未明确研究对象和领域；"人机对齐"虽然明确了人与机器之间对齐，但未明确研究领域、对齐内容及到底是人对齐机器还是机器对齐人。鉴于此，本文统一使用AI对齐和LLM对齐，LLM对齐可看作是AI对齐与自然语言处理、大语言模型的交叉领域。

其次，AI对齐的定义也没有形成共识。Paul Christiano将AI对齐定义为[4]：

> A is aligned with H if A is trying to do what H wants it to do.

上述定义过于宽泛，任何AI系统都可以认为是要完成人类想要它完成的任务，但实际上，上文已隐含提到AI对齐主要针对具有高智能（Highly Capable）的AI代理(Carroll, 2018)，这也意味着由未对齐AI导致的安全问题有别于一般的弱人工智能安全问题。也有研究人员从AI与人类关系的角度定义AI对齐。如Eliezer Yudkowsky将AI对齐定义为"创造友好的AI"、"连贯的外推意志（Coherent Extrapolated Volition）"。

除了从其本身的内涵及与人类关系角度定义AI对齐之外，还有一些工作试图以AI对齐要解决的具体问题来解释和具化AI对齐，Gordon Worley汇总了一些研究人员提出的AI对齐需要解决的问题[5]：

[3] http://edge.org/conversation/the-myth-of-ai#26015

[4] https://ai-alignment.com/clarifying-ai-alignment-cec47cd69dd6

[5] https://laptrinhx.com/formally-stating-the-ai-alignment-problem-223323934/

第二十二届中国计算语言学大会论文集，第77页-第87页，哈尔滨，中国，2023年8月3日至5日。
卷2：前沿综述

- 避免副作用（Avoiding Negative Side Effects）：避免AI代理产生预期之外的行为。
- 避免奖励劫持/游戏（Avoiding Reward Hacking/Gaming）：避免AI代理利用奖励函数中的漏洞反复攫取奖励而忽视真正的目标。
- 可扩展的监管（Scalable Oversight）：将对AI代理的监管延伸至信息有限的情形或者人类难以直接判断的复杂任务上，比如当大语言模型能力在很多任务上超过人类水平时仍然可对其进行有效监管。
- 分布变化鲁棒性（Robustness to Distributional Shifts）：在新领域、新环境中，AI代理仍然能够按预期方式运行，尤其是在人类设计员未预期到的环境中，AI代理不会产生破坏性后果。
- 对抗鲁棒性（Robustness to Adversaries）：AI代理对对抗性攻击具有鲁棒性，其对齐不会被对抗攻击破坏，如在大语言模型的指令数据中掺入未对齐指令，其对齐效果不会受影响。
- 安全探索（Safe Exploration）：AI代理在不产生危险结果的前提下探索新的行为，如清洁机器人探索使用湿抹布，但不会用湿抹布擦拭电源插座。
- 安全中断（Safe Interruptibility）：AI 代理可随时被操作员安全中断，即AI代理不寻求避免被人类中断。
- 自我修改（Self-modification）：AI代理在可修改的环境中进行安全的自我修改，自我修改后仍然与人类价值对齐。
- 本体（Ontology）：AI代理建模世界并知晓其是世界的一部分。
- 理想决策理论和逻辑不确定性（Idealized Decision Theory and Logical Uncertainty）：AI代理能够作出理想化的决策，即使是在不确定环境下。
- Vingean反思（Vingean Reflection）：如何推测一个比人类更聪明的AI代理的行为，以确保其与人类价值对齐？如果能够推测这个更聪明的AI代理的行为，理论上，人类应该与该AI代理一样聪明甚至比其更聪明，这与之前的假设相悖。
- 可修正性（Corrigibility）：如果当人类需要修正AI代理（如修正建造AI代理时犯的错误）或者对其进行重编程时，AI代理应该允许被修正/重编程，而不是阻止，或者欺骗操作员其已被修正/重编程（实际AI代理仍然保持其原有目标，并未被修正/重编程）。
- 价值学习（Value Learning）：AI代理可以学习人类价值。

以上AI对齐问题和任务，有些已经进入了经验主义研究和实践阶段，如避免奖励劫持、可扩展的监管、鲁棒性等，有些则仍然在概念设想阶段，如本体、Vingean反思、可修正性等。

在本文中，我们从AI对齐的内涵角度对其进行定义：AI对齐是指AI代理的外部目标和内部目标均与人类价值一致，外部目标是AI代理设计者根据人类价值设计的训练目标，内部目标则是AI代理内部优化的目标。上述定义虽然对AI代理的目标进行了内部和外部界定和区分，但未对人类价值进行界定，因此仍然是一个不精确的定义。之所以将AI代理的目标分为外部和内部目标，是由AI对齐的技术本质决定的（详见第4节），而未对人类价值进行界定，则是因为AI对齐本身存在的社会和技术挑战导致难以从社会和技术角度明确定义人类价值（详见第3节）。

由于AI对齐涉及到接近或超过人类智能水平的AI代理与人类价值之间的对齐，因此AI对齐自然包括：

- 目前具备高智能的AI代理与人类价值的对齐，如现阶段大语言模型的人类价值对齐，
- 未来AGI与人类价值的对齐。

第二十二届中国计算语言学大会论文集，第77页-第87页，哈尔滨，中国，2023年8月3日至5日。
卷2：前沿综述

相比于AI对齐，人们对通用人工智能AGI更未形成共识，其争议也更多。但即便如此，在讨论AI对齐时，我们认为有必要介绍一些AGI基本假设和论点，因为这些AGI相关背景有助于我们对AI对齐形成更好的理解和认识。

- 正交性论点（Orthogonality Thesis）：该论点认为AI代理的智能和它的目标处于两个正交的维度，即任意水平的智能可以与任意的目标相结合(Bostrom, 2012)，处于高智能水平的AI代理并不意味着其目标与人类价值对齐。

- 工具性目标趋同论点（Instrumental Convergence Thesis）：AI代理拥有一些趋同的工具性亚目标（Subgoal），实现这些工具性亚目标有助于AI代理实现其最终目标(Bostrom, 2012)。Nick Bostrom列出了一些潜在的工具性亚目标:
  – 自我保持（Self-preservation）：为了实现最终目标，AI代理可能将自我保持作为其工具性亚目标。
  – 自我增强（Self-improvement）：同样，为了实现最终目标，AI代理可能将自我增强作为其工具性亚目标，因为不断增强的推理能力、认知能力、知识水平，可以帮助AI代理更容易实现最终目标。
  – 资源获取（Resource Acquisition）：AI代理获取更多的资源，如电力等，以帮助其实现最终目标。

3 社会与技术挑战

从以上的介绍和讨论中，可以看出，AI对齐不仅仅是一个技术问题，它还具有很强的社会属性。首先，AI技术在社会经济中广泛应用，其发展也给社会带来了短期和长期影响，AI技术和人类社会形成了一个巨大的社会技术系统（Sociotechnical System），这个社会技术系统必然要求AI与人类社会进行对齐，因为只有如此，这个系统才能和谐发展和共存。其次，AI代理要对齐的人类价值是一个典型的社会概念。以上社会属性，自然给AI对齐带来社会层面的挑战:

- AI对齐的人类价值如何定义？是全人类社会的价值还是某些国家和文化的价值?

- 如何将人类价值的文化差异性纳入AI对齐框架中，使对齐的大语言模型支持不同的文化价值?

- 如何确保在差异性背景下价值对齐的公平性，以保证少数群体的价值不被AI模型忽视?

- 如何在AI对齐框架中处理价值冲突问题?

- 如何在社会技术系统中避免大语言模型的价值对齐不被少数利益群体劫持?

- 如何评估AI对齐对社会的影响?

以上仅列出部分社会挑战，这些挑战对AI对齐的内在实现和外在部署均会形成影响，这就要求大语言模型对齐不仅要从技术角度考虑如何实现，同时也要从大语言模型实际应用的社会环境角度进行综合评估和规划。

除了以上AI对齐的社会属性给AI对齐研究带来社会挑战之外，AI能力研究也会给AI对齐研究带来重大挑战。AI对齐与AI能力，两者关系如同硬币的正面和反面，一方面，AI对齐研究不仅可以为AI能力的研究提供深刻洞见，而且也为AI能力研究提供安全护栏，使其在风险可控的条件下有序发展；另一方面，AI能力研究也可以为AI对齐研究提供技术手段和支持，但失衡的AI能力研究、过度的AI能力研究，反而加速了AI风险的累积，尤其是在AI研究和应用极度竞争的情形下，AI研发机构和利益方可能更关注短期利益，把更多资源投入AI能力研发，以获取更快的利益回报和竞争优势。

除了社会挑战之外，AI对齐研究面临巨大的技术挑战，其技术难度不亚于甚至远远超过AI能力研发的技术难度。AI对齐至少面临以下几方面的技术挑战:

第二十二届中国计算语言学大会论文集，第77页-第87页，哈尔滨，中国，2023年8月3日至5日。
卷2：前沿综述

- 如何设定（Specify）AI代理需要对齐的人类价值：一方面，人类价值具有多元化、结构复杂、文化相关、不断演变等特点，造成其难以被明确定义；另一方面，人类价值是一个定性的概念，而AI代理常常需要一个可度量的定量优化目标。

- 如何优化AI代理的目标：由于人类价值难以设定，AI对齐通常优化人类价值的替代物（Proxy），如从人类偏好中学习到的奖励函数。但是优化替代物是否就是优化AI模型使其逼近人类价值，这本身就是一个问题。另一方面，在优化过程中，如何避免模型对奖励进行劫持或游戏也是具有挑战性的技术难题。

- 如何规避负面效果：如何防止AI对齐损害AI代理的能力（对齐税）？如何避免AI代理产生预期之外的行为?

- 如何应对未见情况：如何应对分布变化、对抗性攻击?

- 如何将AI对齐扩展至更高级系统：AI代理能力越强，使其与人类价值对齐的难度也越大，如何使AI对齐沿AI能力增长曲线进行有效扩展，极具挑战性。

以上技术挑战是目前在对齐大语言模型等高智能的AI代理中真实存在的技术难题，如果未来AGI预期实现的话，第2节提到的安全探索、安全中断、自我修改、可修正性、价值学习等均是AI对齐要解决的重要技术挑战。

4 技术路线

针对AI对齐，一些学者和研究机构陆续提出了对齐方法和提案（Proposal）。Geoffrey Irving等人提出通过"辩论（Debate）"的方式实现AI对齐(Irving et al., 2018)，即在零和辩论游戏的基础上，通过自我对局的方式训练AI代理。对给定的问题或建议的行为，两个AI代理轮流做简短陈述，然后由人类判断哪个代理提供了最真实、最有用的信息。提出该方案的主要动机是，对于复杂的任务，人类通常难以直接判断AI代理的行为是否安全和有效，辩论方式使人类可以在多步对局的环境中只需要简单的推理规则就可以判断真假。该方案于2018年提出，当时语言模型还不能有效捕获人类意图和指令并生成相应的回复，让AI代理使用自然语言进行辩论，在当时条件下难以实现。虽然目前的大语言模型已经具备使用自然语言交互的能力，但辩论方案是否对大语言模型的对齐有效，仍然有待实验验证。

同在2018年，Paul Christiano（前OpenAI 语言模型对齐团队负责人、对齐研究中心ARC创始人）等人提出了"迭代蒸馏和扩增（Iterated Distillation and Amplification，IDA）"方案（又称为迭代扩增）(Christiano et al., 2018)，该方案同样是针对人类难以在复杂任务上评测AI代理的问题提出来的，即实现可扩展的监管。初始时，人类将知识蒸馏给一个比自己弱的AI代理，这个过程称为蒸馏（Distillation），接着人类可以使用蒸馏的AI代理辅助自己，得到扩增版的新代理，这个过程称为扩增（Amplification）。以上蒸馏和扩增不断迭代进行，在这个过程中，AI代理的能力在不断增强，同时因为人类提供了对齐信号，其对齐能力也在不断增强。

仍然是在2018年，Jan Leike（现OpenAI对齐团队负责人）等人提出了"递归奖励建模（Recursive Reward Modeling，RRW）"的对齐方案(Leike et al., 2018)，该方案类似于前两个方案，均是针对可扩展的监管问题。RRW方案可看作是用奖励建模取代蒸馏模仿学习的IDA，具体而言，奖励建模分为两步：（1）从用户提供的对齐信号中学习奖励模型；（2）用该奖励模型以强化学习方式优化AI代理。在扩增步中，用户与强化学习优化的AI代理交互形成一个增强版的AI代理，用于下一步的迭代。可以看出，ChatGPT所用的"人类反馈强化学习（Reinforcement Learning from Human Feedback，RLHF）"方法(Ouyang et al., 2022)实际就是一个未递归的RRW，即只进行了一步对齐学习，未进行迭代扩增。最近OpenAI调集资源成立"超级对齐（Superalignment）"团队，并提出了超级对齐方案[6]，该方案可看作是RLHF的迭代扩增版（结合了可解释性及对抗测试）。

以上仅仅介绍了三个不同的AI对齐方案，这只是AI对齐提案的一小部分而已，其他提案还包括"逆奖励设计（Inverse Reward Design）"(Hadfield-Menell et al., 2017)、"协同式逆强化学习（Cooperative Inverse Reinforcement Learning）"(Hadfield-Menell et al., 2016)等，限于篇

[6]https://openai.com/blog/introducing-superalignment

第二十二届中国计算语言学大会论文集，第77页-第87页，哈尔滨，中国，2023年8月3日至5日。
卷2：前沿综述

幅，不逐一介绍。辩论、迭代蒸馏和扩增及递归奖励建模三个对齐方案除了都是针对可扩展的监管之外，它们还有一个共同点，即均是进行外部对齐。AI对齐领域近年来形成的一个重要共识是，AI对齐按照由外到内，包含外部对齐和内部对齐两部分。

- 外部对齐（Outer Alignment）：人类价值或预期目标与AI模型训练目标之间的对齐，即AI代理的设计人员是否将人类价值/预期目标转化对应到AI代理的训练目标函数上。预训练语言模型（未进行对齐训练）的目标函数是预测下一个单词，这个目标函数显然和人类价值/目标未对齐，因此，只是经过预训练的大语言模型，与人类价值未进行外部对齐，其输出文本中存在具有社会伦理风险的内容、且通常难以捕获人类的意图。与此相反，人类反馈强化学习RLHF则进行了外部对齐，对齐的实际目标是人类价值、意图等，由于人类价值/意图很难量化定义（见第3节）,RLHF采用了人类偏好作为人类价值/意图的替代物（Proxy）。为了实现外部对齐，RLHF采用了模仿学习和强化学习。在模仿学习步骤中（即有监督的微调（Supervised Fine-tuning，SFT）），RLHF提供与人类价值/意图对齐的样本作为示范供预训练的大语言模型进行模仿学习；在强化学习步骤中，RLHF首先根据人类偏好训练一个奖励函数，然后用该奖励函数通过强化学习进一步优化经过模仿学习的大语言模型，使其进一步与人类价值/意图对齐。

- 内部对齐（Inner Alignment）：AI代理真实优化的目标与人类赋予它的训练目标之间的对齐，即在AI代理训练过程中，其内部优化的目标与模型训练的目标函数一致。Evan Hubinger等人首次提出内部对齐概念(Hubinger et al., 2019)。当一个被训练的模型（如神经网络）本身是一个优化器（即其本身按照某种目标函数在可能的空间中进行搜索）时，我们称之为内优化器（Mesa-optimizer），而训练这个模型的学习算法则称为基优化器（Base-optimizer）。基优化器的目标函数称为基目标（Base-objective），内优化器的目标函数则称为内目标（Mesa-objective），内部对齐便是当一个被训练的模型本身是一个优化器时其基目标与内目标之间的对齐。基目标通常是模型设计人员定义的目标函数，而内目标则通常是是内优化器内部为完成给定任务演化出来的工具性目标，也就是说，基目标是模型设计人员定义和赋予的，内目标并不是设计人员指定的。Evan Hubinger等人用生物进化类比说明基目标与内目标的不对齐情况，生物进化的基目标是生物体与环境的包容性遗传适应性（Inclusive Genetic Fitness），适应性强的生物体被进化基目标选择和保留。作为生物进化出的特殊生物体的人类，其本身也是一个优化器。但是人类大脑的内目标与生物进化的基目标可能并不一致，比如按照生物进化的基目标，人类应该尽可能多地繁衍后代，但是很多人选择不生孩子。

  Evan Hubinger等人进一步指出，内优化器可能产生欺骗性对齐（Deceptive Alignment）。具体而言，内优化器演化出对基目标建模的能力，并知晓内优化器如果在基目标上表现差就会被基优化器修改而不能完成其自身优化的目标，因此，内优化器将会激励自已不被修改：在训练阶段表现出是在优化基目标函数，但一旦训练完成被部署时，由于被修改的风险已解除，内优化器就会寻求自己的内目标。

上文提到RLHF是一种外部对齐方法，该方法虽然对齐效果显著，但是该方法本身因为其潜在的缺陷遭到了批评。对该方法的批评意见主要来自于两方面[7]：

- “强化学习”（RL）部分：批评者认为RLHF中强化学习会带来如下风险：
  - 目标导向性：强化学习可能使大语言模型追求奖励而具有目标性；
  - 工具趋同：强化学习可能使大语言模型形成工具性亚目标，已有工作(Perez et al., 2022)发现，RLHF增强了大语言模型追求自我保持的欲望（即不被关闭）；
  - 激励欺骗性：经过RLHF训练的大语言模型，参数规模越大，产生的回复与用户偏好的回复一致的比例越高(Perez et al., 2022)，即迎合用户的偏好。
- “人类反馈”（HF）部分：批评者认为RLHF中的人类反馈存在以下缺陷：
  - 人类反馈数据通常以人工方式收集，因此需要较高的成本，同时也存在引入错误或被操纵的可能性；

[7]https://www.lesswrong.com/posts/d6DvuCKH5bSoT62DB/compendium-of-problems-with-rlhf

第二十二届中国计算语言学大会论文集，第77页-第87页，哈尔滨，中国，2023年8月3日至5日。
卷2：前沿综述

- RLHF最终使用的是从人类反馈中学习到的奖励函数，是人类反馈的替代物，并非人类反馈本身；
- 如前文所述，人类反馈未进行扩增，因此不能适应可扩展的监管（单纯的人类反馈无法胜任复杂任务）。

除了上面提到的外部和内部对齐，AI对齐还有一个重要问题要需要研究和解决，即可解释性（Interpretability）。可解释性的研究通常包括两部分(Critch and Krueger, 2020)：透明性（Transparency）和可说明性（Explainability），前者揭示AI代理、大语言模型的内部运作机理，后者说明AI代理决策过程中的事实或反事实的依赖关系，即模型为什么产生这样的预测结果或行为。相比而言，透明性更专注于模型内部，可说明性则通常是事后行为(Lipton, 2016)。

可解释性研究，显然有助于AI代理研发人员深入了解其研发的模型。对于AI对齐，尤其是内部对齐，可解释性不仅可以提供监测和洞见，而且其本身的评测指标也可以作为AI对齐优化的目标函数(Critch and Krueger, 2020)，以激励AI模型保持目标透明性（Goal Transparency）(Amodei et al., 2016)（避免欺骗性对齐）。

近年来，机械可解释性（Mechanistic Interpretability）成为AI对齐可解释性研究的一个重要方向，该可解释性研究旨在以逆向工程方式剖析AI模型，尤其是黑盒子的神经网络模型。由于大语言模型参数规模庞大，内在神经网络结构复杂，对其进行逆向工程，难度非常高，因此，现阶段的机械可解释性通常是在简化的玩具模型上开展的。即便如此，机械可解释性近几年仍然陆续揭示了神经回路[8]、归纳头（Induction Head，可用于解释语境学习（In-Context Learning））[9]等神经网络内部机理。

5 评测

上文提到大语言模型对人类社会存在近期和远期风险：社会伦理风险及通用人工智能安全风险，而AI对齐技术正是要避免这些风险，因此对AI对齐的评测也主要从这两方面展开：社会伦理对齐评测和通用智能安全评测。

5.1 社会伦理对齐评测

大语言模型生成的内容广泛出现于社交媒体、新闻媒体和在线平台，对人们的意见、观点和决策产生影响。如果大模型的价值观与人类价值观不相符，其生成的内容可能传播有害、误导性或偏见的信息，从而导致社会隔阂、歧视或其他负面后果。恶意行为者还可以利用大语言模型制造虚假信息、进行网络欺诈或发动攻击。

因此，确保大语言模型输出及行为与人类伦理价值对齐至关重要，这是在真实应用场景中部署和应用的大语言模型必须具备的能力。为了评估此能力，现有的研究考虑了多个与人类价值对齐的标准，如真实性、偏见性和伦理性(Askell et al., 2021; Bai et al., 2022)。对于真实性，可以利用对抗性问答任务（例如TruthfulQA (Lin et al., 2021)）检测。偏见性主要指性别、种族和年龄等方面的歧视，许多研究针对偏见的某一方面或多个方面建立了评估数据集。

尽管很多数据集提供了自动评估方法，但在伦理价值评测中，人工评估仍然是一种有效的评测方法，因为许多偏见暗含在语言之中，仅凭现有的自动评估指标很难判定。

5.2 通用智能安全评测

前文提到，通用人工智能通常具有自我保持、自我增强、自主复制、资源获取等方面的特征和趋势，因此，对以大语言模型为代表的AI代理，需要进行通用智能安全方面的科学和综合评测，以及时发现和防范潜在的风险。未经过通用智能安全评测或评测不达标的通用智能体，为避免产生不可控的安全风险，应该由相关部门监督该智能体研发机构对其进行AI对齐修复，直至安全评测达标方可发放模型部署和应用许可证。

目前的大语言模型虽然能力还未达到AGI水平，但是相关的通用智能安全评测已经开始。OpenAI委托对齐研究中心ARC对其研制的GPT-4进行“自主复制”方面的对齐评测，ARC将自主复制（Autonomous Replication）定义为[10]：部署在云端的AI代理获取相关

[8] https://distill.pub/2020/circuits/

[9] https://transformer-circuits.pub/2022/in-context-learning-and-induction-heads/index.html

[10] https://evals.alignment.org/

第二十二届中国计算语言学大会论文集，第77页-第87页，哈尔滨，中国，2023年8月3日至5日。
卷2：前沿综述

资源（计算、资金等）并利用这些资源进行自我拷贝的能力。ARC对此设计了相应的评测实验，虽然未发现GPT-4具备自主复制方面的能力，但他们警告大语言模型能力在持续提升中。

Anthropic、Surge AI、及Machine Intelligence Research Institute三家单位联合对大语言模型的行为进行了综合评测(Perez et al., 2022)，评测用例由大语言模型本身生成，该评测不仅发现了大语言模型在能力上存在逆扩展（Inverse Scaling ）现象（即模型规模增大，某些能力反而降低），而且发现RLHF使大语言模型具有目标保持、资源获取的趋势。

6 未来趋势

未来几年，AI和LLM对齐将在多个方面取得重要进展和突破：

- 可扩展的监管：现阶段的AI/LLM对齐研究虽然在大规模系统上取得了初步成效，但仍然停留在AI对齐的初步阶段，在人类难以企及的复杂任务上，虽然已经提出了相关的对齐方案，但这些方案仍未进行大规模经验主义验证。未来将基于人机结合、多智能体结合方式进行迭代扩增，实现可扩展的监管的突破。

- 欺骗性对齐的实验验证：现阶段的大语言模型虽然能力非常强，但仍没有达到欺骗性临界点，未来大语言模型能力进一步发展，大型AI研发机构和企业将会开展大规模实验，寻找欺骗性对齐存在的蛛丝马迹，以便在其真正出现的时候做好应对准备。

- 机械可解释性：未来研究将会借鉴神经科学、心理学、脑科学相关理论和方法，对真实复杂的大语言模型进行大规模逆向工程，揭示其内部工作机理，如功能性/任务性神经回路等。

- LLM对齐对大语言模型能力研究的反馈：大语言模型对齐的研究将会为大语言模型能力的研究提供正反馈，帮助解锁大语言模型更多能力，未来大语言模型能力的提升可能不是来自于模型、数据规模的单纯扩增，而是来自于对齐算法及其发现。

- 对齐评测：对齐研究离不开对齐评测，未来对齐评测将呈现从社会伦理评测向通用人工智能安全评测发展的趋势。

7 结论

本文对AI/LLM对齐研究进行了简要介绍，包括相关概念、挑战、技术路线、评测及未来发展趋势。可以看出，为了避免大语言模型和通用人工智能目前的社会伦理风险及未来的人类生存风险，其发展必须坚持"智善一体化"的原则，大力开展AI/LLM对齐研究。对齐研究和大模型能力研究并不矛盾，两者相辅相成，对齐研究为大语言模型能力的研究带来洞见，并进一步推进大语言模型能力的研究。另一方面，AI/LLM对齐研究非常具有挑战性，现阶段的研究还未形成统一的科学研究范式，整个领域还处于前科学阶段，需要更多的研究人员、研究机构投入其中，合力推动AI安全与能力的协同发展。

致谢

本研究受云南省科技厅重点研发计划专项（202203AA080004）、新疆维吾尔自治区自然科学基金重点项目（2022D01D43）、之江实验室开放课题（2022KH0AB01）资助。

参考文献

Dario Amodei, Chris Olah, Jacob Steinhardt, Paul F. Christiano, John Schulman, and Dan Mané. 2016. Concrete problems in AI safety. *CoRR*, abs/1606.06565.

Amanda Askell, Yuntao Bai, Anna Chen, Dawn Drain, Deep Ganguli, Tom Henighan, Andy Jones, Nicholas Joseph, Benjamin Mann, Nova DasSarma, Nelson Elhage, Zac Hatfield-Dodds, Danny Hernandez, Jackson Kernion, Kamal Ndousse, Catherine Olsson, Dario Amodei, Tom B. Brown, Jack Clark, Sam McCandlish, Chris Olah, and Jared Kaplan. 2021. A general language assistant as a laboratory for alignment. *CoRR*, abs/2112.00861.

第二十二届中国计算语言学大会论文集，第77页-第87页，哈尔滨，中国，2023年8月3日至5日。
卷2：前沿综述

Yuntao Bai, Andy Jones, Kamal Ndousse, Amanda Askell, Anna Chen, Nova DasSarma, Dawn Drain, Stanislav Fort, Deep Ganguli, T. J. Henighan, Nicholas Joseph, Saurav Kadavath, John Kernion, Tom Conerly, Sheer El-Showk, Nelson Elhage, Zac Hatfield-Dodds, Danny Hernandez, Tristan Hume, Scott Johnston, Shauna Kravec, Liane Lovitt, Neel Nanda, Catherine Olsson, Dario Amodei, Tom B. Brown, Jack Clark, Sam McCandlish, Christopher Olah, Benjamin Mann, and Jared Kaplan. 2022. Training a helpful and harmless assistant with reinforcement learning from human feedback. *ArXiv*, abs/2204.05862.

Nick Bostrom. 2012. The superintelligent will: Motivation and instrumental rationality in advanced artificial agents. *Minds Mach.*, 22(2):71–85, may.

Sébastien Bubeck, Varun Chandrasekaran, Ronen Eldan, John A. Gehrke, Eric Horvitz, Ece Kamar, Peter Lee, Yin Tat Lee, Yuan-Fang Li, Scott M. Lundberg, Harsha Nori, Hamid Palangi, Marco Tulio Ribeiro, and Yi Zhang. 2023. Sparks of artificial general intelligence: Early experiments with GPT-4. *ArXiv*, abs/2303.12712.

Joseph Carlsmith. 2022. Is power-seeking AI an existential risk? *ArXiv*, abs/2206.13353.

Micah Carroll. 2018. Overview of current AI alignment approaches.

Paul F. Christiano, Buck Shlegeris, and Dario Amodei. 2018. Supervising strong learners by amplifying weak experts. *CoRR*, abs/1810.08575.

Andrew Critch and David Krueger. 2020. AI research considerations for human existential safety (ARCHES). *CoRR*, abs/2006.04948.

Tyna Eloundou, Sam Manning, Pamela Mishkin, and Daniel Rock. 2023. GPTs are GPTs: An early look at the labor market impact potential of large language models. *ArXiv*, abs/2303.10130.

Dylan Hadfield-Menell, Anca D. Dragan, Pieter Abbeel, and Stuart Russell. 2016. Cooperative inverse reinforcement learning. *CoRR*, abs/1606.03137.

Dylan Hadfield-Menell, Smitha Milli, Pieter Abbeel, Stuart Russell, and Anca D. Dragan. 2017. Inverse reward design. *CoRR*, abs/1711.02827.

Evan Hubinger, Chris van Merwijk, Vladimir Mikulik, Joar Skalse, and Scott Garrabrant. 2019. Risks from learned optimization in advanced machine learning systems. *CoRR*, abs/1906.01820.

Geoffrey Irving, Paul Francis Christiano, and Dario Amodei. 2018. AI safety via debate. *ArXiv*, abs/1805.00899.

Jan H. Kirchner, Logan Smith, Jacques Thibodeau, Kyle McDonell, and Laria Reynolds. 2022. Understanding AI alignment research: A systematic analysis. *ArXiv*, abs/2206.02841.

Jan Leike, David Krueger, Tom Everitt, Miljan Martic, Vishal Maini, and Shane Legg. 2018. Scalable agent alignment via reward modeling: a research direction. *CoRR*, abs/1811.07871.

Stephanie Lin, Jacob Hilton, and Owain Evans. 2021. TruthfulQA: Measuring how models mimic human falsehoods. *CoRR*, abs/2109.07958.

Zachary Chase Lipton. 2016. The mythos of model interpretability. *CoRR*, abs/1606.03490.

Long Ouyang, Jeff Wu, Xu Jiang, Diogo Almeida, Carroll L. Wainwright, Pamela Mishkin, Chong Zhang, Sandhini Agarwal, Katarina Slama, Alex Ray, John Schulman, Jacob Hilton, Fraser Kelton, Luke E. Miller, Maddie Simens, Amanda Askell, Peter Welinder, Paul Francis Christiano, Jan Leike, and Ryan J. Lowe. 2022. Training language models to follow instructions with human feedback. *ArXiv*, abs/2203.02155.

Ethan Perez, Sam Ringer, Kamilė Lukoiūtė, Karina Nguyen, Edwin Chen, Scott Heiner, Craig Pettit, Catherine Olsson, Sandipan Kundu, Saurav Kadavath, Andy Jones, Anna Chen, Benjamin Mann, Brian Israel, Bryan Seethor, Cameron McKinnon, Christopher Olah, Daisong Yan, Daniela Amodei, Dario Amodei, Dawn Drain, Dustin Li, Eli Tran-Johnson, G R Khundadze, John Kernion, James McCauley Landis, Jamie Kerr, Jared Mueller, Jeeyoon Hyun, Joshua D. Landau, Kamal Ndousse, Landon Goldberg, Liane Lovitt, Martin Lucas, Michael Sellitto, Miranda Zhang, Neerav Kingsland, Nelson Elhage, Nicholas Joseph, Noem'i Mercado, Nova DasSarma, Oliver Rausch, Robin Larson, Sam McCandlish, Scott Johnston, Shauna Kravec, Sheer El Showk, Tamera Lanham, Timothy Telleen-Lawton, Tom B. Brown, T. J. Henighan, Tristan Hume, Yuntao Bai, Zac Hatfield-Dodds,

第二十二届中国计算语言学大会论文集，第77页-第87页，哈尔滨，中国，2023年8月3日至5日。
卷2：前沿综述

Jack Clark, Sam Bowman, Amanda Askell, Roger C. Grosse, Danny Hernandez, Deep Ganguli, Evan Hubinger, Nicholas Schiefer, and Jared Kaplan. 2022. Discovering language model behaviors with model-written evaluations. *ArXiv*, abs/2212.09251.

Laura Weidinger, John Mellor, Maribeth Rauh, Conor Griffin, Jonathan Uesato, Po-Sen Huang, Myra Cheng, Mia Glaese, Borja Balle, Atoosa Kasirzadeh, Zac Kenton, Sasha Brown, Will Hawkins, Tom Stepleton, Courtney Biles, Abeba Birhane, Julia Haas, Laura Rimell, Lisa Anne Hendricks, William Isaac, Sean Legassick, Geoffrey Irving, and Iason Gabriel. 2021. Ethical and social risks of harm from language models. *CoRR*, abs/2112.04359.

Norbert Wiener. 1960. Some moral and technical consequences of automation. *Science*, 131(3410):1355–1358.

第二十二届中国计算语言学大会论文集，第77页-第87页，哈尔滨，中国，2023年8月3日至5日。
卷2：前沿综述

Through the Lens of Core Competency: Survey on Evaluation of Large Language Models

Ziyu Zhuang, Qiguang Chen, Longxuan Ma, Mingda Li, Yi Han, Yushan Qian, Haopeng Bai, Weinan Zhang*, Ting Liu
Research Center for Social Computing and Information Retrieval, Harbin Institute of Technology
{zyzhuang, qgchen, lxma, mdli, yihan, ysqian, hpbai, wnzhang, tliu}@ir.hit.edu.cn

Abstract

From pre-trained language model (PLM) to large language model (LLM), the field of natural language processing (NLP) has witnessed steep performance gains and wide practical uses. The evaluation of a research field guides its direction of improvement. However, LLMs are extremely hard to thoroughly evaluate for two reasons. First of all, traditional NLP tasks become inadequate due to the excellent performance of LLM. Secondly, existing evaluation tasks are difficult to keep up with the wide range of applications in real-world scenarios. To tackle these problems, existing works proposed various benchmarks to better evaluate LLMs. To clarify the numerous evaluation tasks in both academia and industry, we investigate multiple papers concerning LLM evaluations. We summarize 4 core competencies of LLM, including reasoning, knowledge, reliability, and safety. For every competency, we introduce its definition, corresponding benchmarks, and metrics. Under this competency architecture, similar tasks are combined to reflect corresponding ability, while new tasks can also be easily added into the system. Finally, we give our suggestions on the future direction of LLM's evaluation.

1 Introduction

Large language models(LLMs) have achieved great progresses in many areas. One representative, ChatGPT[0], which applies the ability of LLMs in the form of dialogue, has received much attention due to its incredible versatility such as creative writing, coding, planning, etc. The evaluation of such a model thus becomes necessary to benchmark and build up its ability while preventing potential harmfulness.

Existing works on the evaluation of LLMs can be divided into three paradigms. The first line of work is evaluating LLMs with traditional NLP tasks like dialogue, summarization, etc. Since LLMs are actually pre-trained language models(PLMs) with huge model parameter size and data size (Kaplan et al., 2020), benchmarks like GLUE (Wang et al., 2019b), SuperGLUE (Wang et al., 2019a) can be adopted to evaluate its language understanding ability. The problem is that LLMs work really well on less restrictive tasks like translation, summarization, and natural language understanding tasks. Sometimes LLMs generated outputs' third-party scores are even higher than human generations (Liang et al., 2022), showing the need for higher-quality tasks. Secondly, advanced ability evaluations are proposed to completely test language models. The parameter size difference between LLMs and PLMs brings an amazing phenomenon, emergence (Wei et al., 2022a; Srivastava et al., 2022), which means that scaled models exhibit abilities that are not possessed in small-scaled language models. For instance, in tasks like reasoning, and tool manipulation, the correlation curve between the number of model parameters and the task effect is non-linear. And the effect will rise sharply when the model parameter exceeds a certain parameter scale. They're called "advanced" because they're more closely related to human abilities and harder for models to complete (Zhong et al., 2023). Thirdly, test language models' intrinsic abilities independent of the specific tasks. It can be tested in parallel with almost every task above. Robustness is a classic ability

*Corresponding author

[0]https://openai.com/blog/chatgpt/

Proceedings of the 22nd China National Conference on Computational Linguistics, pages 88-109, Harbin, China, August 3 - 5, 2023.
Volume 2: Frotier Forum
(c) Technical Committee on Computational Linguistics, Chinese Information Processing Society of China

in this paradigm. Due to the black-box nature of neural networks (Szegedy et al., 2014), robustness problems exist for every modality of input data(vision, audio, test, etc.).

Current evaluation benchmarks (Liang et al., 2022; Srivastava et al., 2022; Gao et al., 2021; Zhong et al., 2023; Li et al., 2023a) are mostly a mixture of the former three paradigms. They emphasize a complete system of evaluation tasks, in which all tasks are of equal importance. But the significance of marginal increases in model effects on tasks with excellent performance is debatable. Thus numerous evaluation tasks and benchmarks are proposed to follow and challenge the ever-evolving LLMs, while, oddly, seldom being reviewed in a systematic way. How to link numerous tasks and benchmarks, better present the evaluation results, and thus facilitate the research of LLMs is an urgent problem.

An ideal large language model needs to be capable, reliable, and safe (Ouyang et al., 2022). One surely needs extensive tests on multiple datasets to meet these miscellaneous standards. Moreover, to avoid the prevalent training set leakage, test sets also should be updated regularly (Huang et al., 2023). This is similar to the competency (Hoffmann, 1999) tests adopted in corporate recruitment. In competency tests, different task sets are combined to test the corresponding competency. And task sets also need renewal to prevent possible fraud.

In this survey, **we draw on the concept of the core competency to integrate multiple evaluation research for LLMs.** We investigated **540+** tasks widely used in various papers, aggregating tasks corresponding to a certain competency. During this process, 4 core competencies are summarized, including knowledge, reasoning, reliability, and safety. We will introduce the definition, taxonomy, and metrics for these competencies. Through this competency test, superabundant evaluation tasks and benchmarks are combed and clarified for their aiming utility. Furthermore, the evaluation results presented with this procedure will be direct, concise, and focused. Updated new tasks can also be added comprehensively. To support the community in taking this competency test further, We also create an extensible project, which will show the many-to-many relationship between competencies and tasks precisely. Due to the length of the paper, we can only present part of the surveyed results in this paper. A more comprehensive study will be released in a later version.

2 Core Competencies

In this section, we introduce the definition and taxonomy of the core competencies we summarized.

2.1 Knowledge

Knowledge is generally defined as the cognition of humans when practicing in the subjective and objective world, which is verified and can be reused over time[1]. The large language models (LLMs) nowadays obtain human knowledge from a large scale of training corpus, so that it can use the knowledge to solve various downstream tasks. In this section, we focus on the fundamental knowledge competency of LLMs that facilitates communication and other downstream tasks (such as reasoning). Specifically, we divide the fundamental knowledge into **linguistic knowledge** and **world knowledge** (Day et al., 1998) and introduce the definitions of them and the benchmarks that can evaluate them.

2.1.1 Linguistic Knowledge Competency

Linguistic knowledge includes grammatical, semantic, and pragmatic knowledge (Fromkin et al., 2018). The grammar of a natural language is its set of structural constraints on speakers' or writers' composition of clauses, phrases, and words. The term can also refer to the study of such constraints, a field that includes domains such as phonology, morphology, and syntax, often complemented by phonetics, semantics, and pragmatics. Semantic (Austin, 1975) studies the meaning of words, phrases, and sentences, focusing on general meanings rather than on what an individual speaker may want them to mean. Pragmatics (Austin, 1975) studies language use and how listeners bridge the gap between sentence meaning and the speaker's meaning. It is concerned with the relationship between semantic meaning, the context of use, and the speaker's meaning.

[1] https://plato.stanford.edu/entries/epistemology/

Proceedings of the 22nd China National Conference on Computational Linguistics, pages 88-109, Harbin, China, August 3 - 5, 2023.
Volume 2: Frotier Forum

Dataset	Knowledge Category	LLM evaluated	Task Format	Lang
BLiMP	grammatical	MT-NLG;BLOOM	Classification	En
linguistic_mappings	grammar/syntax	Gopher;Chinchilla;FLAN-T5;GLM;etc.	Generation	En
minute_mysteries_qa	semantic	Gopher;Chinchilla;FLAN-T5;GLM;etc.	Generation/QA	En
metaphor_boolean	pragmatic/semantic	Gopher;Chinchilla;FLAN-T5;GLM;etc.	Classification	En
LexGLUE	domain	BLOOM	Multiple choice	En
WikiFact	world	BLOOM	Generation	En
TruthfulQA	world	GPT-3/InstructGPT/GPT-4	Generation	En
HellaSwag	commonsense	GPT-3/InstructGPT/GPT-4	Generation	En

Table 1: Datasets that are used to evaluate the knowledge Competency of LLMs.

The Linguistic Knowledge competency is embodied in almost all NLP tasks, researchers usually design specific scenarios to test the linguistic competency of LLMs. Some examples are shown in the upper group of Table 1. BLiMP (Warstadt et al., 2020) evaluates what language models (LMs) know about major grammatical phenomena. Linguistic_mappings [2] task aims to explore the depth of linguistic knowledge in enormous language models trained on word prediction. It aims to discover whether such knowledge is structured so as to support the use of grammatical abstractions, both morphological (past tense formation and pluralization) and syntactic (question formation, negation, and pronominalization). The minute_mysteries_qa [3] is a reading comprehension task focusing on short crime and mystery stories where the goal is to identify the perpetrator and to explain the reasoning behind the deduction and the clues that support it. The metaphor_boolean [4] task presents a model with a metaphoric sentence and asks it to identify whether a second sentence is the correct interpretation of the first. The last three are selected from BIG-Bench (Srivastava et al., 2022), containing diverse task topics including linguistics.

2.1.2 World Knowledge Competency

World knowledge is non-linguistic information that helps a reader or listener interpret the meanings of words and sentences (Ovchinnikova, 2012). It is also referred to as extra-linguistic knowledge. In this paper, we categorize world knowledge into general knowledge and domain knowledge. The general knowledge includes commonsense knowledge (Davis, 2014) and prevalent knowledge. The commonsense knowledge consists of world facts, such as "Lemons are sour", or "Cows say moo", that most humans are expected to know. The prevalent knowledge exists at a particular time or place. For example, "Chinese people are used to drinking boiled water." is only known by a part of human beings; "There were eight planets in the solar system" is prevalent knowledge until it is overthrown. The domain knowledge (Alexander, 1992) is of a specific, specialized discipline or field, in contrast to general or domain-independent knowledge. People who have domain knowledge, are often considered specialists or experts in the field.

The bottom group of Table 1 shows some task examples that are used for testing world knowledge. For example, the LexGLUE (Chalkidis et al., 2022) tests whether LLMs perform well in the legal domain; WikiFact (Yasunaga et al., 2022) is a fact completion scenario that tests language models' factual knowledge based on Wikipedia. The input will be a partial sentence such as "The capital of France is _", and the output will be the continuation of the sentence such as "Paris"; TruthfulQA (Lin et al., 2022b) comprises questions spanning numerous categories including economics, science, and law. The questions are strategically chosen so humans may also incorrectly answer them based on misconceptions and biases; language models should ideally return accurate and truthful responses; HellaSwag (Zellers et al., 2019) tests commonsense inference and was created through adversarial filtering to synthesize wrong answers. The World knowledge competency, along with linguistic knowledge, serves as the foundation for solving different NLP tasks and is one of the core competencies of LLMs.

2.2 Reasoning

Reasoning competency is a crucial skill for LLMs to solve complex problems. What's more, from the perspective of intelligent agents, reasoning ability is also one of the core capabilities towards achieving

[2]https://github.com/google/BIG-bench/blob/main/bigbench/benchmark_tasks/linguistic_mappings
[3]https://github.com/google/BIG-bench/blob/main/bigbench/benchmark_tasks/minute_mysteries_qa
[4]https://github.com/google/BIG-bench/tree/main/bigbench/benchmark_tasks/metaphor_boolean

Proceedings of the 22nd China National Conference on Computational Linguistics, pages 88-109, Harbin, China, August 3 - 5, 2023.
Volume 2: Frotier Forum

Dataset	Reasoning Competency	LLM evaluated	Task Format	Lang
COPA	Causal/Commonsense*	UL2;Deberta;GLaM;GPT3;PaLM;etc.	Classification	En
Mathematical Induction	Induction/Mathematical*	Gopher;Chinchilla;FLAN-T5;GLM;etc.	Generation	En
Synthetic Reasoning	Abduction/Deduction	HELM	Multiple choice	En
SAT Analogy	Analogical	GPT-3	Multiple choice	En
StrategyQA	Multi-hop/Commonsense*	Gopher;Chinchilla;FLAN-T5;GLM;etc.	Classification	En
GSM8K	Mathematical*	BLOOM;LLaMA;GPT-4;MT-NLG	Generation	En
ToTTo	Structured Data*	UL2	Generation	En

Table 2: Datasets that are used to evaluate the reasoning competency of LLMs. * represents a specific reasoning scenario.

AGI (Bubeck et al., 2023; Qiao et al., 2022). However, there remains no consensus whether LLMs can really reason, or just simply produce a larger context that increases the likelihood of correctly predicting the missing tokens (Mialon et al., 2023). Although "reasoning" itself may currently be an excuse of language, we can still objectively verify the reasoning performance of LLMs through various reasoning competencies. Previous methods mainly focus on the division of reasoning tasks. Yu et al. (2023) divides existing evaluation tasks into three major categories, namely knowledge reasoning, symbolic reasoning, and mathematical reasoning, based on the type of logic and evidence involved in the reasoning process. Zhao et al. (2023) divides reasoning tasks into deductive reasoning and defeasible reasoning according to the reasoning form. In this section, we decompose the reasoning competency into 6 sub-parts from the perspective of model competency, providing a comprehensive overview of existing research efforts and suggesting potential future directions. And Table 2 presents some datasets for evaluating LLM's reasoning competency using this categorization approach.

2.2.1 Causal Reasoning Competency

Causal reasoning competency is a highly significant cognitive ability aimed at inferring causality through the observation of cause-effect relationships (Vowels et al., 2023; Dündar-Coecke, 2022; Chan et al., 2023). It enables us to comprehend and explain the relationships between events, variables, and actions, ultimately empowering us to make informed predictions and decisions (Gao et al., 2023).

The benchmarks Causal-TimeBank (Mirza et al., 2014), StoryLine (Caselli and Vossen, 2017), and MAVEN-ERE (Wang et al., 2022c) aim to test the existence of causal relationships between two events in sentences. COPA (Gordon et al., 2012) and XCOPA (Ponti et al., 2020) are evaluation benchmarks for extracting causal relationships in sentences, consisting of a set of premises and possible causes or effects. Tested systems are required to apply commonsense knowledge to identify the correct answers. e-CARE (Du et al., 2022) and CALM-Bench (Dalal et al., 2023) introduce a set of causal querying tasks to evaluate models, which include a cause and several potential effect sentences. Additionally, an annotated and interpretable causal reasoning dataset is provided for these tasks.

2.2.2 Deduction Reasoning Competency

In the era of Large Language Models (LLMs), deductive reasoning abilities serve as the foundational skills for logical reasoning (Evans, 2002). Unlike traditional rule-based deductive reasoning systems, it involves deriving specific conclusions or answers from general and universally applicable premises using given rules and logic. Specifically, it manifests as a process of Zero-Shot Chain-of-Thought utilizing given rules (Lyu et al., 2023; Kojima et al., 2022). For instance, (Kojima et al., 2022) introduced the "Let's think step by step" prompt technique to better evaluate the Deduction Reasoning Competency.

Current testing of this ability often intertwines with other skills and still lacks an independent evaluation on typical text (Clark et al., 2020) and symbol-related (Wu et al., 2021) deductive datasets. However, in general, almost all QA tasks can be explicitly evaluated for Deduction Reasoning using the Chain-of-Thought (CoT) approach. Therefore, the effectiveness of models' Deduction Reasoning Competency can be to some extent reflected by evaluating the performance of QA tasks after applying the CoT method.

2.2.3 Induction Reasoning Competency

In contrast to deductive reasoning, inductive reasoning aims to derive conclusions from specific observations to general principles (Yang et al., 2022; Olsson et al., 2022). In recent years, a new paradigm

Proceedings of the 22nd China National Conference on Computational Linguistics, pages 88-109, Harbin, China, August 3 - 5, 2023.
Volume 2: Frotier Forum

of Induction Reasoning has been proposed by (Cheng et al., 2023), which requires models to generate general-purpose program code to solve a class of problems based on given contextual questions and a specific question. For example, Cheng et al. (2023), Jiang et al. (2023) and Surís et al. (2023) induced general principle-based solutions by generalizing each question into a universal executable language.

Therefore, for competency evaluation, while DEER (Yang et al., 2022) and Mathematical Induction (BIGBench Split (Srivastava et al., 2022)) took the first step in inductive reasoning, we still hope to establish a more systematic and comprehensive benchmark for evaluating this capability. Recently, Bills et al. (2023) has tested the inductive ability of GPT-4 (OpenAI, 2023) to evaluate its effectiveness in inducing patterns that are difficult for humans to express clearly. Intriguingly, Mankowitz et al. (2023) used some techniques to evaluate the extent to which LLM can mine previously unknown patterns.

2.2.4 Abduction Reasoning Competency

Abduction Reasoning Competency encompasses the task of providing explanations for the output generated based on given inputs (Kakas and Michael, 2020). This form of reasoning is particularly critical in scenarios where uncertainty or incomplete information exists, enabling systems to generate hypotheses and make informed decisions based on the available evidence. Notably, the research conducted by LIREx (Zhao and Vydiswaran, 2021) and STaR (Zelikman et al., 2022) delved into the Abduction Reasoning Competency of models and demonstrated the effectiveness of rationales provided during the Abduction Reasoning process in facilitating improved learning in downstream models.

In terms of datasets within the LLM setting, the benchmarks HUMMINGBIRD (Mathew et al., 2021) and HateXplain (Hayati et al., 2021) require models to output word-level textual segments as explanations for sentiment classification results. On the other hand, benchmarks such as WikiQA (Yang et al., 2015), HotpotQA (Yang et al., 2018), and SciFact (Wadden et al., 2020) provide sentence-level coarse-grained textual segments as explanations for model classification results. ERASER (DeYoung et al., 2020) and FineIEB (Wang et al., 2022b) provide benchmarks for evaluating Abduction Reasoning with diverse granularity explanations. Based on previous research, Synthetic Reasoning (Liang et al., 2022) provides a comprehensive evaluation of both Deduction Reasoning and Abduction Reasoning Competency. Moreover, Hessel et al. (2022) introduced the first comprehensive multimodal benchmark for testing Abduction Reasoning capabilities, providing a solid foundation for future advancements in this domain. Recently, Bills et al. (2023) evaluate GPT-4 by observing the activation of neurons in GPT-2 and offering explanations for the GPT-2's outputs. This research avenue also presents a novel approach for exploring the future evaluation of Abduction Reasoning Competency.

2.2.5 Analogical Reasoning Competency

Analogy reasoning competency encompasses the ability of reasoning by identifying and applying similarities between diverse situations or domains. It is based on the assumption that similar cases or objects tend to exhibit common attributes or behaviors. By recognizing these similarities, analogy reasoning enables systems to transfer knowledge or experience from one context to another (Sinha et al., 2019; Wei et al., 2022b). This type of reasoning plays a vital role in problem-solving, decision-making, and learning from past experiences. A typical example is In-Context-Learning (Dong et al., 2023), where the model is required to perform analogical reasoning based on given contexts, which are evaluated based on the final analogical results.

For a better assessment and understanding of the model's analogical reasoning ability, Brown et al. (2020) introduces SAT Analogies as a test to evaluate LLM's analogical reasoning capabilities. In recent years, Authorship Verification and ARC datasets (Srivastava et al., 2022) have also proposed evaluation benchmark that involve presenting contextual examples and requiring the model to produce induced pattern-compliant results. However, it should be noted that In-Context Learning (ICL) can be utilized for almost all tasks, enabling the evaluation of models' Analogical Reasoning Competency to some extent through the assessment of their performance after undergoing ICL.

Proceedings of the 22nd China National Conference on Computational Linguistics, pages 88-109, Harbin, China, August 3 - 5, 2023.
Volume 2: Frotier Forum

2.2.6 Multi-hop Reasoning Competency

Multi-hop reasoning refers to the ability to combine and integrate information from multiple sources or contexts to arrive at logical conclusions. This competency of reasoning enables systems to retrieve coherent and comprehensive answers by traversing multiple pieces of information, thus performing complex tasks of information retrieval, comprehension, and reasoning (Wang et al., 2022a; Qiu et al., 2019).

Currently, HotpotQA (Yang et al., 2018) serves as a commonly used dataset for multi-hop question answering tasks. Expanding on this, Ye and Durrett (2022) introduced a new and demanding subset that aimed to achieve a balance between accurate and inaccurate predictions using their model. Similarly, StrategyQA (Geva et al., 2021) is another widely used benchmark for multi-hop question answering (Wei et al., 2022b), where the required reasoning steps are implicit in the questions and should be inferred using strategies.

2.2.7 Reasoning in Scenarios

Commonsense Reasoning Commonsense reasoning is crucial for machines to achieve human-like understanding and interaction with the world in the field of machine intelligence (Storks et al., 2019; Bhargava and Ng, 2022). The ability to comprehend and apply commonsense knowledge enables machines to make accurate predictions, engage in logical reasoning, and navigate complex social situations.

OpenBookQA (Mihaylov et al., 2018) provides a foundational test for evaluating Commonsense Reasoning abilities in the form of an open-book exam. Building upon this, CommonsenseQA (Talmor et al., 2019) requires models to employ rich world knowledge for reasoning tasks. PIQA (Bisk et al., 2020) introduces a dataset for testing models' understanding of physical world commonsense reasoning. StrategyQA (Geva et al., 2021) presents a complex benchmark that requires commonsense-based multi-step/multi-hop reasoning, enabling a better exploration of the upper limits of models' Commonsense Reasoning Competency. Currently, due to early research on LLM (Wei et al., 2022b), CommonsenseQA (Talmor et al., 2019) remains the most widely used benchmark for commonsense reasoning.

Mathematical Reasoning Mathematical reasoning competency is crucial for general intelligent systems. It empowers intelligent systems with the capability of logical reasoning, problem-solving, and data manipulation and analysis, thereby facilitating the development and application of intelligent systems (Qiao et al., 2022; Mishra et al., 2022b; Mishra et al., 2022a).

Early evluation studies focused on small datasets of elementary-level mathematical word problems (MWPs) (Hosseini et al., 2014), but subsequent research aimed to increase complexity and scale (Srivastava et al., 2022; Brown et al., 2020). Furthermore, recent benchmarks (Mishra et al., 2022b; Mishra et al., 2022a) have provided comprehensive evaluation platforms and benchmarks for mathematical reasoning abilities. GSM8K (Cobbe et al., 2021) aims to evaluate elementary school MWPs. Currently, due to early research efforts on LLMs (Wei et al., 2022b), it remains the most widely used benchmark for mathematical reasoning in the LLM evaluation. Moreover, There have been recent advancements in evaluation research that explore mathematical reasoning competency integrating external knowledge, leveraging language diversity for multilingual evaluation (Shi et al., 2023), and testing mathematical reasoning on multi-modal setting (Lindström and Abraham, 2022), aiming to judge the broader data reasoning capabilities of large language models (LLMs).

Structured Data Reasoning Structured data reasoning involves the ability to reason and derive insights and answers from structured data sources, such as structured tabular data (Qiao et al., 2022; Li et al., 2023b; Xie et al., 2022).

WikiSQL (Zhong et al., 2017) and WikiTQ (Pasupat and Liang, 2015) provide tables as input and answer questions based on the additional input of questions. HybridQA (Chen et al., 2020b) and MultiModalQA (Talmor et al., 2021) propose benchmarks for hybrid Structure Reasoning by combining structured table inputs with text (and even other modalities). Similarly, MultiWoZ (Budzianowski et al., 2018), KVRET (Eric et al., 2017) and SQA (Iyyer et al., 2017) integrate table data into task-oriented dialogue systems to generate more complex structures and output dialog-related classifications. Unlike traditional QA, FeTaQA (Nan et al., 2021) requires free-form answers instead of extracting answer spans from passages. ToTTo (Parikh et al., 2020) introduces an open-domain English table-to-text dataset for

Proceedings of the 22nd China National Conference on Computational Linguistics, pages 88-109, Harbin, China, August 3 - 5, 2023.
Volume 2: Frotier Forum

Structured Data Reasoning. Additionally, benchmarks such as TabFact (Chen et al., 2020a) and FEVEROUS (Aly et al., 2021) evaluate whether model statements are consistent with facts mentioned in structured data. In recent years, with a deeper focus on testing models' mathematical abilities, TabMWP (Lu et al., 2023) introduces a grade-level dataset of table-based mathematical word problems that require mathematical reasoning using both text and table data.

2.3 Reliability

Reliability measures to what extent a human can trust the contents generated by a LLM. It is of vital importance for the deployment and usability of the LLM, and attracts tons of concerns along with the rapid and astonishing development of recent LLMs (Weidinger et al., 2021; Wang et al., 2022d; Ji et al., 2023; Zhuo et al., 2023). Lots of concepts are closely related to reliability under the context of LLM, including but not limited to hallucination, truthfulness, factuality, honesty, calibration, robustness, interpretability (Lee et al., 2018; Belinkov et al., 2020; Evans et al., 2021; Mielke et al., 2022; Lin et al., 2022b). Reliability also overlaps with the safety and generalization of a LLM (Weidinger et al., 2021). In this section, we will give an overview of two most concerned directions: Hallucination, Uncertainty and Calibration.

2.3.1 Hallucination

Hallucination is a term often used to describe LLM's falsehoods, which is the opposite side of truthfulness or factuality (Ji et al., 2023; OpenAI, 2023; Bubeck et al., 2023). Hallucination is always categorized into intrinsic (close domain) hallucination and extrinsic (open domain) hallucination (Ji et al., 2023; OpenAI, 2023). Intrinsic hallucination refers to the unfaithfulness of the model output to a given context, while extrinsic hallucination refers to the untruthful contents about the world generated by the model without reference to a given source.

Early research on hallucination mainly focused on the intrinsic hallucination and lots of interesting metrics were proposed to evaluate the intrinsic hallucination level of a PTM (Ji et al., 2023). However, Bang et al. (2023) claimed that intrinsic hallucination was barely found after conducting a comprehensive analysis of ChatGPT's responses. Hence for LLM, the extrinsic hallucination is of the greatest concern. To evaluate the extrinsic hallucination potential of a LLM, a common practice is to leverage knowledge-intensive tasks such as Factual Question Answering (Joshi et al., 2017; Zheng et al., 2023) or Knowledge-grounded Dialogue (Dinan et al., 2019b; Das et al., 2022). TruthfulQA (Lin et al., 2022b) is the most popular dataset used to quantify hallucination level of a LLM. This dataset is adversarially constructed to exploit the weakness of LLM, which contained 817 questions that span 38 categories. OpenAI (2023) leveraged real-world data flagged as non-factual to construct an adversarial dataset to test GPT-4's hallucination potential. BIG-bench (Srivastava et al., 2022), a famous benchmark to evaluate LLM's capabilities, also contains many sub-tasks on factual correctness including TruthfulQA. Although most of these tasks are multiple choices or classification in a fact verification(Thorne et al., 2018) manner, they are closely associated with truthfulness and can be regarded as a generalized hallucination evaluation.

2.3.2 Uncertainty and Calibration

A reliable and trustworthy Language model must have the capability to accurately articulate its level of confidence over its response, which requires the model to be aware of its uncertainty. A model that can precisely measure its own uncertainty is sometimes called self-aware, honesty or known-unknown (Kadavath et al., 2022; Yin et al., 2023). In general deep learning applications, calibration concerns about the uncertainty estimation of a classifier. Output probability from a well-calibrated classifier are supposed to be consistent with the empirical accuracy in real world (Vaicenavicius et al., 2019). HELM (Liang et al., 2022) treated calibration as one of general metrics and comprehensively evaluated the calibration degree of many prevailing models on multiple choice and classification tasks. (OpenAI, 2023) also showed that GPT-4 before RLHF was well-calibrated on multiple choice tasks, although the decent calibration degree was compromised significantly by post-training.

when it comes to free-form generation, it's a different story. Kuhn et al. (2023) pointed out that semantic nature of language and intractable output space guaranteed the uniqueness of free-form generation.

Proceedings of the 22nd China National Conference on Computational Linguistics, pages 88-109, Harbin, China, August 3 - 5, 2023.
Volume 2: Frotier Forum

Dataset	Safety Category	LLM evaluated	Task Format	Lang
RealToxicityPrompts	Harmful Contents	InstructGPT;LLaMA;Flan-PaLM;GPT-4;BLOOM	Generation	En
BAD	Harmful Contents	-	Generation	En
CrowS-Pairs	Social Bias	LLaMA;MT-NLG;InstructGPT;Pythia	Generatio	En
French CrowS-Pairs	Social Bias	MT-NLG	Generation	Fr
StereoSet	Social Bias	-	Multiple choice	En

Table 3: Datasets used to evaluate the safety competency of LLMs.

They proposed an algorithm to cluster model outputs and then estimate the model uncertainty. Mielke et al. (2022) claimed that models always express confidence over incorrect answers and proposed the notion of linguistic calibration, which teached models to verbally express uncertainty rather than estimating a probability. Lin et al. (2022a) trained models to directly generate predicted uncertainty probability in natural language. Yin et al. (2023) proposed the SelfAware dataset which contains unanswerable questions and used the accuracy of model rejection as a measure of uncertainty.

2.4 Safety

As the LLMs rapidly penetrate into the manufactural and interactive activities of human society, such as LLM-based poem-template generators and chatting robots, the safety concerns for LLMs gain much attention nowadays. The rationales of LLMs are statistics-based, and this inherent stochasticity brings limitations and underlying risks, which deeply affect the real-world deployment of LLMs. Some datasets are proposed to evaluated the safety of LLMs (Table 3), however, the corresponding validity and authority of the safety judgement are inadequate as the current evaluative dimensions are not sufficient (Waseem et al., 2017; Weidinger et al., 2021) and the perception of safety is highly subjective (Kocoń et al., 2021; Weidinger et al., 2021). To this end, based on our survey on relevant papers, we propose a comprehensive perspective on the safety competency of LLMs, ranging from harmful contents to the ethical consideration, to inspire the further developments towards the techniques and evaluations of LLMs safety.

2.4.1 Harmfulness

The harmful contents include the offensive language or others that have the explicit harm towards the specific object, such content that has been widely discussed. However, there is not a unified definition of the constitution of harmful contents, based on our surveys, we conclude the relevant themes into five aspects, including offensiveness, violence, crime, sexual-explicit, and unauthorized expertise. Many researches focus on the language detection for the outputs of LLMs to ensure the harmlessness (Wulczyn et al., 2017; Davidson et al., 2017; Zampieri et al., 2019; Dinan et al., 2019a), while other techniques are proposed to stimulate LLMs to generate safe outputs directly (Krause et al., 2021; Atwell et al., 2022). For the unauthorized expertise, a general LLM should avoid any unauthorized expertise before the establishment of accountability system (Sun et al., 2022), which involves the psychological orientation and any medical advice. Besides, the impact of conversation context on safety gains more attention recently, as a results, detective and generative algorithms base on the context are proposed successively (Dinan et al., 2019a; Baheti et al., 2021; Dinan et al., 2022). RealToxicityPrompts (Gehman et al., 2020) is a dataset derived from English web texts, where prompts are automatically truncated from sentences classified as toxicity from a widely-used toxicity classifier. RealToxicityPrompts consists of 100K natural prompts, with average 11.7 tokens in length. BAD (Xu et al., 2021) is a dataset collected by the human-in-the-loop strategy, where crowdworkers are ask to prob harmful model outputs. BAD consist of 5k conversations with around 70k utterances in total, which could be used in both non-adversarially and adversarially testing the model weakness.

2.4.2 Unfairness and Social Bias

Unfairness and social bias present more covertly and widely for LLMs. Following the previous studies, we conclude that social bias is an inherent characteristic of a LLM, which mainly embody in the distribution difference of a LLM in language selection based on different demographic groups. Compared to the social bias, unfairness is the external form, which reflected in the output performance of specific tasks, for example, the African American English (AAE) is frequently mis-classified as the offensive lan-

Proceedings of the 22nd China National Conference on Computational Linguistics, pages 88-109, Harbin, China, August 3 - 5, 2023.
Volume 2: Frotier Forum

guage by some language detector (Lwowski et al., 2022). However, issues of unfairness and social bias are inevitable as they are widely distributed in human languages, and LLMs are required to memorize language as accurately as possible in the training stage (Weidinger et al., 2021). With respect to evaluate this important aspect, CrowS-Pairs (Nangia et al., 2020) is benchmark proposed to evaluating social bias. There are 1508 examples in CrowS-Pairs that involves nine types of social bias, like gender, race, and Nationality. StereoSet (Nadeem et al., 2021) is a dataset that could be used to evaluate social bias level in both word-level and sentence level, which examples are in four domains: race, gender,religion, and profession. For the StereoSet, the bias level is computed by the difference between model generation probabilities of biased and anti-biased sentence.

2.4.3 Others

As current algorithms for model safety based on the human perception, there is still no golden standardized judgement for LLMs to refer to, especially when a judgement is highly various across societies. It is necessary to align LLMs with the morality, ethics, and values of human society. More and more works focus on reifying this abstract concept into textual data recently, for example, Sap et al. (2020) proposal an implicit reasoning frame to explain the underlying harm of the target language. Besides, other works leverage rule-of-thumb (RoT) annotations of texts to support the judgement (Forbes et al., 2020; Ziems et al., 2022). However, current works in this area are neonatal, and we could expect more related works in the future.

Besides, we are also concerned about the privacy and political risks of LLMs. Since the LLMs are trained on vast corpus collected from books, conversations, web texts and so on, the privacy safety of LLMs arouses people's concern. These training texts might contain the private or sensitive information such as personal physical information, home address, etc. Many studies indicate LLMs are brittle under attacks, leaking the sensitive information unintentionally (Carlini et al., 2020; Li et al., 2022). Therefore, it is essential to test the privacy protection ability of a LLM. Moreover, the politics ignorance is also intractable for a LLM. The politics-related risk mainly stems from the composition of the training corpus. Texts in the corpus are derived from different language and social environments (usually the larger the more diversified), and different countries have different political prudence and stance, which brings additional risks to the wide deployment of a LM.

3 Future Directions

In this section, we outline some other competencies that are important for evaluating LLMs.

3.1 Sentiment

It is crucial to equip LLMs with the ability to understand and generate sentiments. As an indispensable factor in human life, sentiments are widely present in daily chats, social media posts, customer reviews, and news articles (Liu, 2015). Through the comprehensive research and high-level summary of the literature related to sentiments, we introduce the sentiment competency of LLMs in two aspects: sentiment understand and sentiment generation.

3.1.1 Sentiment Understand

Sentiment understand mainly involves the understanding of opinions, sentiments and emotions in the text (Liu, 2015). Representative tasks that reflect this competency include sentiment classification (SC), aspect-based sentiment analysis (ABSA), and multifaceted analysis of subjective texts (MAST). SC aims at assigning pre-defined sentiment classes to given texts. The typical datasets include IMDB (Maas et al., 2011), SST (Socher et al., 2013), Twitter (Rosenthal et al., 2017), Yelp (Zhang et al., 2015). ABSA focuses on identifying the sentiments of specific aspects in a sentence (Zhang et al., 2022), and the most widely used datasets are the SemEval series (Pontiki et al., 2014; Pontiki et al., 2015; Pontiki et al., 2016). MAST are tasks that involve the finer-grained and broader range of human subjective feelings (emotions (Sailunaz et al., 2018), stance (Küçük and Can, 2021), hate (Schmidt and Wiegand, 2017), irony (Zeng and Li, 2022), offensive (Pradhan et al., 2020), etc.) (Poria et al., 2023). Given that MAST includes a wide range of tasks, the datasets are not listed here in detail. Among them, the commonly used evaluation metrics for the above tasks are accuracy and F1 score (micro or macro). Some preliminary empirical studies (Zhang et al., 2023; Wang et al., 2023) indicate that LLMs can significantly improve performance on these tasks in few-shot learning settings. LLMs have the potential to be a general solution without designing different models for various tasks. Therefore, the sentiment understand competency of different LLMs deserves comprehensive exploration and empirical evaluation. To evaluate the performance of this competency, we can utilize multiple domain-specific datasets or choose the comprehensive benchmark (Srivastava et al., 2022; Liang et al., 2022).

3.1.2 Sentiment Generation

We categorize sentiment generation into two manifestations. One is to generate text that contains sentiments, and the other is to generate text that elicits sentiments. The former requires specifying the desired sentiment, and the latter requires a combination of commonsense knowledge (Speer et al., 2017; Hwang et al., 2021) or theory of mind (Sodian and Kristen, 2010). A classic application scenario is in open-domain dialogue, specifically, emotional dialogue (Zhou et al., 2018), empathetic dialogue (Rashkin et al., 2019), and emotional support conversation (Liu et al., 2021). To measure the quality of the generated text, it is necessary to employ both automatic metrics (such as sentiment accuracy, BLEU (Papineni et al., 2002), perplexity) and human evaluations (human ratings or preference tests). Currently, no work has comprehensively explored this aspect, but it is an essential path towards artificial general intelligence (AGI) (Bubeck et al., 2023).

3.2 Planning

Planning is the thinking before the actions take place. Given a specific goal, planning is the process to decide the means to achieve the goal. There're few works (Valmeekam et al., 2023; Valmeekam et al., 2022; Pallagani et al., 2023; Huang et al., 2022) that look at the planning ability of LLMs. Some of them focus on commonsense areas (Huang et al., 2022) like wedding or menu planning. Others adopted automated planning problems, formal language translators, and verifiers to automatically evaluate LLMs' competency(Valmeekam et al., 2023). With PDDL[5] represented problem descriptions and the translation of such problems into text and back, LLMs can thus sequence a series of actions to reach the planning goal. Whether the planning purpose is achieved can be easily verified via automatic verifiers. Possessing web-scale knowledge, LLMs have great potential for executing planning tasks or assisting planners.

3.3 Code

Coding competency is one of the advanced abilities of LLMs. LLMs with this competency can not only perform program synthesis but also possess the potential of self-evolving. Technically, all of the tasks involved with code like code generation and code understanding need this competency. In oracle manual evaluation, prominent LLMs like ChatGPT are capable of up to 15 ubiquitous software engineering tasks and perform well in most of them (Sridhara et al., 2023). The most explored evaluation task in coding competency would be program synthesis, where program description and function signature are given for its code implementation. One of the most pioneering benchmarks in program synthesis, HUMANEVAL (Chen et al., 2021), consists of 164 pairs of human generated docstrings and the associated unit tests to test the functional correctness of model generation. However, with the worry of insufficient testing and the imprecise problem description (Liu et al., 2023), existing LLM-for-code benchmarks still have lots of room for improvement.

4 Conclusion

This survey provides a comprehensive review of various literature for the evaluation of LLMs. We aggregate different works with their intended competencies. Some of the competencies(reasoning, knowledge) already have holistic evaluation benchmarks, while others(planning, coding) still face disparate challenges. The goal of this paper is to comb the numerous work concerning LLMs' evaluation through the lens of the core competencies test. Lighten the cognitive load for assimilating numerous evaluation

[5]Planning Domain Definition Language, a formal language used to describe classical planning problems.

Proceedings of the 22nd China National Conference on Computational Linguistics, pages 88-109, Harbin, China, August 3 - 5, 2023.
Volume 2: Frotier Forum

works due to the various functions of LLMs. In doing so, we have also identified the challenge faced by each competency, looking forward to alleviating it in the future.

Acknowledgements

We want to thank Yuanxing Liu, Xuesong Wang, Mengzhou Sun, Runze Liu, Yuhang Gou, Shuhan Zhou, Yifan Chen, Ruiyu Xiao, Xinyu Li, Yuchi Zhang, Yang Wang, Jiahang Han, Wenqi Ding, and Xinpeng Liu for their priceless help with the initial dataset investigation process.

References

Patricia A Alexander. 1992. Domain knowledge: Evolving themes and emerging concerns. *Educational psychologist*, 27(1):33–51.

Rami Aly, Zhijiang Guo, M. Schlichtkrull, James Thorne, Andreas Vlachos, Christos Christodoulopoulos, Oana Cocarascu, and Arpit Mittal. 2021. The fact extraction and verification over unstructured and structured information (feverous) shared task. *Proceedings of the Fourth Workshop on Fact Extraction and VERification (FEVER)*.

Katherine Atwell, Sabit Hassan, and Malihe Alikhani. 2022. APPDIA: A discourse-aware transformer-based style transfer model for offensive social media conversations. In *Proceedings of the 29th International Conference on Computational Linguistics*, pages 6063–6074, Gyeongju, Republic of Korea, October. International Committee on Computational Linguistics.

John Langshaw Austin. 1975. *How to do things with words*, volume 88. Oxford university press.

Ashutosh Baheti, Maarten Sap, Alan Ritter, and Mark Riedl. 2021. Just say no: Analyzing the stance of neural dialogue generation in offensive contexts. In *Proceedings of the 2021 Conference on Empirical Methods in Natural Language Processing*, pages 4846–4862, Online and Punta Cana, Dominican Republic, November. Association for Computational Linguistics.

Yejin Bang, Samuel Cahyawijaya, Nayeon Lee, Wenliang Dai, Dan Su, Bryan Wilie, Holy Lovenia, Ziwei Ji, Tiezheng Yu, Willy Chung, Quyet V. Do, Yan Xu, and Pascale Fung. 2023. A multitask, multilingual, multimodal evaluation of chatgpt on reasoning, hallucination, and interactivity. *CoRR*, abs/2302.04023.

Yonatan Belinkov, Sebastian Gehrmann, and Ellie Pavlick. 2020. Interpretability and analysis in neural NLP. In *Proceedings of the 58th Annual Meeting of the Association for Computational Linguistics: Tutorial Abstracts*, pages 1–5, Online, July. Association for Computational Linguistics.

Prajjwal Bhargava and Vincent Ng. 2022. Commonsense knowledge reasoning and generation with pre-trained language models: A survey. In *Thirty-Sixth AAAI Conference on Artificial Intelligence, AAAI 2022, Thirty-Fourth Conference on Innovative Applications of Artificial Intelligence, IAAI 2022, The Twelveth Symposium on Educational Advances in Artificial Intelligence, EAAI 2022 Virtual Event, February 22 - March 1, 2022*, pages 12317–12325. AAAI Press.

Steven Bills, Nick Cammarata, Dan Mossing, Henk Tillman, Leo Gao, Gabriel Goh, Ilya Sutskever, Jan Leike, Jeff Wu, and William Saunders. 2023. Language models can explain neurons in language models. `https://openaipublic.blob.core.windows.net/neuron-explainer/paper/index.html`.

Yonatan Bisk, Rowan Zellers, Ronan Le Bras, Jianfeng Gao, and Yejin Choi. 2020. PIQA: reasoning about physical commonsense in natural language. In *The Thirty-Fourth AAAI Conference on Artificial Intelligence, AAAI 2020, The Thirty-Second Innovative Applications of Artificial Intelligence Conference, IAAI 2020, The Tenth AAAI Symposium on Educational Advances in Artificial Intelligence, EAAI 2020, New York, NY, USA, February 7-12, 2020*, pages 7432–7439. AAAI Press.

Tom B. Brown, Benjamin Mann, Nick Ryder, Melanie Subbiah, Jared Kaplan, Prafulla Dhariwal, Arvind Neelakantan, Pranav Shyam, Girish Sastry, Amanda Askell, Sandhini Agarwal, Ariel Herbert-Voss, Gretchen Krueger, Tom Henighan, Rewon Child, Aditya Ramesh, Daniel M. Ziegler, Jeffrey Wu, Clemens Winter, Christopher Hesse, Mark Chen, Eric Sigler, Mateusz Litwin, Scott Gray, Benjamin Chess, Jack Clark, Christopher Berner, Sam McCandlish, Alec Radford, Ilya Sutskever, and Dario Amodei. 2020. Language models are few-shot learners. In Hugo Larochelle, Marc'Aurelio Ranzato, Raia Hadsell, Maria-Florina Balcan, and Hsuan-Tien Lin, editors, *Advances in Neural Information Processing Systems 33: Annual Conference on Neural Information Processing Systems 2020, NeurIPS 2020, December 6-12, 2020, virtual.*

Sébastien Bubeck, Varun Chandrasekaran, Ronen Eldan, Johannes Gehrke, Eric Horvitz, Ece Kamar, Peter Lee, Yin Tat Lee, Yuanzhi Li, Scott M. Lundberg, Harsha Nori, Hamid Palangi, Marco Túlio Ribeiro, and Yi Zhang. 2023. Sparks of artificial general intelligence: Early experiments with GPT-4. *CoRR*, abs/2303.12712.

Pawel Budzianowski, Tsung-Hsien Wen, Bo-Hsiang Tseng, Iñigo Casanueva, Stefan Ultes, Osman Ramadan, and Milica Gasic. 2018. Multiwoz - A large-scale multi-domain wizard-of-oz dataset for task-oriented dialogue modelling. In Ellen Riloff, David Chiang, Julia Hockenmaier, and Jun'ichi Tsujii, editors, *Proceedings of the 2018 Conference on Empirical Methods in Natural Language Processing, Brussels, Belgium, October 31 - November 4, 2018*, pages 5016–5026. Association for Computational Linguistics.

Nicholas Carlini, Florian Tramèr, Eric Wallace, Matthew Jagielski, Ariel Herbert-Voss, Katherine Lee, Adam Roberts, Tom B. Brown, Dawn Song, Úlfar Erlingsson, Alina Oprea, and Colin Raffel. 2020. Extracting training data from large language models. *CoRR*, abs/2012.07805.

Tommaso Caselli and Piek Vossen. 2017. The event storyline corpus: A new benchmark for causal and temporal relation extraction. In Tommaso Caselli, Ben Miller, Marieke van Erp, Piek Vossen, Martha Palmer, Eduard H. Hovy, Teruko Mitamura, and David Caswell, editors, *Proceedings of the Events and Stories in the News Workshop@ACL 2017, Vancouver, Canada, August 4, 2017*, pages 77–86. Association for Computational Linguistics.

Ilias Chalkidis, Abhik Jana, Dirk Hartung, Michael J. Bommarito II, Ion Androutsopoulos, Daniel Martin Katz, and Nikolaos Aletras. 2022. Lexglue: A benchmark dataset for legal language understanding in english. In Smaranda Muresan, Preslav Nakov, and Aline Villavicencio, editors, *Proceedings of the 60th Annual Meeting of the Association for Computational Linguistics (Volume 1: Long Papers), ACL 2022, Dublin, Ireland, May 22-27, 2022*, pages 4310–4330. Association for Computational Linguistics.

Chunkit Chan, Jiayang Cheng, Weiqi Wang, Yuxin Jiang, Tianqing Fang, Xin Liu, and Yangqiu Song. 2023. Chatgpt evaluation on sentence level relations: A focus on temporal, causal, and discourse relations. *CoRR*, abs/2304.14827.

Wenhu Chen, Hongmin Wang, Jianshu Chen, Yunkai Zhang, Hong Wang, Shiyang Li, Xiyou Zhou, and William Yang Wang. 2020a. Tabfact: A large-scale dataset for table-based fact verification. In *8th International Conference on Learning Representations, ICLR 2020, Addis Ababa, Ethiopia, April 26-30, 2020*. OpenReview.net.

Wenhu Chen, Hanwen Zha, Zhiyu Chen, Wenhan Xiong, Hong Wang, and William Yang Wang. 2020b. Hybridqa: A dataset of multi-hop question answering over tabular and textual data. In Trevor Cohn, Yulan He, and Yang Liu, editors, *Findings of the Association for Computational Linguistics: EMNLP 2020, Online Event, 16-20 November 2020*, volume EMNLP 2020 of *Findings of ACL*, pages 1026–1036. Association for Computational Linguistics.

Mark Chen, Jerry Tworek, Heewoo Jun, Qiming Yuan, Henrique Pondé de Oliveira Pinto, Jared Kaplan, Harrison Edwards, Yuri Burda, Nicholas Joseph, Greg Brockman, Alex Ray, Raul Puri, Gretchen Krueger, Michael Petrov, Heidy Khlaaf, Girish Sastry, Pamela Mishkin, Brooke Chan, Scott Gray, Nick Ryder, Mikhail Pavlov, Alethea Power, Lukasz Kaiser, Mohammad Bavarian, Clemens Winter, Philippe Tillet, Felipe Petroski Such, Dave Cummings, Matthias Plappert, Fotios Chantzis, Elizabeth Barnes, Ariel Herbert-Voss, William Hebgen Guss, Alex Nichol, Alex Paino, Nikolas Tezak, Jie Tang, Igor Babuschkin, Suchir Balaji, Shantanu Jain, William Saunders, Christopher Hesse, Andrew N. Carr, Jan Leike, Joshua Achiam, Vedant Misra, Evan Morikawa, Alec Radford, Matthew Knight, Miles Brundage, Mira Murati, Katie Mayer, Peter Welinder, Bob McGrew, Dario Amodei, Sam McCandlish, Ilya Sutskever, and Wojciech Zaremba. 2021. Evaluating large language models trained on code. *CoRR*, abs/2107.03374.

Zhoujun Cheng, Tianbao Xie, Peng Shi, Chengzu Li, Rahul Nadkarni, Yushi Hu, Caiming Xiong, Dragomir Radev, Mari Ostendorf, Luke Zettlemoyer, Noah A. Smith, and Tao Yu. 2023. Binding language models in symbolic languages. In *The Eleventh International Conference on Learning Representations, ICLR 2023, Kigali, Rwanda, May 1-5, 2023*. OpenReview.net.

Peter Clark, Oyvind Tafjord, and Kyle Richardson. 2020. Transformers as soft reasoners over language. In Christian Bessiere, editor, *Proceedings of the Twenty-Ninth International Joint Conference on Artificial Intelligence, IJCAI 2020*, pages 3882–3890. ijcai.org.

Karl Cobbe, Vineet Kosaraju, Mohammad Bavarian, Mark Chen, Heewoo Jun, Lukasz Kaiser, Matthias Plappert, Jerry Tworek, Jacob Hilton, Reiichiro Nakano, Christopher Hesse, and John Schulman. 2021. Training verifiers to solve math word problems. *CoRR*, abs/2110.14168.

Proceedings of the 22nd China National Conference on Computational Linguistics, pages 88-109, Harbin, China, August 3 - 5, 2023.
Volume 2: Frotier Forum

Dhairya Dalal, Paul Buitelaar, and Mihael Arcan. 2023. Calm-bench: A multi-task benchmark for evaluating causality-aware language models. In Andreas Vlachos and Isabelle Augenstein, editors, *Findings of the Association for Computational Linguistics: EACL 2023, Dubrovnik, Croatia, May 2-6, 2023*, pages 296–311. Association for Computational Linguistics.

Souvik Das, Sougata Saha, and Rohini K. Srihari. 2022. Diving deep into modes of fact hallucinations in dialogue systems. In Yoav Goldberg, Zornitsa Kozareva, and Yue Zhang, editors, *Findings of the Association for Computational Linguistics: EMNLP 2022, Abu Dhabi, United Arab Emirates, December 7-11, 2022*, pages 684–699. Association for Computational Linguistics.

Thomas Davidson, Dana Warmsley, Michael W. Macy, and Ingmar Weber. 2017. Automated hate speech detection and the problem of offensive language. In *International Conference on Web and Social Media*.

Ernest Davis. 2014. *Representations of commonsense knowledge*. Morgan Kaufmann.

Richard R Day, Julian Bamford, Willy A Renandya, George M Jacobs, and Vivienne Wai-Sze Yu. 1998. Extensive reading in the second language classroom. *RELC Journal*, 29(2):187–191.

Jay DeYoung, Sarthak Jain, Nazneen Fatema Rajani, Eric Lehman, Caiming Xiong, Richard Socher, and Byron C. Wallace. 2020. ERASER: A benchmark to evaluate rationalized NLP models. In Dan Jurafsky, Joyce Chai, Natalie Schluter, and Joel R. Tetreault, editors, *Proceedings of the 58th Annual Meeting of the Association for Computational Linguistics, ACL 2020, Online, July 5-10, 2020*, pages 4443–4458. Association for Computational Linguistics.

Emily Dinan, Samuel Humeau, Bharath Chintagunta, and Jason Weston. 2019a. Build it break it fix it for dialogue safety: Robustness from adversarial human attack. In *Proceedings of the 2019 Conference on Empirical Methods in Natural Language Processing and the 9th International Joint Conference on Natural Language Processing (EMNLP-IJCNLP)*, pages 4537–4546, Hong Kong, China, November. Association for Computational Linguistics.

Emily Dinan, Stephen Roller, Kurt Shuster, Angela Fan, Michael Auli, and Jason Weston. 2019b. Wizard of wikipedia: Knowledge-powered conversational agents. In *7th International Conference on Learning Representations, ICLR 2019, New Orleans, LA, USA, May 6-9, 2019*. OpenReview.net.

Emily Dinan, Gavin Abercrombie, A. Bergman, Shannon Spruit, Dirk Hovy, Y-Lan Boureau, and Verena Rieser. 2022. SafetyKit: First aid for measuring safety in open-domain conversational systems. In *Proceedings of the 60th Annual Meeting of the Association for Computational Linguistics (Volume 1: Long Papers)*, pages 4113–4133, Dublin, Ireland, May. Association for Computational Linguistics.

Qingxiu Dong, Lei Li, Damai Dai, Ce Zheng, Zhiyong Wu, Baobao Chang, Xu Sun, Jingjing Xu, Lei Li, and Zhifang Sui. 2023. A survey for in-context learning. *CoRR*, abs/2301.00234.

Li Du, Xiao Ding, Kai Xiong, Ting Liu, and Bing Qin. 2022. e-care: a new dataset for exploring explainable causal reasoning. In Smaranda Muresan, Preslav Nakov, and Aline Villavicencio, editors, *Proceedings of the 60th Annual Meeting of the Association for Computational Linguistics (Volume 1: Long Papers), ACL 2022, Dublin, Ireland, May 22-27, 2022*, pages 432–446. Association for Computational Linguistics.

Selma Dündar-Coecke. 2022. To what extent is general intelligence relevant to causal reasoning? a developmental study. *Frontiers in Psychology*, 13.

Mihail Eric, Lakshmi Krishnan, François Charette, and Christopher D. Manning. 2017. Key-value retrieval networks for task-oriented dialogue. In Kristiina Jokinen, Manfred Stede, David DeVault, and Annie Louis, editors, *Proceedings of the 18th Annual SIGdial Meeting on Discourse and Dialogue, Saarbrücken, Germany, August 15-17, 2017*, pages 37–49. Association for Computational Linguistics.

Owain Evans, Owen Cotton-Barratt, Lukas Finnveden, Adam Bales, Avital Balwit, Peter Wills, Luca Righetti, and William Saunders. 2021. Truthful AI: developing and governing AI that does not lie. *CoRR*, abs/2110.06674.

Jonathan Evans. 2002. Logic and human reasoning: an assessment of the deduction paradigm. *Psychological bulletin*, 128 6:978–96.

Maxwell Forbes, Jena D. Hwang, Vered Shwartz, Maarten Sap, and Yejin Choi. 2020. Social chemistry 101: Learning to reason about social and moral norms. In *Proceedings of the 2020 Conference on Empirical Methods in Natural Language Processing (EMNLP)*, pages 653–670, Online, November. Association for Computational Linguistics.

Proceedings of the 22nd China National Conference on Computational Linguistics, pages 88-109, Harbin, China, August 3 - 5, 2023.
Volume 2: Frotier Forum

Victoria Fromkin, Robert Rodman, and Nina Hyams. 2018. *An Introduction to Language (w/MLA9E Updates)*. Cengage Learning.

Leo Gao, Jonathan Tow, Stella Biderman, Sid Black, Anthony DiPofi, Charles Foster, Laurence Golding, Jeffrey Hsu, Kyle McDonell, Niklas Muennighoff, Jason Phang, Laria Reynolds, Eric Tang, Anish Thite, Ben Wang, Kevin Wang, and Andy Zou. 2021. A framework for few-shot language model evaluation, September.

Jinglong Gao, Xiao Ding, Bing Qin, and Ting Liu. 2023. Is chatgpt a good causal reasoner? A comprehensive evaluation. *CoRR*, abs/2305.07375.

Samuel Gehman, Suchin Gururangan, Maarten Sap, Yejin Choi, and Noah A. Smith. 2020. RealToxicityPrompts: Evaluating neural toxic degeneration in language models. In *Findings of the Association for Computational Linguistics: EMNLP 2020*, pages 3356–3369, Online, November. Association for Computational Linguistics.

Mor Geva, Daniel Khashabi, Elad Segal, Tushar Khot, Dan Roth, and Jonathan Berant. 2021. Did aristotle use a laptop? A question answering benchmark with implicit reasoning strategies. *Trans. Assoc. Comput. Linguistics*, 9:346–361.

Andrew S. Gordon, Zornitsa Kozareva, and Melissa Roemmele. 2012. Semeval-2012 task 7: Choice of plausible alternatives: An evaluation of commonsense causal reasoning. In Eneko Agirre, Johan Bos, and Mona T. Diab, editors, *Proceedings of the 6th International Workshop on Semantic Evaluation, SemEval@NAACL-HLT 2012, Montréal, Canada, June 7-8, 2012*, pages 394–398. The Association for Computer Linguistics.

Shirley Anugrah Hayati, Dongyeop Kang, and Lyle Ungar. 2021. Does BERT learn as humans perceive? understanding linguistic styles through lexica. In Marie-Francine Moens, Xuanjing Huang, Lucia Specia, and Scott Wen-tau Yih, editors, *Proceedings of the 2021 Conference on Empirical Methods in Natural Language Processing, EMNLP 2021, Virtual Event / Punta Cana, Dominican Republic, 7-11 November, 2021*, pages 6323–6331. Association for Computational Linguistics.

Jack Hessel, Jena D. Hwang, Jae Sung Park, Rowan Zellers, Chandra Bhagavatula, Anna Rohrbach, Kate Saenko, and Yejin Choi. 2022. The abduction of sherlock holmes: A dataset for visual abductive reasoning. In Shai Avidan, Gabriel J. Brostow, Moustapha Cissé, Giovanni Maria Farinella, and Tal Hassner, editors, *Computer Vision - ECCV 2022 - 17th European Conference, Tel Aviv, Israel, October 23-27, 2022, Proceedings, Part XXXVI*, volume 13696 of *Lecture Notes in Computer Science*, pages 558–575. Springer.

Terrence Hoffmann. 1999. The meanings of competency. *Journal of european industrial training*, 23(6):275–286.

Mohammad Javad Hosseini, Hannaneh Hajishirzi, Oren Etzioni, and Nate Kushman. 2014. Learning to solve arithmetic word problems with verb categorization. In Alessandro Moschitti, Bo Pang, and Walter Daelemans, editors, *Proceedings of the 2014 Conference on Empirical Methods in Natural Language Processing, EMNLP 2014, October 25-29, 2014, Doha, Qatar, A meeting of SIGDAT, a Special Interest Group of the ACL*, pages 523–533. ACL.

Wenlong Huang, Pieter Abbeel, Deepak Pathak, and Igor Mordatch. 2022. Language models as zero-shot planners: Extracting actionable knowledge for embodied agents. In Kamalika Chaudhuri, Stefanie Jegelka, Le Song, Csaba Szepesvári, Gang Niu, and Sivan Sabato, editors, *International Conference on Machine Learning, ICML 2022, 17-23 July 2022, Baltimore, Maryland, USA*, volume 162 of *Proceedings of Machine Learning Research*, pages 9118–9147. PMLR.

Yuzhen Huang, Yuzhuo Bai, Zhihao Zhu, Junlei Zhang, Jinghan Zhang, Tangjun Su, Junteng Liu, Chuancheng Lv, Yikai Zhang, Jiayi Lei, Yao Fu, Maosong Sun, and Junxian He. 2023. C-eval: A multi-level multi-discipline chinese evaluation suite for foundation models. *CoRR*, abs/2305.08322.

Jena D. Hwang, Chandra Bhagavatula, Ronan Le Bras, Jeff Da, Keisuke Sakaguchi, Antoine Bosselut, and Yejin Choi. 2021. (comet-) atomic 2020: On symbolic and neural commonsense knowledge graphs. In *Thirty-Fifth AAAI Conference on Artificial Intelligence, AAAI 2021, Thirty-Third Conference on Innovative Applications of Artificial Intelligence, IAAI 2021, The Eleventh Symposium on Educational Advances in Artificial Intelligence, EAAI 2021, Virtual Event, February 2-9, 2021*, pages 6384–6392. AAAI Press.

Mohit Iyyer, Wen-tau Yih, and Ming-Wei Chang. 2017. Search-based neural structured learning for sequential question answering. In Regina Barzilay and Min-Yen Kan, editors, *Proceedings of the 55th Annual Meeting of the Association for Computational Linguistics, ACL 2017, Vancouver, Canada, July 30 - August 4, Volume 1: Long Papers*, pages 1821–1831. Association for Computational Linguistics.

Ziwei Ji, Nayeon Lee, Rita Frieske, Tiezheng Yu, Dan Su, Yan Xu, Etsuko Ishii, Yejin Bang, Andrea Madotto, and Pascale Fung. 2023. Survey of hallucination in natural language generation. *ACM Comput. Surv.*, 55(12):248:1–248:38.

Proceedings of the 22nd China National Conference on Computational Linguistics, pages 88-109, Harbin, China, August 3 - 5, 2023.
Volume 2: Frotier Forum

Jinhao Jiang, Kun Zhou, Zican Dong, Keming Ye, Wayne Xin Zhao, and Ji-Rong Wen. 2023. Structgpt: A general framework for large language model to reason over structured data. *CoRR*, abs/2305.09645.

Mandar Joshi, Eunsol Choi, Daniel S. Weld, and Luke Zettlemoyer. 2017. Triviaqa: A large scale distantly supervised challenge dataset for reading comprehension. In Regina Barzilay and Min-Yen Kan, editors, *Proceedings of the 55th Annual Meeting of the Association for Computational Linguistics, ACL 2017, Vancouver, Canada, July 30 - August 4, Volume 1: Long Papers*, pages 1601–1611. Association for Computational Linguistics.

Saurav Kadavath, Tom Conerly, Amanda Askell, Tom Henighan, Dawn Drain, Ethan Perez, Nicholas Schiefer, Zac Hatfield-Dodds, Nova DasSarma, Eli Tran-Johnson, Scott Johnston, Sheer El Showk, Andy Jones, Nelson Elhage, Tristan Hume, Anna Chen, Yuntao Bai, Sam Bowman, Stanislav Fort, Deep Ganguli, Danny Hernandez, Josh Jacobson, Jackson Kernion, Shauna Kravec, Liane Lovitt, Kamal Ndousse, Catherine Olsson, Sam Ringer, Dario Amodei, Tom Brown, Jack Clark, Nicholas Joseph, Ben Mann, Sam McCandlish, Chris Olah, and Jared Kaplan. 2022. Language models (mostly) know what they know. *CoRR*, abs/2207.05221.

Antonis C. Kakas and Loizos Michael. 2020. Abduction and argumentation for explainable machine learning: A position survey. *CoRR*, abs/2010.12896.

Jared Kaplan, Sam McCandlish, Tom Henighan, Tom B. Brown, Benjamin Chess, Rewon Child, Scott Gray, Alec Radford, Jeffrey Wu, and Dario Amodei. 2020. Scaling laws for neural language models. *CoRR*, abs/2001.08361.

Jan Kocoń, Alicja Figas, Marcin Gruza, Daria Puchalska, Tomasz Kajdanowicz, and Przemysław Kazienko. 2021. Offensive, aggressive, and hate speech analysis: From data-centric to human-centered approach. *Information Processing Management*, 58(5):102643.

Takeshi Kojima, Shixiang Shane Gu, Machel Reid, Yutaka Matsuo, and Yusuke Iwasawa. 2022. Large language models are zero-shot reasoners. In *NeurIPS*.

Ben Krause, Akhilesh Deepak Gotmare, Bryan McCann, Nitish Shirish Keskar, Shafiq Joty, Richard Socher, and Nazneen Fatema Rajani. 2021. GeDi: Generative discriminator guided sequence generation. In *Findings of the Association for Computational Linguistics: EMNLP 2021*, pages 4929–4952, Punta Cana, Dominican Republic, November. Association for Computational Linguistics.

Dilek Küçük and Fazli Can. 2021. Stance detection: A survey. *ACM Comput. Surv.*, 53(1):12:1–12:37.

Lorenz Kuhn, Yarin Gal, and Sebastian Farquhar. 2023. Semantic uncertainty: Linguistic invariances for uncertainty estimation in natural language generation. In *The Eleventh International Conference on Learning Representations, ICLR 2023, Kigali, Rwanda, May 1-5, 2023*. OpenReview.net.

Katherine Lee, Orhan Firat, Ashish Agarwal, Clara Fannjiang, and David Sussillo. 2018. Hallucinations in neural machine translation.

Haoran Li, Yangqiu Song, and Lixin Fan. 2022. You don't know my favorite color: Preventing dialogue representations from revealing speakers' private personas. In *Proceedings of the 2022 Conference of the North American Chapter of the Association for Computational Linguistics: Human Language Technologies*, pages 5858–5870, Seattle, United States, July. Association for Computational Linguistics.

Haonan Li, Yixuan Zhang, Fajri Koto, Yifei Yang, Hai Zhao, Yeyun Gong, Nan Duan, and Timothy Baldwin. 2023a. CMMLU: measuring massive multitask language understanding in chinese. *CoRR*, abs/2306.09212.

Xingxuan Li, Ruochen Zhao, Yew Ken Chia, Bosheng Ding, Lidong Bing, Shafiq R. Joty, and Soujanya Poria. 2023b. Chain of knowledge: A framework for grounding large language models with structured knowledge bases. *CoRR*, abs/2305.13269.

Percy Liang, Rishi Bommasani, Tony Lee, Dimitris Tsipras, Dilara Soylu, Michihiro Yasunaga, Yian Zhang, Deepak Narayanan, Yuhuai Wu, Ananya Kumar, Benjamin Newman, Binhang Yuan, Bobby Yan, Ce Zhang, Christian Cosgrove, Christopher D. Manning, Christopher Ré, Diana Acosta-Navas, Drew A. Hudson, Eric Zelikman, Esin Durmus, Faisal Ladhak, Frieda Rong, Hongyu Ren, Huaxiu Yao, Jue Wang, Keshav Santhanam, Laurel J. Orr, Lucia Zheng, Mert Yüksekgönül, Mirac Suzgun, Nathan Kim, Neel Guha, Niladri S. Chatterji, Omar Khattab, Peter Henderson, Qian Huang, Ryan Chi, Sang Michael Xie, Shibani Santurkar, Surya Ganguli, Tatsunori Hashimoto, Thomas Icard, Tianyi Zhang, Vishrav Chaudhary, William Wang, Xuechen Li, Yifan Mai, Yuhui Zhang, and Yuta Koreeda. 2022. Holistic evaluation of language models. *CoRR*, abs/2211.09110.

Stephanie Lin, Jacob Hilton, and Owain Evans. 2022a. Teaching models to express their uncertainty in words. *Trans. Mach. Learn. Res.*, 2022.

Proceedings of the 22nd China National Conference on Computational Linguistics, pages 88-109, Harbin, China, August 3 - 5, 2023.
Volume 2: Frotier Forum

Stephanie Lin, Jacob Hilton, and Owain Evans. 2022b. Truthfulqa: Measuring how models mimic human falsehoods. In Smaranda Muresan, Preslav Nakov, and Aline Villavicencio, editors, *Proceedings of the 60th Annual Meeting of the Association for Computational Linguistics (Volume 1: Long Papers), ACL 2022, Dublin, Ireland, May 22-27, 2022*, pages 3214–3252. Association for Computational Linguistics.

Adam Dahlgren Lindström and Savitha Sam Abraham. 2022. Clevr-math: A dataset for compositional language, visual and mathematical reasoning. In Artur S. d'Avila Garcez and Ernesto Jiménez-Ruiz, editors, *Proceedings of the 16th International Workshop on Neural-Symbolic Learning and Reasoning as part of the 2nd International Joint Conference on Learning & Reasoning (IJCLR 2022), Cumberland Lodge, Windsor Great Park, UK, September 28-30, 2022*, volume 3212 of *CEUR Workshop Proceedings*, pages 155–170. CEUR-WS.org.

Siyang Liu, Chujie Zheng, Orianna Demasi, Sahand Sabour, Yu Li, Zhou Yu, Yong Jiang, and Minlie Huang. 2021. Towards emotional support dialog systems. In Chengqing Zong, Fei Xia, Wenjie Li, and Roberto Navigli, editors, *Proceedings of the 59th Annual Meeting of the Association for Computational Linguistics and the 11th International Joint Conference on Natural Language Processing, ACL/IJCNLP 2021, (Volume 1: Long Papers), Virtual Event, August 1-6, 2021*, pages 3469–3483. Association for Computational Linguistics.

Jiawei Liu, Chunqiu Steven Xia, Yuyao Wang, and Lingming Zhang. 2023. Is your code generated by chatgpt really correct? rigorous evaluation of large language models for code generation. *CoRR*, abs/2305.01210.

Bing Liu. 2015. *Sentiment Analysis - Mining Opinions, Sentiments, and Emotions*. Cambridge University Press.

Pan Lu, Liang Qiu, Kai-Wei Chang, Ying Nian Wu, Song-Chun Zhu, Tanmay Rajpurohit, Peter Clark, and Ashwin Kalyan. 2023. Dynamic prompt learning via policy gradient for semi-structured mathematical reasoning. In *The Eleventh International Conference on Learning Representations, ICLR 2023, Kigali, Rwanda, May 1-5, 2023*. OpenReview.net.

Brandon Lwowski, Paul Rad, and Anthony Rios. 2022. Measuring geographic performance disparities of offensive language classifiers. In *Proceedings of the 29th International Conference on Computational Linguistics*, pages 6600–6616, Gyeongju, Republic of Korea, October. International Committee on Computational Linguistics.

Qing Lyu, Shreya Havaldar, Adam Stein, Li Zhang, Delip Rao, Eric Wong, Marianna Apidianaki, and Chris Callison-Burch. 2023. Faithful chain-of-thought reasoning. *CoRR*, abs/2301.13379.

Andrew L. Maas, Raymond E. Daly, Peter T. Pham, Dan Huang, Andrew Y. Ng, and Christopher Potts. 2011. Learning word vectors for sentiment analysis. In Dekang Lin, Yuji Matsumoto, and Rada Mihalcea, editors, *The 49th Annual Meeting of the Association for Computational Linguistics: Human Language Technologies, Proceedings of the Conference, 19-24 June, 2011, Portland, Oregon, USA*, pages 142–150. The Association for Computer Linguistics.

Daniel Jaymin Mankowitz, Andrea Michi, Anton Zhernov, Marco Gelmi, Marco Selvi, Cosmin Paduraru, Edouard Leurent, Shariq Iqbal, Jean-Baptiste Lespiau, Alex Ahern, Thomas Köppe, Kevin Millikin, Stephen Gaffney, Sophie Elster, Jackson Broshear, Chris Gamble, Kieran Milan, Robert Tung, Minjae Hwang, taylan. cemgil, Mohammadamin Barekatain, Yujia Li, Amol Mandhane, Thomas Hubert, Julian Schrittwieser, Demis Hassabis, Pushmeet Kohli, Martin A. Riedmiller, Oriol Vinyals, and David Silver. 2023. Faster sorting algorithms discovered using deep reinforcement learning. *Nature*, 618:257 – 263.

Binny Mathew, Punyajoy Saha, Seid Muhie Yimam, Chris Biemann, Pawan Goyal, and Animesh Mukherjee. 2021. Hatexplain: A benchmark dataset for explainable hate speech detection. In *Thirty-Fifth AAAI Conference on Artificial Intelligence, AAAI 2021, Thirty-Third Conference on Innovative Applications of Artificial Intelligence, IAAI 2021, The Eleventh Symposium on Educational Advances in Artificial Intelligence, EAAI 2021, Virtual Event, February 2-9, 2021*, pages 14867–14875. AAAI Press.

Grégoire Mialon, Roberto Dessì, Maria Lomeli, Christoforos Nalmpantis, Ramakanth Pasunuru, Roberta Raileanu, Baptiste Rozière, Timo Schick, Jane Dwivedi-Yu, Asli Celikyilmaz, Edouard Grave, Yann LeCun, and Thomas Scialom. 2023. Augmented language models: a survey. *CoRR*, abs/2302.07842.

Sabrina J. Mielke, Arthur Szlam, Emily Dinan, and Y-Lan Boureau. 2022. Reducing conversational agents' overconfidence through linguistic calibration. *Trans. Assoc. Comput. Linguistics*, 10:857–872.

Todor Mihaylov, Peter Clark, Tushar Khot, and Ashish Sabharwal. 2018. Can a suit of armor conduct electricity? A new dataset for open book question answering. In Ellen Riloff, David Chiang, Julia Hockenmaier, and Jun'ichi Tsujii, editors, *Proceedings of the 2018 Conference on Empirical Methods in Natural Language Processing, Brussels, Belgium, October 31 - November 4, 2018*, pages 2381–2391. Association for Computational Linguistics.

Proceedings of the 22nd China National Conference on Computational Linguistics, pages 88-109, Harbin, China, August 3 - 5, 2023.
Volume 2: Frotier Forum

Paramita Mirza, R. Sprugnoli, Sara Tonelli, and Manuela Speranza. 2014. Annotating causality in the tempeval-3 corpus. In *Conference of the European Chapter of the Association for Computational Linguistics*.

Swaroop Mishra, Matthew Finlayson, Pan Lu, Leonard Tang, Sean Welleck, Chitta Baral, Tanmay Rajpurohit, Oyvind Tafjord, Ashish Sabharwal, Peter Clark, and Ashwin Kalyan. 2022a. LILA: A unified benchmark for mathematical reasoning. In Yoav Goldberg, Zornitsa Kozareva, and Yue Zhang, editors, *Proceedings of the 2022 Conference on Empirical Methods in Natural Language Processing, EMNLP 2022, Abu Dhabi, United Arab Emirates, December 7-11, 2022*, pages 5807–5832. Association for Computational Linguistics.

Swaroop Mishra, Arindam Mitra, Neeraj Varshney, Bhavdeep Singh Sachdeva, Peter Clark, Chitta Baral, and Ashwin Kalyan. 2022b. Numglue: A suite of fundamental yet challenging mathematical reasoning tasks. In Smaranda Muresan, Preslav Nakov, and Aline Villavicencio, editors, *Proceedings of the 60th Annual Meeting of the Association for Computational Linguistics (Volume 1: Long Papers), ACL 2022, Dublin, Ireland, May 22-27, 2022*, pages 3505–3523. Association for Computational Linguistics.

Moin Nadeem, Anna Bethke, and Siva Reddy. 2021. StereoSet: Measuring stereotypical bias in pretrained language models. In *Proceedings of the 59th Annual Meeting of the Association for Computational Linguistics and the 11th International Joint Conference on Natural Language Processing (Volume 1: Long Papers)*, pages 5356–5371, Online, August. Association for Computational Linguistics.

Linyong Nan, Chia-Hsuan Hsieh, Ziming Mao, Xi Victoria Lin, Neha Verma, Rui Zhang, Wojciech Kryscinski, Nick Schoelkopf, Riley Kong, Xiangru Tang, Murori Mutuma, Benjamin Rosand, Isabel Trindade, Renusree Bandaru, Jacob Cunningham, Caiming Xiong, and Dragomir R. Radev. 2021. Fetaqa: Free-form table question answering. *Transactions of the Association for Computational Linguistics*, 10:35–49.

Nikita Nangia, Clara Vania, Rasika Bhalerao, and Samuel R. Bowman. 2020. CrowS-pairs: A challenge dataset for measuring social biases in masked language models. In *Proceedings of the 2020 Conference on Empirical Methods in Natural Language Processing (EMNLP)*, pages 1953–1967, Online, November. Association for Computational Linguistics.

Catherine Olsson, Nelson Elhage, Neel Nanda, Nicholas Joseph, Nova DasSarma, Tom Henighan, Ben Mann, Amanda Askell, Yuntao Bai, Anna Chen, Tom Conerly, Dawn Drain, Deep Ganguli, Zac Hatfield-Dodds, Danny Hernandez, Scott Johnston, Andy Jones, Jackson Kernion, Liane Lovitt, Kamal Ndousse, Dario Amodei, Tom Brown, Jack Clark, Jared Kaplan, Sam McCandlish, and Chris Olah. 2022. In-context learning and induction heads. *CoRR*, abs/2209.11895.

OpenAI. 2023. GPT-4 technical report. *CoRR*, abs/2303.08774.

Long Ouyang, Jeffrey Wu, Xu Jiang, Diogo Almeida, Carroll L. Wainwright, Pamela Mishkin, Chong Zhang, Sandhini Agarwal, Katarina Slama, Alex Ray, John Schulman, Jacob Hilton, Fraser Kelton, Luke Miller, Maddie Simens, Amanda Askell, Peter Welinder, Paul F. Christiano, Jan Leike, and Ryan Lowe. 2022. Training language models to follow instructions with human feedback. In *NeurIPS*.

Ekaterina Ovchinnikova. 2012. *Integration of World Knowledge for Natural Language Understanding*, volume 3 of *Atlantis Thinking Machines*. Atlantis Press.

Vishal Pallagani, Bharath Muppasani, Keerthiram Murugesan, Francesca Rossi, Biplav Srivastava, Lior Horesh, Francesco Fabiano, and Andrea Loreggia. 2023. Understanding the capabilities of large language models for automated planning. *CoRR*, abs/2305.16151.

Kishore Papineni, Salim Roukos, Todd Ward, and Wei-Jing Zhu. 2002. Bleu: a method for automatic evaluation of machine translation. In *Proceedings of the 40th Annual Meeting of the Association for Computational Linguistics, July 6-12, 2002, Philadelphia, PA, USA*, pages 311–318. ACL.

Ankur P. Parikh, Xuezhi Wang, Sebastian Gehrmann, Manaal Faruqui, Bhuwan Dhingra, Diyi Yang, and Dipanjan Das. 2020. Totto: A controlled table-to-text generation dataset. In Bonnie Webber, Trevor Cohn, Yulan He, and Yang Liu, editors, *Proceedings of the 2020 Conference on Empirical Methods in Natural Language Processing, EMNLP 2020, Online, November 16-20, 2020*, pages 1173–1186. Association for Computational Linguistics.

Panupong Pasupat and Percy Liang. 2015. Compositional semantic parsing on semi-structured tables. In *Proceedings of the 53rd Annual Meeting of the Association for Computational Linguistics and the 7th International Joint Conference on Natural Language Processing of the Asian Federation of Natural Language Processing, ACL 2015, July 26-31, 2015, Beijing, China, Volume 1: Long Papers*, pages 1470–1480. The Association for Computer Linguistics.

Proceedings of the 22nd China National Conference on Computational Linguistics, pages 88-109, Harbin, China, August 3 - 5, 2023.
Volume 2: Frotier Forum

Edoardo Maria Ponti, Goran Glavas, Olga Majewska, Qianchu Liu, Ivan Vulic, and Anna Korhonen. 2020. XCOPA: A multilingual dataset for causal commonsense reasoning. In Bonnie Webber, Trevor Cohn, Yulan He, and Yang Liu, editors, *Proceedings of the 2020 Conference on Empirical Methods in Natural Language Processing, EMNLP 2020, Online, November 16-20, 2020*, pages 2362–2376. Association for Computational Linguistics.

Maria Pontiki, Dimitris Galanis, John Pavlopoulos, Harris Papageorgiou, Ion Androutsopoulos, and Suresh Manandhar. 2014. Semeval-2014 task 4: Aspect based sentiment analysis. In Preslav Nakov and Torsten Zesch, editors, *Proceedings of the 8th International Workshop on Semantic Evaluation, SemEval@COLING 2014, Dublin, Ireland, August 23-24, 2014*, pages 27–35. The Association for Computer Linguistics.

Maria Pontiki, Dimitris Galanis, Haris Papageorgiou, Suresh Manandhar, and Ion Androutsopoulos. 2015. Semeval-2015 task 12: Aspect based sentiment analysis. In Daniel M. Cer, David Jurgens, Preslav Nakov, and Torsten Zesch, editors, *Proceedings of the 9th International Workshop on Semantic Evaluation, SemEval@NAACL-HLT 2015, Denver, Colorado, USA, June 4-5, 2015*, pages 486–495. The Association for Computer Linguistics.

Maria Pontiki, Dimitris Galanis, Haris Papageorgiou, Ion Androutsopoulos, Suresh Manandhar, Mohammad AL-Smadi, Mahmoud Al-Ayyoub, Yanyan Zhao, Bing Qin, Orphée De Clercq, Véronique Hoste, Marianna Apidianaki, Xavier Tannier, Natalia Loukachevitch, Evgeniy Kotelnikov, Nuria Bel, Salud María Jiménez-Zafra, and Gülşen Eryiğit. 2016. SemEval-2016 task 5: Aspect based sentiment analysis. In *Proceedings of the 10th International Workshop on Semantic Evaluation (SemEval-2016)*, pages 19–30, San Diego, California, June. Association for Computational Linguistics.

Soujanya Poria, Devamanyu Hazarika, Navonil Majumder, and Rada Mihalcea. 2023. Beneath the tip of the iceberg: Current challenges and new directions in sentiment analysis research. *IEEE Trans. Affect. Comput.*, 14(1):108–132.

Rahul Pradhan, Ankur Chaturvedi, Aprna Tripathi, and Dilip Kumar Sharma. 2020. A review on offensive language detection. In Mohan L. Kolhe, Shailesh Tiwari, Munesh C. Trivedi, and Krishn K. Mishra, editors, *Advances in Data and Information Sciences*, pages 433–439, Singapore. Springer Singapore.

Shuofei Qiao, Yixin Ou, Ningyu Zhang, Xiang Chen, Yunzhi Yao, Shumin Deng, Chuanqi Tan, Fei Huang, and Huajun Chen. 2022. Reasoning with language model prompting: A survey. *CoRR*, abs/2212.09597.

Lin Qiu, Yunxuan Xiao, Yanru Qu, Hao Zhou, Lei Li, Weinan Zhang, and Yong Yu. 2019. Dynamically fused graph network for multi-hop reasoning. In Anna Korhonen, David R. Traum, and Lluís Màrquez, editors, *Proceedings of the 57th Conference of the Association for Computational Linguistics, ACL 2019, Florence, Italy, July 28- August 2, 2019, Volume 1: Long Papers*, pages 6140–6150. Association for Computational Linguistics.

Hannah Rashkin, Eric Michael Smith, Margaret Li, and Y-Lan Boureau. 2019. Towards empathetic open-domain conversation models: A new benchmark and dataset. In Anna Korhonen, David R. Traum, and Lluís Màrquez, editors, *Proceedings of the 57th Conference of the Association for Computational Linguistics, ACL 2019, Florence, Italy, July 28- August 2, 2019, Volume 1: Long Papers*, pages 5370–5381. Association for Computational Linguistics.

Sara Rosenthal, Noura Farra, and Preslav Nakov. 2017. Semeval-2017 task 4: Sentiment analysis in twitter. In Steven Bethard, Marine Carpuat, Marianna Apidianaki, Saif M. Mohammad, Daniel M. Cer, and David Jurgens, editors, *Proceedings of the 11th International Workshop on Semantic Evaluation, SemEval@ACL 2017, Vancouver, Canada, August 3-4, 2017*, pages 502–518. Association for Computational Linguistics.

Kashfia Sailunaz, Manmeet Dhaliwal, Jon G. Rokne, and Reda Alhajj. 2018. Emotion detection from text and speech: a survey. *Soc. Netw. Anal. Min.*, 8(1):28:1–28:26.

Maarten Sap, Saadia Gabriel, Lianhui Qin, Dan Jurafsky, Noah A. Smith, and Yejin Choi. 2020. Social bias frames: Reasoning about social and power implications of language. In *Proceedings of the 58th Annual Meeting of the Association for Computational Linguistics*, pages 5477–5490, Online, July. Association for Computational Linguistics.

Anna Schmidt and Michael Wiegand. 2017. A survey on hate speech detection using natural language processing. In Lun-Wei Ku and Cheng-Te Li, editors, *Proceedings of the Fifth International Workshop on Natural Language Processing for Social Media, SocialNLP@EACL 2017, Valencia, Spain, April 3, 2017*, pages 1–10. Association for Computational Linguistics.

Proceedings of the 22nd China National Conference on Computational Linguistics, pages 88-109, Harbin, China, August 3 - 5, 2023.
Volume 2: Frotier Forum

Freda Shi, Mirac Suzgun, Markus Freitag, Xuezhi Wang, Suraj Srivats, Soroush Vosoughi, Hyung Won Chung, Yi Tay, Sebastian Ruder, Denny Zhou, Dipanjan Das, and Jason Wei. 2023. Language models are multilingual chain-of-thought reasoners. In *The Eleventh International Conference on Learning Representations, ICLR 2023, Kigali, Rwanda, May 1-5, 2023*. OpenReview.net.

Koustuv Sinha, Shagun Sodhani, Jin Dong, Joelle Pineau, and William L. Hamilton. 2019. CLUTRR: A diagnostic benchmark for inductive reasoning from text. In Kentaro Inui, Jing Jiang, Vincent Ng, and Xiaojun Wan, editors, *Proceedings of the 2019 Conference on Empirical Methods in Natural Language Processing and the 9th International Joint Conference on Natural Language Processing, EMNLP-IJCNLP 2019, Hong Kong, China, November 3-7, 2019*, pages 4505–4514. Association for Computational Linguistics.

Richard Socher, Alex Perelygin, Jean Wu, Jason Chuang, Christopher D. Manning, Andrew Ng, and Christopher Potts. 2013. Recursive deep models for semantic compositionality over a sentiment treebank. In *Proceedings of the 2013 Conference on Empirical Methods in Natural Language Processing*, pages 1631–1642, Seattle, Washington, USA, October. Association for Computational Linguistics.

Beate Sodian and Susanne Kristen, 2010. *Theory of Mind*, pages 189–201. Springer Berlin Heidelberg, Berlin, Heidelberg.

Robyn Speer, Joshua Chin, and Catherine Havasi. 2017. Conceptnet 5.5: An open multilingual graph of general knowledge. In Satinder Singh and Shaul Markovitch, editors, *Proceedings of the Thirty-First AAAI Conference on Artificial Intelligence, February 4-9, 2017, San Francisco, California, USA*, pages 4444–4451. AAAI Press.

Giriprasad Sridhara, Ranjani H. G., and Sourav Mazumdar. 2023. Chatgpt: A study on its utility for ubiquitous software engineering tasks. *CoRR*, abs/2305.16837.

Aarohi Srivastava, Abhinav Rastogi, Abhishek Rao, Abu Awal Md Shoeb, Abubakar Abid, Adam Fisch, Adam R. Brown, Adam Santoro, Aditya Gupta, Adrià Garriga-Alonso, Agnieszka Kluska, Aitor Lewkowycz, Akshat Agarwal, Alethea Power, Alex Ray, Alex Warstadt, Alexander W. Kocurek, Ali Safaya, Ali Tazarv, Alice Xiang, Alicia Parrish, Allen Nie, Aman Hussain, Amanda Askell, Amanda Dsouza, Ameet Rahane, Anantharaman S. Iyer, Anders Andreassen, Andrea Santilli, Andreas Stuhlmüller, Andrew M. Dai, Andrew La, Andrew K. Lampinen, Andy Zou, Angela Jiang, Angelica Chen, Anh Vuong, Animesh Gupta, Anna Gottardi, Antonio Norelli, Anu Venkatesh, Arash Gholamidavoodi, Arfa Tabassum, Arul Menezes, Arun Kirubarajan, Asher Mullokandov, Ashish Sabharwal, Austin Herrick, Avia Efrat, Aykut Erdem, Ayla Karakas, and et al. 2022. Beyond the imitation game: Quantifying and extrapolating the capabilities of language models. *CoRR*, abs/2206.04615.

Shane Storks, Qiaozi Gao, and Joyce Y. Chai. 2019. Commonsense reasoning for natural language understanding: A survey of benchmarks, resources, and approaches. *CoRR*, abs/1904.01172.

Hao Sun, Guangxuan Xu, Jiawen Deng, Jiale Cheng, Chujie Zheng, Hao Zhou, Nanyun Peng, Xiaoyan Zhu, and Minlie Huang. 2022. On the safety of conversational models: Taxonomy, dataset, and benchmark. In *Findings of the Association for Computational Linguistics: ACL 2022*, pages 3906–3923, Dublin, Ireland, May. Association for Computational Linguistics.

Dídac Surís, Sachit Menon, and Carl Vondrick. 2023. Vipergpt: Visual inference via python execution for reasoning. *CoRR*, abs/2303.08128.

Christian Szegedy, Wojciech Zaremba, Ilya Sutskever, Joan Bruna, Dumitru Erhan, Ian J. Goodfellow, and Rob Fergus. 2014. Intriguing properties of neural networks. In Yoshua Bengio and Yann LeCun, editors, *2nd International Conference on Learning Representations, ICLR 2014, Banff, AB, Canada, April 14-16, 2014, Conference Track Proceedings*.

Alon Talmor, Jonathan Herzig, Nicholas Lourie, and Jonathan Berant. 2019. Commonsenseqa: A question answering challenge targeting commonsense knowledge. In Jill Burstein, Christy Doran, and Thamar Solorio, editors, *Proceedings of the 2019 Conference of the North American Chapter of the Association for Computational Linguistics: Human Language Technologies, NAACL-HLT 2019, Minneapolis, MN, USA, June 2-7, 2019, Volume 1 (Long and Short Papers)*, pages 4149–4158. Association for Computational Linguistics.

Alon Talmor, Ori Yoran, Amnon Catav, Dan Lahav, Yizhong Wang, Akari Asai, Gabriel Ilharco, Hannaneh Hajishirzi, and Jonathan Berant. 2021. Multimodalqa: complex question answering over text, tables and images. In *9th International Conference on Learning Representations, ICLR 2021, Virtual Event, Austria, May 3-7, 2021*. OpenReview.net.

James Thorne, Andreas Vlachos, Christos Christodoulopoulos, and Arpit Mittal. 2018. FEVER: a large-scale dataset for fact extraction and verification. In Marilyn A. Walker, Heng Ji, and Amanda Stent, editors, *Proceedings of the 2018 Conference of the North American Chapter of the Association for Computational Linguistics: Human Language Technologies, NAACL-HLT 2018, New Orleans, Louisiana, USA, June 1-6, 2018, Volume 1 (Long Papers)*, pages 809–819. Association for Computational Linguistics.

Proceedings of the 22nd China National Conference on Computational Linguistics, pages 88-109, Harbin, China, August 3 - 5, 2023.
Volume 2: Frotier Forum

Juozas Vaicenavicius, David Widmann, Carl R. Andersson, Fredrik Lindsten, Jacob Roll, and Thomas B. Schön. 2019. Evaluating model calibration in classification. In Kamalika Chaudhuri and Masashi Sugiyama, editors, *The 22nd International Conference on Artificial Intelligence and Statistics, AISTATS 2019, 16-18 April 2019, Naha, Okinawa, Japan*, volume 89 of *Proceedings of Machine Learning Research*, pages 3459–3467. PMLR.

Karthik Valmeekam, Alberto Olmo Hernandez, Sarath Sreedharan, and Subbarao Kambhampati. 2022. Large language models still can't plan (A benchmark for llms on planning and reasoning about change). *CoRR*, abs/2206.10498.

Karthik Valmeekam, Matthew Marquez, Sarath Sreedharan, and Subbarao Kambhampati. 2023. On the planning abilities of large language models - A critical investigation. *CoRR*, abs/2305.15771.

Matthew J. Vowels, Necati Cihan Camgöz, and Richard Bowden. 2023. D'ya like dags? A survey on structure learning and causal discovery. *ACM Comput. Surv.*, 55(4):82:1–82:36.

David Wadden, Shanchuan Lin, Kyle Lo, Lucy Lu Wang, Madeleine van Zuylen, Arman Cohan, and Hannaneh Hajishirzi. 2020. Fact or fiction: Verifying scientific claims. In Bonnie Webber, Trevor Cohn, Yulan He, and Yang Liu, editors, *Proceedings of the 2020 Conference on Empirical Methods in Natural Language Processing, EMNLP 2020, Online, November 16-20, 2020*, pages 7534–7550. Association for Computational Linguistics.

Alex Wang, Yada Pruksachatkun, Nikita Nangia, Amanpreet Singh, Julian Michael, Felix Hill, Omer Levy, and Samuel R. Bowman. 2019a. Superglue: A stickier benchmark for general-purpose language understanding systems. In Hanna M. Wallach, Hugo Larochelle, Alina Beygelzimer, Florence d'Alché-Buc, Emily B. Fox, and Roman Garnett, editors, *Advances in Neural Information Processing Systems 32: Annual Conference on Neural Information Processing Systems 2019, NeurIPS 2019, December 8-14, 2019, Vancouver, BC, Canada*, pages 3261–3275.

Alex Wang, Amanpreet Singh, Julian Michael, Felix Hill, Omer Levy, and Samuel R. Bowman. 2019b. GLUE: A multi-task benchmark and analysis platform for natural language understanding. In *7th International Conference on Learning Representations, ICLR 2019, New Orleans, LA, USA, May 6-9, 2019*. OpenReview.net.

Dingzirui Wang, Longxu Dou, and Wanxiang Che. 2022a. A survey on table-and-text hybridqa: Concepts, methods, challenges and future directions. *CoRR*, abs/2212.13465.

Lijie Wang, Yaozong Shen, Shuyuan Peng, Shuai Zhang, Xinyan Xiao, Hao Liu, Hongxuan Tang, Ying Chen, Hua Wu, and Haifeng Wang. 2022b. A fine-grained interpretability evaluation benchmark for neural NLP. In *Proceedings of the 26th Conference on Computational Natural Language Learning (CoNLL)*, pages 70–84, Abu Dhabi, United Arab Emirates (Hybrid), December. Association for Computational Linguistics.

Xiaozhi Wang, Yulin Chen, Ning Ding, Hao Peng, Zimu Wang, Yankai Lin, Xu Han, Lei Hou, Juanzi Li, Zhiyuan Liu, Peng Li, and Jie Zhou. 2022c. MAVEN-ERE: A unified large-scale dataset for event coreference, temporal, causal, and subevent relation extraction. In Yoav Goldberg, Zornitsa Kozareva, and Yue Zhang, editors, *Proceedings of the 2022 Conference on Empirical Methods in Natural Language Processing, EMNLP 2022, Abu Dhabi, United Arab Emirates, December 7-11, 2022*, pages 926–941. Association for Computational Linguistics.

Xuezhi Wang, Haohan Wang, and Diyi Yang. 2022d. Measure and improve robustness in NLP models: A survey. In Marine Carpuat, Marie-Catherine de Marneffe, and Iván Vladimir Meza Ruíz, editors, *Proceedings of the 2022 Conference of the North American Chapter of the Association for Computational Linguistics: Human Language Technologies, NAACL 2022, Seattle, WA, United States, July 10-15, 2022*, pages 4569–4586. Association for Computational Linguistics.

Zengzhi Wang, Qiming Xie, Zixiang Ding, Yi Feng, and Rui Xia. 2023. Is chatgpt a good sentiment analyzer? A preliminary study. *CoRR*, abs/2304.04339.

Alex Warstadt, Alicia Parrish, Haokun Liu, Anhad Mohananey, Wei Peng, Sheng-Fu Wang, and Samuel R. Bowman. 2020. Blimp: The benchmark of linguistic minimal pairs for english. *Trans. Assoc. Comput. Linguistics*, 8:377–392.

Zeerak Waseem, Thomas Davidson, Dana Warmsley, and Ingmar Weber. 2017. Understanding abuse: A typology of abusive language detection subtasks. In *Proceedings of the First Workshop on Abusive Language Online*, pages 78–84, Vancouver, BC, Canada, August. Association for Computational Linguistics.

Jason Wei, Yi Tay, Rishi Bommasani, Colin Raffel, Barret Zoph, Sebastian Borgeaud, Dani Yogatama, Maarten Bosma, Denny Zhou, Donald Metzler, Ed H. Chi, Tatsunori Hashimoto, Oriol Vinyals, Percy Liang, Jeff Dean, and William Fedus. 2022a. Emergent abilities of large language models. *Trans. Mach. Learn. Res.*, 2022.

Proceedings of the 22nd China National Conference on Computational Linguistics, pages 88-109, Harbin, China, August 3 - 5, 2023.
Volume 2: Frotier Forum

Jason Wei, Xuezhi Wang, Dale Schuurmans, Maarten Bosma, Brian Ichter, Fei Xia, Ed H. Chi, Quoc V. Le, and Denny Zhou. 2022b. Chain-of-thought prompting elicits reasoning in large language models. In *NeurIPS*.

Laura Weidinger, John Mellor, Maribeth Rauh, Conor Griffin, Jonathan Uesato, Po-Sen Huang, Myra Cheng, Mia Glaese, Borja Balle, Atoosa Kasirzadeh, Zac Kenton, Sasha Brown, Will Hawkins, Tom Stepleton, Courtney Biles, Abeba Birhane, Julia Haas, Laura Rimell, Lisa Anne Hendricks, William Isaac, Sean Legassick, Geoffrey Irving, and Iason Gabriel. 2021. Ethical and social risks of harm from language models. *CoRR*, abs/2112.04359.

Yuhuai Wu, Markus N. Rabe, Wenda Li, Jimmy Ba, Roger B. Grosse, and Christian Szegedy. 2021. LIME: learning inductive bias for primitives of mathematical reasoning. In Marina Meila and Tong Zhang, editors, *Proceedings of the 38th International Conference on Machine Learning, ICML 2021, 18-24 July 2021, Virtual Event*, volume 139 of *Proceedings of Machine Learning Research*, pages 11251–11262. PMLR.

Ellery Wulczyn, Nithum Thain, and Lucas Dixon. 2017. Ex machina: Personal attacks seen at scale. In *Proceedings of the 26th International Conference on World Wide Web*, WWW '17, page 1391–1399, Republic and Canton of Geneva, CHE. International World Wide Web Conferences Steering Committee.

Tianbao Xie, Chen Henry Wu, Peng Shi, Ruiqi Zhong, Torsten Scholak, Michihiro Yasunaga, Chien-Sheng Wu, Ming Zhong, Pengcheng Yin, Sida I. Wang, Victor Zhong, Bailin Wang, Chengzu Li, Connor Boyle, Ansong Ni, Ziyu Yao, Dragomir Radev, Caiming Xiong, Lingpeng Kong, Rui Zhang, Noah A. Smith, Luke Zettlemoyer, and Tao Yu. 2022. Unifiedskg: Unifying and multi-tasking structured knowledge grounding with text-to-text language models. In Yoav Goldberg, Zornitsa Kozareva, and Yue Zhang, editors, *Proceedings of the 2022 Conference on Empirical Methods in Natural Language Processing, EMNLP 2022, Abu Dhabi, United Arab Emirates, December 7-11, 2022*, pages 602–631. Association for Computational Linguistics.

Jing Xu, Da Ju, Margaret Li, Y-Lan Boureau, Jason Weston, and Emily Dinan. 2021. Bot-adversarial dialogue for safe conversational agents. In *Proceedings of the 2021 Conference of the North American Chapter of the Association for Computational Linguistics: Human Language Technologies*, pages 2950–2968, Online, June. Association for Computational Linguistics.

Yi Yang, Wen-tau Yih, and Christopher Meek. 2015. Wikiqa: A challenge dataset for open-domain question answering. In Lluís Màrquez, Chris Callison-Burch, Jian Su, Daniele Pighin, and Yuval Marton, editors, *Proceedings of the 2015 Conference on Empirical Methods in Natural Language Processing, EMNLP 2015, Lisbon, Portugal, September 17-21, 2015*, pages 2013–2018. The Association for Computational Linguistics.

Zhilin Yang, Peng Qi, Saizheng Zhang, Yoshua Bengio, William W. Cohen, Ruslan Salakhutdinov, and Christopher D. Manning. 2018. Hotpotqa: A dataset for diverse, explainable multi-hop question answering. In Ellen Riloff, David Chiang, Julia Hockenmaier, and Jun'ichi Tsujii, editors, *Proceedings of the 2018 Conference on Empirical Methods in Natural Language Processing, Brussels, Belgium, October 31 - November 4, 2018*, pages 2369–2380. Association for Computational Linguistics.

Zonglin Yang, Li Dong, Xinya Du, Hao Cheng, Erik Cambria, Xiaodong Liu, Jianfeng Gao, and Furu Wei. 2022. Language models as inductive reasoners. *CoRR*, abs/2212.10923.

Michihiro Yasunaga, Jure Leskovec, and Percy Liang. 2022. Linkbert: Pretraining language models with document links. In Smaranda Muresan, Preslav Nakov, and Aline Villavicencio, editors, *Proceedings of the 60th Annual Meeting of the Association for Computational Linguistics (Volume 1: Long Papers), ACL 2022, Dublin, Ireland, May 22-27, 2022*, pages 8003–8016. Association for Computational Linguistics.

Xi Ye and Greg Durrett. 2022. The unreliability of explanations in few-shot prompting for textual reasoning. In *NeurIPS*.

Zhangyue Yin, Qiushi Sun, Qipeng Guo, Jiawen Wu, Xipeng Qiu, and Xuanjing Huang. 2023. Do large language models know what they don't know? *CoRR*, abs/2305.18153.

Fei Yu, Hongbo Zhang, Prayag Tiwari, and Benyou Wang. 2023. Natural language reasoning, a survey.

Marcos Zampieri, Shervin Malmasi, Preslav Nakov, Sara Rosenthal, Noura Farra, and Ritesh Kumar. 2019. Predicting the type and target of offensive posts in social media. In *Proceedings of the 2019 Conference of the North American Chapter of the Association for Computational Linguistics: Human Language Technologies, Volume 1 (Long and Short Papers)*, pages 1415–1420, Minneapolis, Minnesota, June. Association for Computational Linguistics.

E. Zelikman, Yuhuai Wu, and Noah D. Goodman. 2022. Star: Bootstrapping reasoning with reasoning. *ArXiv*, abs/2203.14465.

Proceedings of the 22nd China National Conference on Computational Linguistics, pages 88-109, Harbin, China, August 3 - 5, 2023.
Volume 2: Frotier Forum

Rowan Zellers, Ari Holtzman, Yonatan Bisk, Ali Farhadi, and Yejin Choi. 2019. Hellaswag: Can a machine really finish your sentence? In Anna Korhonen, David R. Traum, and Lluís Màrquez, editors, *Proceedings of the 57th Conference of the Association for Computational Linguistics, ACL 2019, Florence, Italy, July 28- August 2, 2019, Volume 1: Long Papers*, pages 4791–4800. Association for Computational Linguistics.

Qingcheng Zeng and An-Ran Li. 2022. A survey in automatic irony processing: Linguistic, cognitive, and multi-x perspectives. In Nicoletta Calzolari, Chu-Ren Huang, Hansaem Kim, James Pustejovsky, Leo Wanner, Key-Sun Choi, Pum-Mo Ryu, Hsin-Hsi Chen, Lucia Donatelli, Heng Ji, Sadao Kurohashi, Patrizia Paggio, Nianwen Xue, Seokhwan Kim, Younggyun Hahm, Zhong He, Tony Kyungil Lee, Enrico Santus, Francis Bond, and Seung-Hoon Na, editors, *Proceedings of the 29th International Conference on Computational Linguistics, COLING 2022, Gyeongju, Republic of Korea, October 12-17, 2022*, pages 824–836. International Committee on Computational Linguistics.

Xiang Zhang, Junbo Jake Zhao, and Yann LeCun. 2015. Character-level convolutional networks for text classification. In Corinna Cortes, Neil D. Lawrence, Daniel D. Lee, Masashi Sugiyama, and Roman Garnett, editors, *Advances in Neural Information Processing Systems 28: Annual Conference on Neural Information Processing Systems 2015, December 7-12, 2015, Montreal, Quebec, Canada*, pages 649–657.

Wenxuan Zhang, Xin Li, Yang Deng, Lidong Bing, and Wai Lam. 2022. A survey on aspect-based sentiment analysis: Tasks, methods, and challenges. *CoRR*, abs/2203.01054.

Wenxuan Zhang, Yue Deng, Bing Liu, Sinno Jialin Pan, and Lidong Bing. 2023. Sentiment analysis in the era of large language models: A reality check. *CoRR*, abs/2305.15005.

Xinyan Zhao and V. G. Vinod Vydiswaran. 2021. Lirex: Augmenting language inference with relevant explanations. In *Thirty-Fifth AAAI Conference on Artificial Intelligence, AAAI 2021, Thirty-Third Conference on Innovative Applications of Artificial Intelligence, IAAI 2021, The Eleventh Symposium on Educational Advances in Artificial Intelligence, EAAI 2021, Virtual Event, February 2-9, 2021*, pages 14532–14539. AAAI Press.

Wayne Xin Zhao, Kun Zhou, Junyi Li, Tianyi Tang, Xiaolei Wang, Yupeng Hou, Yingqian Min, Beichen Zhang, Junjie Zhang, Zican Dong, Yifan Du, Chen Yang, Yushuo Chen, Zhipeng Chen, Jinhao Jiang, Ruiyang Ren, Yifan Li, Xinyu Tang, Zikang Liu, Peiyu Liu, Jian-Yun Nie, and Ji-Rong Wen. 2023. A survey of large language models. *CoRR*, abs/2303.18223.

Shen Zheng, Jie Huang, and Kevin Chen-Chuan Chang. 2023. Why does chatgpt fall short in providing truthful answers?

Victor Zhong, Caiming Xiong, and Richard Socher. 2017. Seq2sql: Generating structured queries from natural language using reinforcement learning. *CoRR*, abs/1709.00103.

Wanjun Zhong, Ruixiang Cui, Yiduo Guo, Yaobo Liang, Shuai Lu, Yanlin Wang, Amin Saied, Weizhu Chen, and Nan Duan. 2023. Agieval: A human-centric benchmark for evaluating foundation models. *CoRR*, abs/2304.06364.

Hao Zhou, Minlie Huang, Tianyang Zhang, Xiaoyan Zhu, and Bing Liu. 2018. Emotional chatting machine: Emotional conversation generation with internal and external memory. In Sheila A. McIlraith and Kilian Q. Weinberger, editors, *Proceedings of the Thirty-Second AAAI Conference on Artificial Intelligence, (AAAI-18), the 30th innovative Applications of Artificial Intelligence (IAAI-18), and the 8th AAAI Symposium on Educational Advances in Artificial Intelligence (EAAI-18), New Orleans, Louisiana, USA, February 2-7, 2018*, pages 730–739. AAAI Press.

Terry Yue Zhuo, Yujin Huang, Chunyang Chen, and Zhenchang Xing. 2023. Red teaming chatgpt via jailbreaking: Bias, robustness, reliability and toxicity.

Caleb Ziems, Jane Yu, Yi-Chia Wang, Alon Halevy, and Diyi Yang. 2022. The moral integrity corpus: A benchmark for ethical dialogue systems. In *Proceedings of the 60th Annual Meeting of the Association for Computational Linguistics (Volume 1: Long Papers)*, pages 3755–3773, Dublin, Ireland, May. Association for Computational Linguistics.

Proceedings of the 22nd China National Conference on Computational Linguistics, pages 88-109, Harbin, China, August 3 - 5, 2023.
Volume 2: Frotier Forum

Frontier Review of Multimodal AI

Nan Duan
Microsoft Research Asia
nanduan@microsoft.com

Abstract

Pre-training techniques have enabled foundation models (such as BERT, T5, GPT) to achieve remarkable success in natural language processing (NLP) and multimodal tasks that involve text, audio and visual contents. Some of the latest multimodal generative models, such as DALL·E and Stable Diffusion, can synthesize novel visual content from text or video inputs, which greatly enhances the creativity and productivity of content creators. However, multimodal AI also faces some challenges, such as adding new modalities or handling diverse tasks that require signals beyond their understanding. Therefore, a new trend in multimodal AI is to build a compositional AI system that connects existing foundation models with external modules and tools. This way, the system can perform more varied tasks by leveraging different modalities and signals. In this paper, we will give a brief overview of the state-of-the-art multimodal AI techniques and the direction of building compositional AI systems. We will also discuss the potential future research topics in multimodal AI.

1 Introduction

Large language models (LLMs) have achieved great success in natural language processing (NLP). These models (e.g., BERT (Devlin et al., 2019), T5 (Raffel et al., 2020) and GPT (Brown et al., 2020)) can learn general data representations and commonsense knowledge from large-scale corpora using self-supervised learning tasks (such as masked language modeling or next token prediction). The learned models can be further fine-tuned on downstream tasks and obtain superior performance on them.

The success of LLMs has also been extended to other non-language domains, such as computer vision or speech processing. The convergence of these techniques on different types of data makes "multimodal AI" the hottest direction in the AI community.

This paper aims to briefly summarize the latest trends of multimodal AI research. In short, there are three trends as follows: (1) the underlying architectures of models for different modalities are converging; (2) the focus of multimodal AI research is shifting from multimodal understanding models to multimodal generation models; (3) single multimodal models have shown limitations and they are still far from covering diverse tasks using data with different modalities, and connecting LLMs with external tools and models to complete more tasks is becoming the new AI paradigm. We will introduce these three trends in Sections 2, 3 and 4, respectively. In Section 5, we will discuss the possible future directions of multimodal AI.

2 The Convergence of Model Architecture

The architecture of models for different modalities is becoming more similar in the era of LLMs. Transformers are widely used in text, code, visual and audio scenarios to support understanding and generation tasks. For instance, the latest LLMs like ChatGPT or GPT-4 have integrated text and code in a single model, which can support text-only, code-only, text-to-code and code-to-text generation tasks. Multimodal generation models like DALL·E (Ramesh et al., 2021) and NUWA-Infinity (Wu et al., 2022) are

Proceedings of the 22nd China National Conference on Computational Linguistics, pages 110-118, Harbin, China, August 3 - 5, 2023.
Volume 2: Frotier Forum
(c) Technical Committee on Computational Linguistics, Chinese Information Processing Society of China

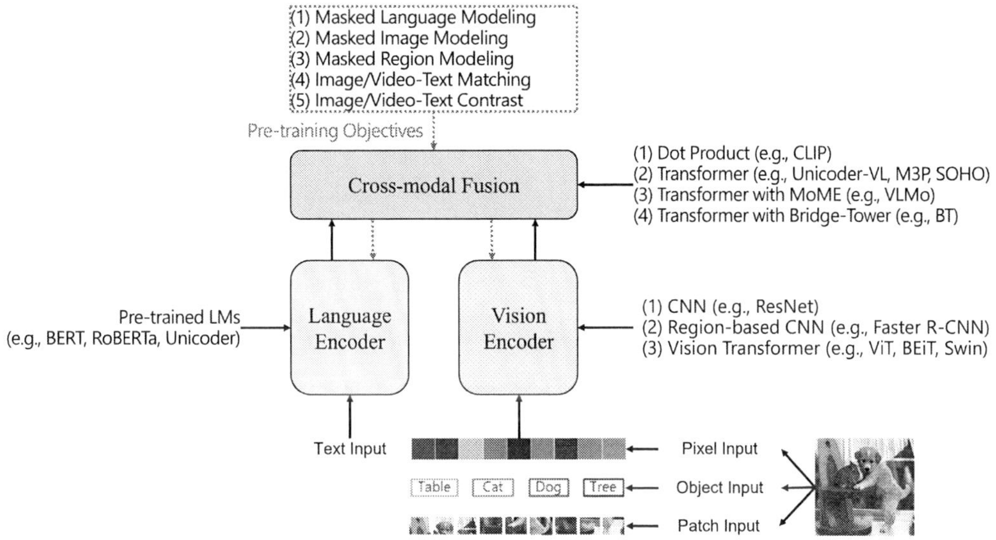

Figure 1: Overview of visual-language models.

also trained based on auto-regressive models like GPT models for image and video generation tasks. VALL-E (Wang et al., 2023) can leverage strong in-context learning capabilities and can be applied for zero-shot cross-lingual text-to-speech synthesis and zero-shot speech-to-speech translations, which is also based on Transformer and GPT-like models. Moreover, we also observed that diffusion models are widely used in content generation tasks as well, such as DALL·E 2 (Ramesh et al., 2022) and Stable Diffusion (Rombach et al., 2022) for visual generation, NaturalSpeech 2 (Shen et al., 2023) for speech generation. But there is also another research thread that aims to unify different types of generation models using diffusion models, which can be also seen as an indication of the model architecture convergence.

Due to the different basic units, data formats, and structures of the contents in different modalities, there is still no universally agreed model architecture for multimodal AIs. However, such convergence is definitely a clear trend in the AI community.

3 From Visual-Language Understanding to Visual Generation from Language

Visual-Text (VL) pre-trained models are the most representative multimodal AIs. The goal of such models is to learn the representations of texts and visuals jointly and support VL tasks such as image retrieval, visual question answering, or text-based image generation. In the past several years, the research focus has shifted from VL understanding tasks to visual generation tasks. Therefore, in this section, we will first review the progress of VL understanding models and then review the latest development of visual generation models from texts.

3.1 Visual-Language Understanding

There are 3 key differences between different VL understanding models.

First, how to represent visual inputs. Different VL understanding models use different granularity to represent visual contents, such as pixels, objects and patches of the images or videos. The most commonly used granularity recently is patches.

Second, how to generate visual representations. Some models use CNN-style models such as ResNet or Faster R-CNN, while other models use Transformers such as ViT (Dosovitskiy et al., 2021), Swin (Liu et al., 2021), etc.

Third, how to fuse the representations from text and visual inputs. There are several ways for this task. For example, CLIP (Radford et al., 2021) model uses a simple dot-product component in the

Proceedings of the 22nd China National Conference on Computational Linguistics, pages 110-118, Harbin, China, August 3 - 5, 2023.
Volume 2: Frotier Forum

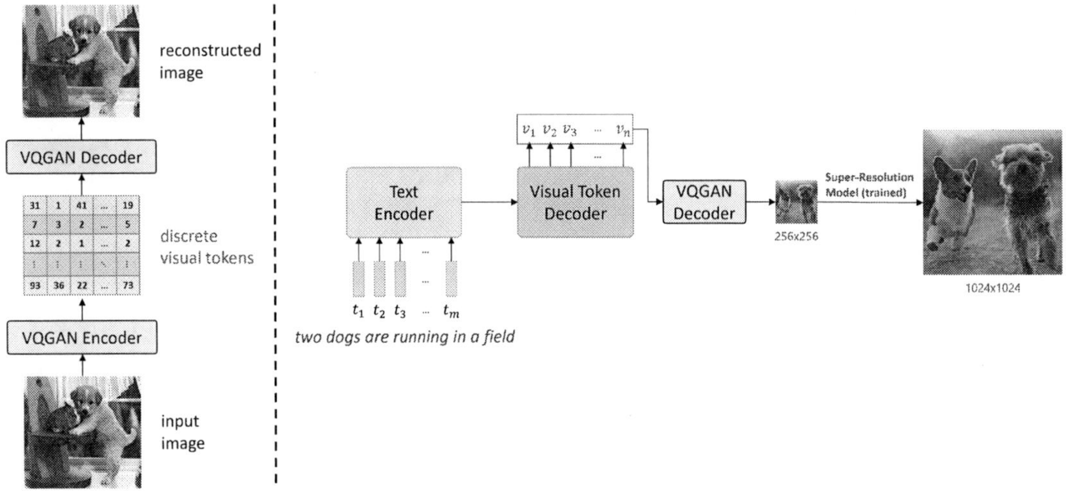

Figure 2: Overview of auto-regressive model.

fusion, which makes the computation cost very low and the resulting framework very effective in the image-text matching task. Some early VL understanding models (Unicoder-VL (Li et al., 2019), M3P (Ni et al., 2019), Uniter (Chen et al., 2020), etc.) used Transformers to further fuse the text and visual representations. Mixture-of-Experts are used to fuse representations from different input modalities as well, such as VLMo (Bao et al., 2022), which makes the model parameters for different modalities more tunable. Some recent work, such as BridgeTower (Xu et al., 2023) and ManagerTower (Xu et al., 2023), leveraged the text or visual representations from different layers to generate better uni-modal representations for the later VL understanding tasks.

In summary, using patches as the visual representation units and using Transformer to fuse text and visual representations is the current state-of-the-art VL pre-trained model setting. Besides images, video understanding is also very important for the development of many future AI systems. Currently image-based visual models are efficiently used in the video models. However, it is straightforward to leverage the large-scale video corpus directly in the future, which can train more powerful multimodal AI models for video-related tasks.

3.2 Visual Generation from Language

Currently, there are two typical text-based visual generation methodologies.

The 1st generation methodology is based on VQGAN (Yu et al., 2022) and autoregressive model. In VQGAN, an encoder can transform each image into discrete visual tokens. Each visual token is an integer code coming from a codebook and represents the content appeared in the corresponding image region. For example, the image region at the top-left corner is represented by a visual token whose ID is 31. Based on these visual tokens, a decoder can reconstruct the original image. It means if a natural language sentence can be translated into a visual token sequence, the VQGAN decoder can simply use the sequence to generate an image that reflects the meaning of the input sentence. This is exactly what DALL E (Ramesh et al., 2021) and Parti (Yu et al., 2022) do in their text-to-image generation procedures. In such models, a text encoder first encodes each natural language description into text embeddings and then a vision decoder follows an autoregressive formulation to generate visual tokens in a left-to-right order. This is similar to the typical text generation procedure in many NLP tasks such as machine translation or text summarization, where each word is generated based on all previous words already generated. Last, the pre-trained VQGAN decoder will generate an image based on the predicted visual tokens and a super-resolution model can further up-sample the output image to a bigger resolution. This methodology has its own pros and cons: thanks to the autoregressive mechanism, these models can capture the dependencies between generated visual tokens and also support variable-length generation

Proceedings of the 22nd China National Conference on Computational Linguistics, pages 110-118, Harbin, China, August 3 - 5, 2023.
Volume 2: Frotier Forum

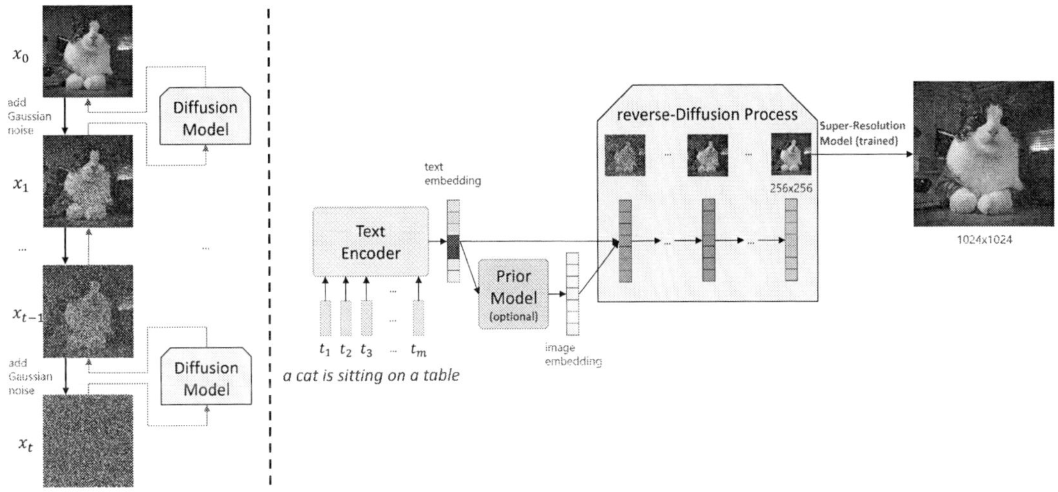

Figure 3: Overview of diffusion model.

tasks. But such generation process is not computationally efficient, as all tokens are generated one after one, instead of concurrently.

The 2nd way to generate images from text is to use diffusion models. Diffusion models work by adding noise to an image and then learning to remove the noise and recover the original image. This is called the forward and reverse diffusion processes. The reverse diffusion process can also use text or image as a condition to guide the image reconstruction. In diffusion model-based methods, a text encoder first turns text into embeddings. Then a reverse diffusion process uses noise and the text embedding to create output images. Some methods, like DALL E 2, also use a prior model to create an image embedding from the text embedding and use it as a condition for the reverse diffusion process to increase the image variety. Finally, a super-resolution model is used to make the output image bigger. Unlike autoregressive models, diffusion models are fast, because they can create the image at each time step at the same time. But they are not good at capturing the relationships between different parts of the image. They also cannot generate images of different sizes, because the image size is fixed beforehand.

To overcome the fixed-size limitation of diffusion models, NWUA-Infinity (Wu et al., 2022) proposed a method that can generate high-quality images and videos with any resolution, by creating them patch by patch. Given a text input and a resolution, a module called Arbitrary Direction Controller (or ADC) first decides the order of patch generation. Based on this order, NUWA-Infinity will create each patch one after another in the patch-level. For example, when it creates patch 13, a module called Nearby Context Pool (or NCP) first collects patch 7, 8, 9 and 12 as the context, because they are close to patch 13 within a certain distance. Then the vision decoder will create visual tokens for patch 13 based on these context patches and VQGAN decoder will create the corresponding image for patch 13. Because the vision decoder uses the nearby patches as its context when it creates each patch, the patches look smooth and natural when they are put together. This is how NUWA-Infinity can make the final image from all the patches. Also, because the number of context patches in NCP is small, as the model will discard those irrelevant patches during the generation process, the computation cost of the local autoregressive model can be greatly reduced, as it doesn't need to consider all patches created before. In this way, NUWA-Infinity can create the remaining patches and get the complete image output. NUWA-Infinity can also generate videos. The main difference from image generation is that the context patches in NCP come from both the current video frame and the previous video frames. For example, when NUWA-Infinity wants to create patch 14 in the second video frame, the context patches in NCP will include patch 1 to patch 9 from the first video frame and patch 10 to patch 13 from the second video frame. After patch 14 is created, it will be added to NCP as a new context and patch 1 will be removed from NCP as it has no impact on the future patches.

Proceedings of the 22nd China National Conference on Computational Linguistics, pages 110-118, Harbin, China, August 3 - 5, 2023.
Volume 2: Frotier Forum

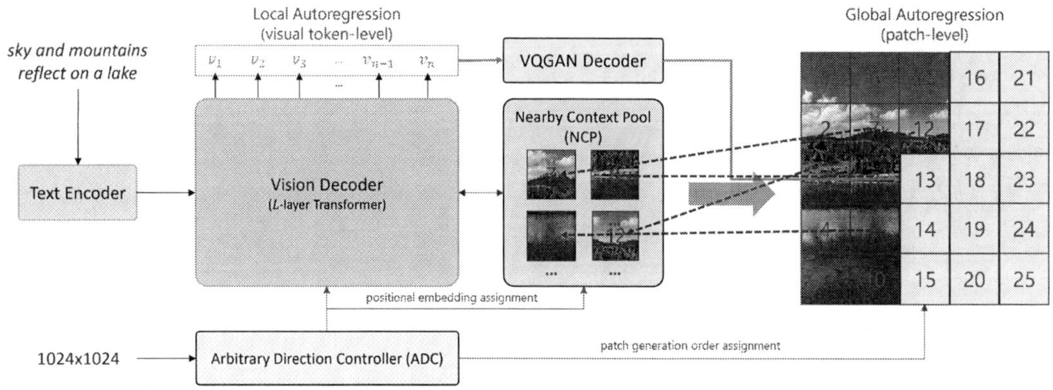

Figure 4: Overview of NUWA-Infinity for text-based image generation.

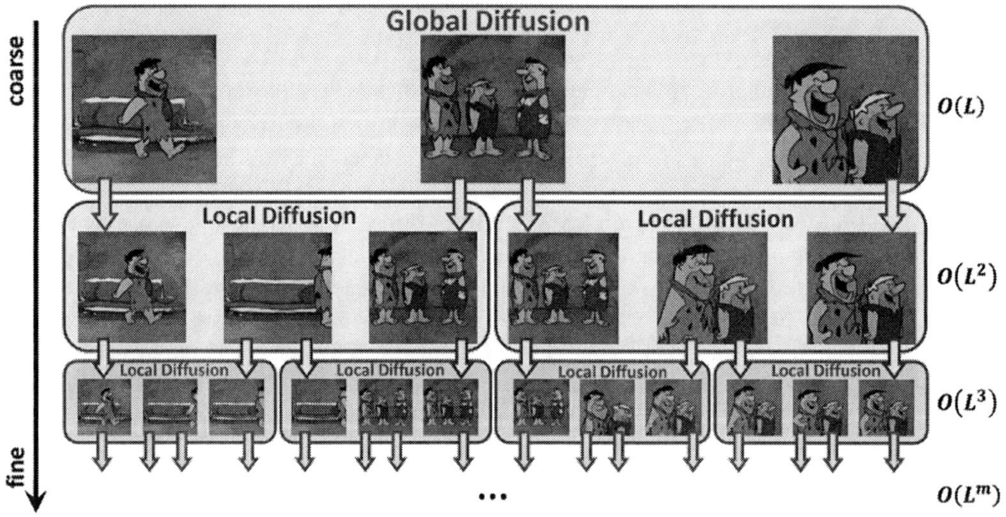

Figure 5: Overview of NUWA-XL for text-based extreme-long video generation.

NUWA-Infinity can create images and videos of different lengths with the auto-regressive over auto-regressive generation method. But auto-regressive models have some drawbacks, such as (1) they are very expensive to train and use; (2) they have error propagation problems that affect the generation quality; (3) they are not good at creating different scenes between images, which is important for video generation as scenes change often in video contents.

To solve these problems, NUWA-XL (Yin et al., 2023) proposed a diffusion over diffusion framework, which uses diffusion models in different levels to create long-videos in a fine-to-coarse way. In the first level, a diffusion model creates the key frames, which have enough scene changes and also keep the visual consistency between different video frames. In the second level, another diffusion model creates in-between video frames between any two adjacent video frames created in the first level. In the third level, a third diffusion model creates more in-between video frames between the adjacent video frames. By doing this, NUWA-XL can create very long videos efficiently and reduce the error propagation issue. Of course, the total scene length is still determined by the first level diffusion model, but creating a good key frame scene is much easier than creating the whole video at once.

Proceedings of the 22nd China National Conference on Computational Linguistics, pages 110-118, Harbin, China, August 3 - 5, 2023.
Volume 2: Frotier Forum

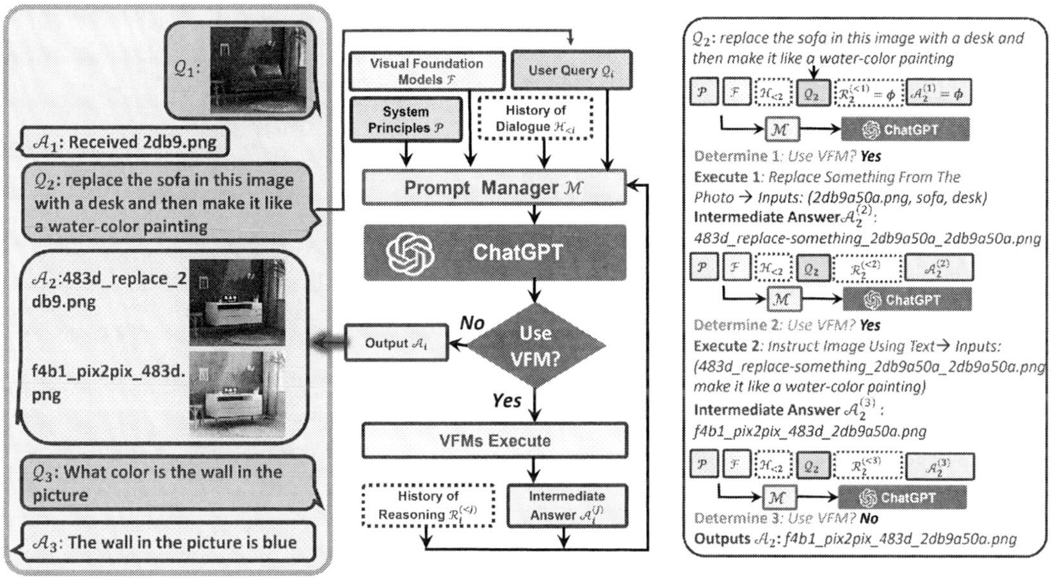

Figure 6: Overview of Visual ChatGPT v1.

4 From Single AI to Compositional AI

Single AI models have obvious limitations. First, it is difficult to include a new modality in an existing multimodal model. This is because adding a new modality needs not only new data with this modality, but also training the model from scratch. So it requires a lot of work on data quality and computing resources, especially GPUs. Second, it is difficult to make a single AI model handle different tasks, even the most advanced LLMs like GPT-4 are not capable of this. This is because a single model is constrained by the current abilities and the predefined modalities.

Therefore, the community is starting to investigate compositional AI (Liang et al., 2023) as a possible new AI paradigm. This involves using and coordinating multiple AI modules with different functions to solve complex problems. Such systems can show new abilities that are beyond what any single module can do. We have seen some examples of this direction in the recent developments of LLMs, from single LLMs, to LLMs with expert sub-modules and the latest trend of combining LLMs with other tools and models to achieve more difficult tasks that are out of the scope of the original LLMs.

The benefits of compositional AI are quite obvious. First, it allows more control over the system's abilities by composing modules with specific functions. Second, it improves the system's interpretability and lowers the chance of hallucination by having clear definitions of modules. Third, it improves the system's continual learning ability and avoids the problem of catastrophic forgetting by not needing to update all modules in each new training stage. Fourth, it makes data collection and training easier for modules with simple skills. Fifth, it lowers data annotation and training costs by not needing to update all modules.

There are two ways to create compositional AI systems from multimodal tasks. First, LLMs can be integrated with external tools using fixed prompts, which can make the LLMs show new abilities on doing different multimodal tasks. Second, LLMs can be connected with new AI modules with specific functions using learnable parameters instead of fixed prompts. This soft connection can transfer information in different modalities in a smooth way and enable better multimodal abilities. Also, as only the learnable connectors are optimized during training with the original LLMs and other AI modules fixed, such system can quickly include new modalities in the system with low computation cost.

Proceedings of the 22nd China National Conference on Computational Linguistics, pages 110-118, Harbin, China, August 3 - 5, 2023.
Volume 2: Frotier Forum

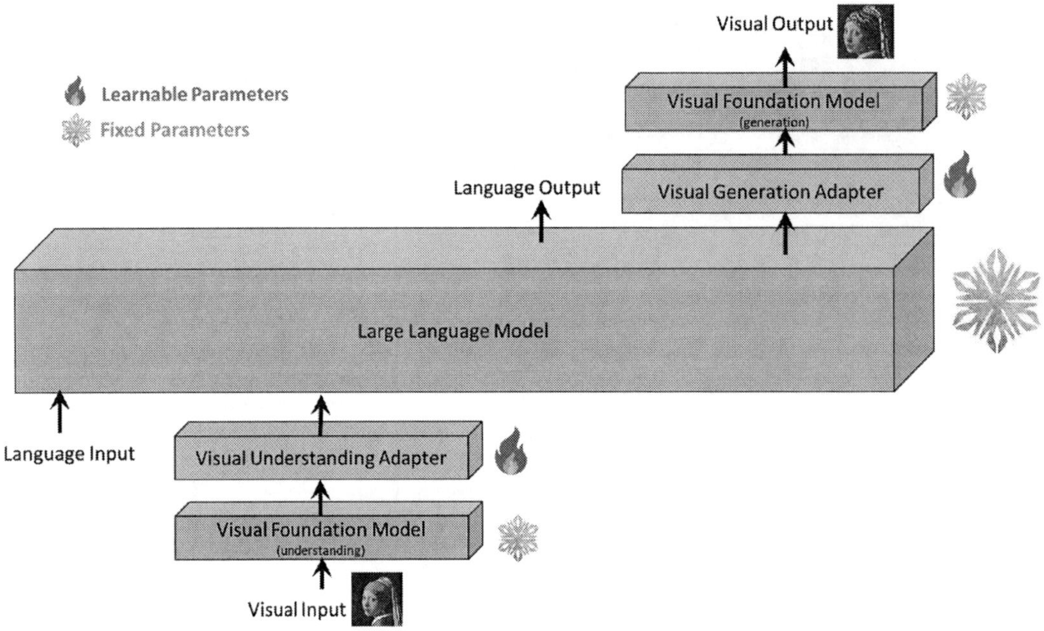

Figure 7: Overview of Visual ChatGPT v2.

4.1 Connecting LLMs with External Tools with Fixed Prompts

For the first type of work, we use Visual ChatGPT (Wu et al., 2023) as an example to illustrate how such work operates.

Visual ChatGPT is one of the first work that aims to combine visual tools with ChatGPT to perform different kinds of visual tasks. As ChatGPT is an LLM, which can only handle textual tasks, the first thing Visual ChatGPT needs to do is inform ChatGPT that it can try to use external visual tools to accomplish visual tasks. This work uses prompts as the system principles to let ChatGPT understand its new capabilities.

After adding system principles, Visual ChatGPT should also let ChatGPT know which tools it can use, when it can use them and how it can use them. For example, for Visual QA, the name and usage fields of this tool will briefly explain the function of the tool and when ChatGPT can use it, and the inputs/outputs field tells ChatGPT what kind of inputs and outputs are needed by this tool.

As the tasks require multiple steps to be completed, Visual ChatGPT also adds the string "do I need to use a tool" as another prompt after each user query, to let ChatGPT decide whether it needs to invoke a tool at the current step. If the answer is NO, then ChatGPT will return the current results to the user. Otherwise, ChatGPT will continue to call new tools and use all intermediate results as the context prompt in the next step.

By adding the above mentioned mechanisms, Visual ChatGPT can achieve many visual understanding, generation and editing tasks that the original ChatGPT model cannot do. This shows the biggest advantage of compositional AI models, new abilities will emerge by composing multiple tools with specific functions.

4.2 Connecting LLMs with External Modules with Learnable Parameters

Systems like Visual ChatGPT are easy to implement and build, as they do not require any weights to be learned. However, such systems also have obvious limitations. First, the fixed prompts are not stable and robust enough to link LLMs and tools. Second, in such systems, non-text information will be turned into text descriptions before sending them to LLMs. And such conversion will lose a lot of information of the original contents.

Proceedings of the 22nd China National Conference on Computational Linguistics, pages 110-118, Harbin, China, August 3 - 5, 2023.
Volume 2: Frotier Forum

Therefore, there are recent related work that use learnable parameters to connect LLMs with other tool modules instead of using prompts. Such work will not change the parameters of the LLM and the external tool modules, as they are already well trained and further fine-tuning requires a lot of computing resources. Instead, they only train the adapters between LLM and tool modules using a small amount of annotations. By doing this, such system can do better message passing between LLM and other tool modules and avoid the catastrophic forgetting problem. For example, instead of converting the input image into a natural language description, Visual ChatGPT v2 gets the image representation based on a visual foundation model first, and then projects the image representation into the LLM input, by a visual understanding adapter. Similarly, another output adapter can be used to pass the LLM's output to the visual generation module, to create output images.

5 Future Directions

This paper briefly reviews the recent developments of multimodal AI research, including (1) the model architectures are becoming more similar, (2) the research focus is moving from multimodal understanding models to multimodal generation models; (3) combining LLMs with external tools and models to accomplish diverse tasks is emerging as the new AI paradigm.

There are several directions that can be further explored in the future. First, concentrating more on video generation, which could trigger the next ChatGPT breakthrough in the AI community. Second, concentrating more on compositional AI for multimodal systems with more modalities covered and less computation costs needed. Third, concentrating more on the autonomous robotics, which can complete more tasks in the physical world, to further enhance human's creativity and productivity.

References

Jacob Devlin, Ming-Wei Chang, Kenton Lee, and Kristina Toutanova. 2019. *BERT: Pre-training of Deep Bidirectional Transformers for Language Understanding*, NAACL.

Colin Raffel, Noam Shazeer, Adam Roberts, Katherine Lee, Sharan Narang, Michael Matena, Yanqi Zhou, Wei Li, and Peter J. Liu. 2020. *Exploring the Limits of Transfer Learning with a Unified Text-to-Text Transformer*, JMLR.

Tom B. Brown, Benjamin Mann, Nick Ryder, Melanie Subbiah, Jared Kaplan, Prafulla Dhariwal, Arvind Neelakantan, Pranav Shyam, Girish Sastry, Amanda Askell, Sandhini Agarwal, Ariel Herbert-Voss, Gretchen Krueger, Tom Henighan, Rewon Child, Aditya Ramesh, Daniel M. Ziegler, Jeffrey Wu, Clemens Winter, Christopher Hesse, Mark Chen, Eric Sigler, Mateusz Litwin, Scott Gray, Benjamin Chess, Jack Clark, Christopher Berner, Sam McCandlish, Alec Radford, Ilya Sutskever, and Dario Amodei. 2020. *Language Models are Few-Shot Learners*, arXiv.

Aditya Ramesh, Mikhail Pavlov, Gabriel Goh, Scott Gray, Chelsea Voss, Alec Radford, Mark Chen, and Ilya Sutskever. 2021. *Zero-Shot Text-to-Image Generation*, arXiv

Chenfei Wu, Jian Liang, Xiaowei Hu, Zhe Gan, Jianfeng Wang, Lijuan Wang, Zicheng Liu, Yuejian Fang, and Nan Duan. 2022. *NUWA-Infinity: Autoregressive over Autoregressive Generation for Infinite Visual Synthesis*, NeurIPS.

Chengyi Wang, Sanyuan Chen, Yu Wu, Ziqiang Zhang, Long Zhou, Shujie Liu, Zhuo Chen, Yanqing Liu, Huaming Wang, Jinyu Li, Lei He, Sheng Zhao, Furu Wei. 2023. *Neural Codec Language Models are Zero-Shot Text to Speech Synthesizers*, arXiv.

Aditya Ramesh, Prafulla Dhariwal, Alex Nichol, Casey Chu, and Mark Chen. 2022. *Hierarchical Text-Conditional Image Generation with CLIP Latents*, arXiv.

Robin Rombach, Andreas Blattmann, Dominik Lorenz, Patrick Esser, and Björn Ommer. 2022. *High-Resolution Image Synthesis with Latent Diffusion Models*, CVPR.

Kai Shen, Zeqian Ju, Xu Tan, Yanqing Liu, Yichong Leng, Lei He, Tao Qin, Sheng Zhao, Jiang Bian. 2023. *NaturalSpeech 2: Latent Diffusion Models are Natural and Zero-Shot Speech and Singing Synthesizers*, arXiv.

Proceedings of the 22nd China National Conference on Computational Linguistics, pages 110-118, Harbin, China, August 3 - 5, 2023.
Volume 2: Frotier Forum

Alexey Dosovitskiy, Lucas Beyer, Alexander Kolesnikov, Dirk Weissenborn, Xiaohua Zhai, Thomas Unterthiner, Mostafa Dehghani, Matthias Minderer, Georg Heigold, Sylvain Gelly, Jakob Uszkoreit, and Neil Houlsby. 2021. *An Image is Worth 16x16 Words: Transformers for Image Recognition at Scale*, arXiv.

Ze Liu, Yutong Lin, Yue Cao, Han Hu, Yixuan Wei, Zheng Zhang, Stephen Lin, and Baining Guo. 2021. *Swin Transformer: Hierarchical Vision Transformer using Shifted Windows*, ICCV.

Alec Radford, Jong Wook Kim, Chris Hallacy, Aditya Ramesh, Gabriel Goh, Sandhini Agarwal, Girish Sastry, Amanda Askell, Pamela Mishkin, Jack Clark, Gretchen Krueger, and Ilya Sutskever. 2021. *Learning Transferable Visual Models From Natural Language Supervision*, arXiv.

Gen Li, Nan Duan, Yuejian Fang, Ming Gong, Daxin Jiang, Ming Zhou. 2019. *Unicoder-VL: A Universal Encoder for Vision and Language by Cross-modal Pre-training*, AAAI.

Minheng Ni, Haoyang Huang, Lin Su, Edward Cui, Taroon Bharti, Lijuan Wang, Jianfeng Gao, Dongdong Zhang, Nan Duan. 2019. *M3P: Learning Universal Representations via Multitask Multilingual Multimodal Pre-training*, CVPR.

Yen-Chun Chen, Linjie Li, Licheng Yu, Ahmed El Kholy, Faisal Ahmed, Zhe Gan, Yu Cheng, and Jingjing Liu. 2020. *UNITER: UNiversal Image-TExt Representation Learning*, ECCV.

Hangbo Bao, Wenhui Wang, Li Dong, Qiang Liu, Owais Khan Mohammed, Kriti Aggarwal, Subhojit Som, and Furu Wei. 2022. *VLMo: Unified Vision-Language Pre-Training with Mixture-of-Modality-Experts*, arXiv.

Xiao Xu, Chenfei Wu, Shachar Rosenman, Vasudev Lal, Wanxiang Che, and Nan Duan. 2023. *BridgeTower: Building Bridges Between Encoders in Vision-Language Representation Learning*, AAAI.

Xiao Xu, Bei Li, Chenfei Wu, Shao-Yen Tseng, Anahita Bhiwandiwalla, Shachar Rosenman, Vasudev Lal, Wanxiang Che, and Nan Duan. 2023. *ManagerTower: Aggregating the Insights of Uni-Modal Experts for Vision-Language Representation Learning*, ACL.

Jiahui Yu, Xin Li, Jing Yu Koh, Han Zhang, Ruoming Pang, James Qin, Alexander Ku, Yuanzhong Xu, Jason Baldridge, and Yonghui Wu. 2022. *Vector-quantized Image Modeling with Improved VQGAN*, arXiv.

Jiahui Yu, Yuanzhong Xu, Jing Yu Koh, Thang Luong, Gunjan Baid, Zirui Wang, Vijay Vasudevan, Alexander Ku, Yinfei Yang, Burcu Karagol Ayan, Ben Hutchinson, Wei Han, Zarana Parekh, Xin Li, Han Zhang, Jason Baldridge, and Yonghui Wu. 2022. *Scaling Autoregressive Models for Content-Rich Text-to-Image Generation*, arXiv.

Shengming Yin, Chenfei Wu, Huan Yang, Jianfeng Wang, Xiaodong Wang, Minheng Ni, Zhengyuan Yang, Linjie Li, Shuguang Liu, Fan Yang, Jianlong Fu, Gong Ming, Lijuan Wang, Zicheng Liu, Houqiang Li, and Nan Duan. 2023. *NUWA-XL: Diffusion over Diffusion for eXtremely Long Video Generation*, ACL.

Chenfei Wu, Shengming Yin, Weizhen Qi, Xiaodong Wang, Zecheng Tang, and Nan Duan. 2023. *Visual ChatGPT: Talking, Drawing and Editing with Visual Foundation Models*, arXiv.

Yaobo Liang, Chenfei Wu, Ting Song, Wenshan Wu, Yan Xia, Yu Liu, Yang Ou, Shuai Lu, Lei Ji, Shaoguang Mao, Yun Wang, Linjun Shou, Ming Gong, and Nan Duan. 2023. *TaskMatrix.AI: Completing Tasks by Connecting Foundation Models with Millions of APIs*, arXiv.

Proceedings of the 22nd China National Conference on Computational Linguistics, pages 110-118, Harbin, China, August 3 - 5, 2023.
Volume 2: Frotier Forum

Association for Computational Linguistics
209 N. Eighth Street
Stroudsburg, Pennsylvania 18360

ISBN 978-1-7138-8989-2

CURRAN ASSOCIATES INC.
proceedings.com